Sell Yourself
Without Selling
Your Soul

Sell Yourself Without Selling Your Soul

A Woman's Guide to Promoting Herself,
Her Business, Her Product, or Her Cause
with Integrity and Spirit

Susan Harrow

HarperResource
An Imprint of HarperCollins*Publishers*

Grateful acknowledgment is made to the following for granting permission to use their work in this book.

Excerpted from *Media Smart: How to Handle a Reporter* by Dennis Stauffer. Ann Keeler Evans for the "Rite to Remember Fact Sheet." Suzanne Jackson for the "Paynet Fact Sheet." © 1997 by Sharon Salzberg/Shambhala Publications, Inc., Boston, www.shambhala.com; reprinted by arrangement with the publisher. "Say It Better" quiz courtesy of Kare Anderson. Excerpted from page 295 from *Stories of the Spirit, Stories of the Heart* by Christina Feldman; © 1991 by Christina Feldman and Jack Kornfield; reprinted by permission of HarperCollins Publishers. Linda Weltner for her excerpt from the January 2000 *Writer's Digest* interview "Ever So Humble" by Cynthia G. LaFerle. Reprinted with permission by SARK © 1991; excerpted from page 37 of *A Creative Companion*, published by Celestial Arts, P. O. Box 7123, Berkeley, CA 94707. Various quotes reprinted with permission from WHYY—Terry Gross's show *Fresh Air*. André Bacard sample pitch letter adapted from *The Computer Privacy Handbook*. "News You Can Use" newsletter courtesy of Joe Vitale. "The Publicity Hound" newsletter courtesy of Joan Stewart, a.k.a. the Publicity Hound. From *Feeling the Shoulder of the Lion* by Rumi, translated by Coleman Barks; © 1991 by Coleman Barks; reprinted by arrangement with Shambhala Publications, Inc., Boston, www.shambhala.com. Kat Albrecht, founder of PEThunters® pet detectives, for her publicity success story "Persevere."

HarperCollins books may be purchased for educational, business, or sales promotional use. For information please write: Special Markets Department, HarperCollins Publishers Inc., 10 East 53rd Street, New York, NY 10022.

FIRST EDITION

Designed by Joseph Rutt

Printed on acid-free paper

Library of Congress Cataloging-in-Publication Data

Harrow, Susan, 1957–
    Sell yourself without selling your soul : a woman's guide to promoting herself, her business, her product, or her cause with integrity and spirit / Susan Harrow.—1st ed.
        p.   cm.
    Includes index
    ISBN 0-06-019880-X
    1. Advertising.   2. Publicity.   3. Success in business.   I. Title.

HF5811 .H28   2002
659.1—dc21

                                    2001039673

02 03 04 05 06 QW 10 9 8 7 6 5 4 3 2 1

To Scorpio Dog Man

Let the beauty we love be what we do.
There are hundreds of ways to kneel and kiss the ground.

—RUMI

CONTENTS

ACKNOWLEDGMENTS

Robert Cardellino for cracking my heart wide open so Brett could get in; Dominick LaGatta for showing me how to really look into a lover's eyes; Terry Lewis, my dear Terrantule, who has been there through it all with me with kind words, showing me how to go easy, natural-like, when I'm pushing through; Sheila Kapur for being such a good friend even at a distance, her persistence in meditation, healing, and passion and her delight in food; Diana Meistrell for her pissed-off spirit and fearlessness and fun-loving daredeviletteness; Marc Louria for his wild unruly heart and his commitment to write no matter what, and his surly sweetness; Nancy Lewis for her yellow eyes, for the ease in being with her, and for being one of my oldest and dearest friends; Roberta and Irving Lewis for my first example of what a romantic love-bird relationship looks like at the beginning, in the middle, and at the end.

Marcia Urbin Raymond for her Buddhahood in all its complexity and fierceness; David Raymond for his love of the image, of art, and his passion for artists and their art; Mary Rich for her faith, for her ability to pray and hold what's dear, and for being an indefatigable seeker of art and beauty; David and Colleen Newlin for believing that anything is possible and then making it so.

Buddhishka for her how-to-chill-out wisdom and gracious dignity and Tati for going her own way and her mischievous, all-I-want-to-do-is-play nature; for their constant companionship and good mood, examples I so often don't follow.

My parents, Noreen Harrow, who taught me how to trust my gut, be insatiably curious, and find beauty in all things used; and Herman Harrow, for his practical nature, the humorous twinkle in his eye, his perseverance and GDI (goddamn independent) spirit, which helped me keep on going even when I thought I couldn't; my brothers, Joshua Horowitz, for his big wide heart, for finding what's funny in the most hideous situations, and for his incredible focus and ability to make beautiful music even with an accordion; and James Harrow, for his crazy toothpick sculpture, his sweet and generous nature, and his nut-wild thinking.

John Grimes, whose humor, intelligence, and belief in me at the beginning helped me become a publicist; Robin Chin for her amazing lesson in being open to whatever mentor shows up and absorbing it all without ego; Theresa Armada for her crazy sharp wit, her bodily strength that's hard to fathom, and her willingness to teach our youth about the beauty of the English language; Nina Glaser with her incredible Israeli stoicism and commitment to live the artist's life even while holding on to the short end of the stick and making moving memorial portraits of her friends dying of AIDS; Zillie Bahar for her dusty-dry wit and way of looking at the world in her way-out way; Jim Vaccaro and Sophia.

Sylvia Sharenow for loving me and showing me how warm a mom can be; Ira Sharenow for his wit, drive, musicality, and smarts, which he passed on to his sons; Dean Sharenow for beating to his own drum, for Webmastering with patience and precision, and for his knifely tongue; Wendi Rogers for her charm and beauty and gilded words.

Laurie Wagner, seeker of truth on the hard road, warrior mom, for her piercing honesty; Joyce Freedman, who reminds me that poetry is real and chewy, and how to shop without a penny; Margo Hackett for her fierce protection of the underdog, passionate gardening, and food-goddess-ness; Susan Pomeroy for her mystery and hidden sides, and "where do they come from?" stories. Sepha Schiffman for her softness and the melodious way she has about her; Joan Logghe for her brilliant teachings and willingness to write where it hurts; Cecile Moochnek for her eye for beauty and stubborn insistence that it can be found everywhere; Donna Levin for her searing insight, hilarious wit, chutzpah, and the guts to wear long hair at her age (I love it!); Jane Staw for her ability to see what counts in a mess of words.

Christian de la Huerta for his wonderful example of a social monk, his calm presence and willingness to say the hard things; Andy Zimmerman for his reminder of what right work is and to remember always not to let that deep well fill with dark stuff; Daniel Killar for saying what he said at my birthday party; Felix Lutz for his sniffer and for that mellifluous voice of his; Mary O'Connor for being the redhead she is; Larry Magid for his big heart and fast mouth; Scott Benjamin for knowing where to put the alligator and being a word lover; Deidre Sommers for her bear-mama coziness and need to go deep wherever that may lead; Laura Blaszkiewicz for her sauciness and crooked finger.

Gabe Ortiz for his gentleness and softness, and Stephanie Ortiz for her wild mouth and guts to stand up to the ugly things that happen; SARK for reminding me that there are over 100 ways to change the shape of a hanger.

Deb Brancato, Dave Lechuga, Chloe and Nico, for their amazing martial-arts minds and bodies, and creative wackiness; Nana Fulgenzi for the damn stubbornness I've inherited from her, her magical greens, potatoes, and garlic, her Italianness; all my ancestors and relatives alive and dead for sharing the spirit we do; Nancy Gerber for her warm support, guidance, and ability to see what's needed now; Maggie Oman Shannon for her contemplative nature and bright eyes, and for giving me the lingam water. Dean Gamburd for his amazing teaching ability, sensitive attunement, and melancholy moods. Diana Ho for her graceful artistic ability to make beautiful art with a few rubber stamps and paper, and her zest for food and life.

All the people who helped me heal my back, my sorrows, my heart: Julia Boudakian, Dr. Sherie Viencek, Dr. Alan and Gillian Creed, Serena Smith, Jill Goldreyer, Tammy Throne, Dr. Ann Stevens, Jaymi Devans, Bronwyn Falcona, Derek Love, Dr. Barbara Berkeley, Dr. Alice Charap, Ruby Gold, Dr. Jialing Yu, Dr. Ching Chun Ou, Vega Rozenberg, and Lisa McClenahan.

Kitzi Tanner, Dan Marchant, and their boys; Mary Hubbell; Larry Tritten; Lulu Vasquez; Charlotte Welty; Tim O'Hern; Nathan Wiesenfeld; Birgit Wick; Carol Adrienne; Sue, Jim, Guy, and Dani Hager; Glen Gold; Mike McCoy; Victoria Moran; Miriam Hospodar; Kelli Fox; Susan Bremer; Jennifer Bernhart; Mary Scott; Judi and Eddie Hays; Morty and Irwin Horowitz; Rebecca Paoletti; Steve Brown; Lynn Morris and Julie Hastings, Marlene and Ron Buono; Laurie Fox; Mary Takacs; Jeff Bondy; the crew at Pacific Bell Directory.

Terry Gross for being the best interviewer alive today, for her insightful interviews on NPR's *Fresh Air,* for finding all the fascinating people who should be known even if they aren't.

All my author and spiritual mentors dead and alive. To Elana Maggal a real whippersnapper for seeing a class in an article and supporting my ideas, and the staff at the Learning Annex of San Francisco. To all the students who have attended my classes, the women and men who have come to my talks and workshops, the people and friends whom I interviewed for this book, and my clients, from whom I've learned most of what I know, I hold my candle up to you. I am grateful to all of you and to you and you, whom I haven't met, who are reading this book. I wish you a long list of people and experiences for which to be grateful.

Patti Breitman for her no-poke-holes honesty and optimism, for her gift for gab, and for making this book possible; Ayesha Pande for her thoughtful editing and heartfelt way of being in the world; Nick Darrell for his enthusiasm and patience; Megan Newman for having the faith and foresight to buy this book; HarperCollins/HarperResource for doing me the honor of publishing it. Half of my library consists of their books. I have always wanted them as my publisher. Funny how things work out.

And finally, Brett Sharenow for his love of roses, his joie de vivre, his editing and organizational wizardry and patience, his unfailing belief in me, and most of all for his love, our love. Scorpio Dog Man, you're where it's at.

Grateful appreciation is made to the following people for their time, stories, or help in creating this book:

Rose Offner, author of *Journal to the Soul; Journal to Intimacy; Journal to the Soul for Teenagers; www.roseoffner.com:roseoffner@aol.com;* (510) 538-5074

Lee Glickstein, author of *Be Heard Now! Tap into Your Inner Speaker and Communicate With Ease* (Broadway Books, 1998).

Marlene Buono for Bambi's
    Epitaph
Laurie Wagner
Victoria Moran
Dana May Casperson
Hannah Onstadt Latham/
    Peachpit Press/
    Division of Pearson education
Karen Ginsberg Wood
Hale Dwoskin/
    Sedona Training Associates
Sally Richards
Andrea Siegel
Joe Sabah
Jane Swigart
Natalie Rogers
Kelli Fox
Leslie Rossman/
    Open Book Publicity

Jenai Lane
Dottie Walters/
    Walters Speakers Services
Debbie Gisonni
Zillah Bahar
Joan Logghe
Carol Adrienne
Carmen McKay
Katherine Geller Myers
Stephen Hall Harrison
Susan RoAne
Sandra Miller
Daniel Janal
Colleen Newlin
Robert Dickman
Diane de Castro
Josepha Schiffman

*The First and Only Marketing and Publicity Book for Women
That Shows You How to Promote Yourself, Your Business,
Product, or Cause with Integrity and Spirit*

Dare to be yourself

Author Victoria Moran and I settled into my couch to review the video of her latest talk show. As we watched her interacting with the host, it was obvious that she was poised and spoke her points succinctly with great animation. But something was off. I asked her what she thought it was. "I am trying too hard," she said.

"Why?" I asked.

"Because I think I need to be bigger than life to reach my audience."

In the next hour of our media-coaching session I showed Victoria ways to make her message clear while connecting with her host and audience using her face, body, and words. She quickly learned to relax into her natural self, to "be" without trying.

The next week she called me excitedly. She had just finished taping another big talk show. At the end of the interview all the cameramen and crew stood up and applauded. What had she done differently? "I allowed myself to be me. Nothing more, nothing less," she said. "And that was enough."

My wish in writing *Sell Yourself Without Selling Your Soul* is that you will embark on your marketing and publicity program exactly as you are, nothing more, nothing less. You will also discover how to work with the skills and personality you already have to achieve the results you want.

Promote yourself whether you're eager or reluctant

When I'm speaking, I often ask the audience, "How many of you feel like doing publicity is equivalent in some way to prostituting yourself?" Two-thirds of the people raise their hands. I think that the other third is lying. Except for the unabashed extroverts, most people harbor secret fears of being seen as a flasher or a fake. This book is for those of you who believe that promoting yourself is in some way whoring, bragging, or begging.

Sell Yourself Without Selling Your Soul is filled with secrets to promote yourself, your business, book, product, or your cause with integrity and spirit. It shows you that you don't need to compromise your values, go beyond your boundaries, or change yourself in some fundamental way to get what you want. For those eager or reluctant this book will give you specific ways to make any publicity and marketing campaign simple, manageable, attainable, pleasurable . . . and fun.

What this book can do for you

Once you complete the process outlined in this book, you will feel secure and ready to launch whatever you are promoting. You will find out how you can effortlessly honor your self-set limits and maximize your positive qualities.

In this book you will learn how to

1. Be yourself.

2. Know your message.

3. Practice presenting your points.

4. Remain true to yourself.

5. Become the message you want to give.

6. Persevere.

These are the six main areas that are of utmost importance to women.

Be great without cheating

Perhaps I came to my job as a media coach and marketing consultant to balance my need for deep inner reflection and outward expression. For over a decade I have faced my own ambivalence about promoting others. However, not until I began promoting myself did those feelings become truly personal. This book began a serious exploration of what it means to move from the comfort of private person to the unknown territory of public personality.

In my twenties I believed I needed to train myself out of my more thoughtful nature into someone more outgoing. I took jobs that demanded extroversion. The first job I sought was in sales. My manager took me aside one day and told me that I'd never be a truly great salesperson because I didn't have enough larceny in my heart. That phrase haunted me for a long time because I wanted to be great, but I didn't want to cheat to get there.

Most women don't want to cheat to get where they want to go.

Why this book is different

When I tell women that this book isn't like other sales, marketing, and publicity books that sometimes use duplicitous means and industry jargon along with sex, sports, or war metaphors to express how they are supposed to accomplish their goals, they let out a little cheer. Phrases like "crush the competition," "attack your workload," "batten down the hatches," "penetrate," "nail them," "put out," and "beat them to a pulp" offend me. You may feel the same way.

What I am offering you on the following pages is a book that is free of that kind of language. I believe that by changing the way we speak, we change our patterns of thought, actions, and results. Our words carry our intentions.

There are already many good books on publicity and marketing that tell you how to get something cheap, for free, or for a small fee. They tell you about tricks, techniques, and shortcuts to help you scramble your way to the top.

But there is another way.

This book will show you how you can use the strategies of professional publicists and marketing experts by practicing principles that embody deep inner reflection, honesty, business smarts, and artistic beauty—while gracefully gliding to the top. In return you will receive fame and fortune—however you define that. Not liking the traditional description, author Rose Offner created her own credo for success: "It is to be able to make a difference in the world through your art, your gift, your presence, spirit, or words. It is the ability to walk your talk."

In walking their talk one of the most important things to most women is to promote community not consumerism. We want to build meaningful relationships based on respect, trust, and equity. Publicity and marketing are all about building relationships. When I first conceived of this book, I had this notion in mind. I specifically sought out examples of people who were using their gifts to add vitality to the lives of others. Following that initial impulse, I have carefully chosen the people and resources in this book for their special appeal and interest to women. These are the people who are asking the question "How can I be of use?" instead of "How can I use?"

Be the change you want to see in the world

Gandhi is a good example of how to accomplish this wish. Famous for saying, "My life is my message," he was a true manifestation of his teaching. For me, my daily practice is living a life that is my message. I say "practice" because I so often fail. Yet, I will continue to practice every day, over and over again, and you can, too. Becoming the message you want to give, integrating your life, work, and being, is the kind of "marketing" that is at the heart of this book.

For the past thirteen years I have used Gandhi's practice as my guide for working with people in many different professions, including executives, best-selling authors, and successful entrepreneurs in many different fields and elite e-businesses. I have media-coached people who have appeared on *60 Minutes, Oprah*, E! The Entertainment Channel, CBS, NBC, CNN, and many others. My clients have been reviewed and interviewed in the top national radio and TV shows and publications in the United States.

In addition I have interviewed thousands of potential salespeople for corporations and assessed them for skills necessary to do the job. I bring to you the knowledge and experience I have gained from working with many talented and wise clients.

My promise to you is that I have given all that I can at this moment, nothing held back. You have in your hands the pages that contain profiles of men and women who are employed by corporations, own their own businesses, work as free agents, or play at a hobby. All of them have implemented the strategies I have outlined in this book. By reading about them you'll benefit from their mistakes and victories.

You'll also discover prototypes of modern-day authors, artists, entrepreneurs, speakers, and corporate business people who have made some contribution to the betterment of society with their information, products, or presence. They are regular people like you and me.

In addition I have included stories of famous and ingenious historical and political figures, artists, actors, spiritual masters, and saints whose fascinating tales will help you discover your own hidden talents. You can look forward to doing the same once you've finished following the principles outlined in this book.

How to make the most of this book

In the pages that follow you will find

- Suggestions of things to think about or do, designed to encourage insights.
- *Invitations* or exercises that give you step-by-step instructions to put you into action. (Note: While you don't need to complete all the invitations if you don't feel inclined, you'll move forward faster if you do. Read with a pen in hand [unless you've borrowed this from the library] to make notes in the margins and to underline the things that are important to you. Go at your own pace, relax, and enjoy the process.)

- **HOT TIP!** Bonuses. Insider secrets to explore within various chapters that will help spark new ideas.

- Signs to alert you to dangers particular to women.

They will help you avoid common mistakes and save you time and grief.

- A resource section at the back of the book with contact information for people, organizations, books, products, and Web sites, to help you access knowledge and people who will speak to you. (To make it simple the Harrow Kiss of Approval appears whenever I personally endorse a product, person, or cause.)

- Please note that throughout the book I've used the pronoun "he" instead of "she" or "he/she" for clarity when referring to members of the media. This was a decision made after long pondering and based purely on practicality and ease of use for you.

What you can expect after experiencing this book

By the end of this book you will have the tools to get your message out under any circumstance or condition. You will have learned how to be flexible and go with the flow.

As you incorporate these strategies into your life, you'll feel better—happier and more centered. You'll find that you're more connected to who you really are and you'll know what matters most to you.

And then something surprising will happen. You'll begin to draw the right opportunities and people to you; the publications and shows you want to be a part of will materialize. Dramatic shifts will happen in your personal and professional life. Sometimes beyond anything you ever imagined.

What I learned studying with spiritual masters over twenty years ago is that everything flows through compassion and generosity of spirit. By focusing on the value of giving you will receive what you want and need. Whether you are an introvert or an extrovert, a performer or a monk, someone who won't leave the house without a hat, or someone who won't leave the house at all, I invite you to join me in sharing your delightful innate talents with the world at large.

Cellist and humanist Pablo Casals said, "It takes courage for a person to listen to their own goodness and act on it. Do we dare be ourselves? This is the question that counts." Together we'll explore how you can promote whatever it is you desire by daring to be yourself without selling your soul.

No matter what you have to give, the world is waiting. It is my wish that you live your life by doing all that you have come here to do. The experiences we will explore together in the following pages will make a big space for your wild, generous spirit. I offer you my hand for whatever this dance may become.

PART I

Achieve Your Goals and Dreams with Publicity

~~~ ~~~ ~~~

Understand What Publicity Is and What It Can Give You

L ast week I got a call from a woman who said, "I had one taste of publicity and I want more. One article in the newspaper got me more clients than I've ever had before in my entire career. Can you help me?" My phone rings all day long. My voice mail box is full of messages from people who have no idea what publicity is or how it works, but who know they want some.

What is publicity and how can you enjoy some of your own? Publicity happens when a person from the media writes about whatever you are promoting in a publication or on the Internet, or interviews you for radio or TV. Sometimes they find out about you on their own. Most of the time you have sent them a press release or a one-page description of why whatever you are promoting is newsworthy right now. (More about how to write press materials in chapter 4.)

They choose to profile you, your business, book, product, or cause because it in some way serves their audience. If their audience finds value in what you do, say, are, or have, they will do any number of things: hire you for your service, buy your product, support your cause, or tell others about you. In addition other media people will find you relevant to their audiences, and your publicity ball will begin rolling.

Publicity is a powerful means to get your message into the public eye. You never know how it is going to affect you or your career or what form it may take. Whether you are looking for credibility, prestige, recognition, fame, fortune, health, harmony, or happiness, follow the guidelines in this book and you will find your measure. Here are a few ways that publicity can give you what you want and make your career and your life an adventure.

Publicity markets your services more effectively than advertising or your parents

Your parents love you. They think you are the best thing that ever walked this earth. And they're right. They're also biased. And everyone knows that. So when they say great things about you to anyone who will listen, those people's eyes tend to get that opaque and uninterested glaze. A similar thing happens when an audience reads or sees advertisements. Even when someone is looking for a specific product or service, they know that anyone who has the money can purchase a showcase for whatever they sell. Advertisers buy space to plug their products. All they need is money to get their names in a magazine or newspaper. That is their bias. "For advertising you pay; for publicity you pray," says veteran publicist Alyson Dutch, whose client accounts include *The Lion King*.

After all those prayers, planning, and promotion, when a journalist writes a story about you, your business, book, product, or cause, you are already one step ahead of those people who choose advertising. Why? You have literally and symbolically passed through a gate-keeper—the editor or producer who has judged that you have something of value for his audience.

Publicity gives you instant credibility

On one level people perceive the journalist or producer as an unbiased source of information. Even though, as a reader or a member of an audience, you know this isn't true, some part of you still believes it. The person who is included in an article or is on a radio or TV show has passed through a journalist's or producer's screen. We credit the media with knowing a good story when they see one. You can't buy the kind of prestige that puts you on the front page of a major newspaper.

You get instant credibility because a publication or show believes that you deserve attention. Once you get that attention, it can lead to many surprising places, as it did for one of my very first clients, Missy Park, president of Title 9 Sports in Berkeley, California. Over ten years ago Missy was running her catalog business with a single employee out of one room stuffed with sports clothing for women. We were developing a campaign on Missy's core audience by focusing on women's sports magazines as well as consumer publications.

We decided that her hometown newspaper would also be interested in her growing success. After we sent the *Greensboro Times* our press release, they ran a story. That article was syndicated to dozens of newspapers all across the country, which resulted in over $20,000 in sales in a few weeks. That is a lot of sports bras and socks! Today Missy has over 100 employees and a retail store and is the fifth-largest sports bra retailer in the country.

Publicity sells your products for you

Since 1995 Girl Tech, a company that makes technical toys for girls, has relied on media attention to help sell their line of products. Their lead item, Password Journal, became a number-one-selling hit in the youth electronics category the year it was released, resulting from founder Janese Swanson's dozens of TV and radio appearances and feature articles written about her and her company. "We couldn't have made the effect in society or change in perceptions without the help of the written and spoken word in public," she notes.

In addition to helping her sell her products, publicity gave her the means to rise up from poverty to plenty, and to share her wealth and knowledge. Forty-two-year-old Janese grew up so poor that at times during her childhood her family lived in the back of a truck and didn't have enough to eat. Today she has reaped the rewards of selling her company to toy giant Radica Games, Ltd. She has bought her mom a house, has bought her family homes, and continues to remain active in bringing awareness that girls have technical talent just like boys.

Publicity encourages customers or clients to give you ideas for products, services, or books they want you to develop

Steven Covey wrote his second big-selling book, *First Things First,* as a result of public demand based on feedback he received from people who were having trouble with the time management portion of his first book, *The Seven Habits of Highly Effective People.* Covey expanded one chapter into an entire book.

Rose Offner, author of *Journal to the Soul: The Art of Sacred Journal Keeping,* a gorgeously lavish place to write innermost thoughts, developed this illustrated book after students begged her for years to put her classes into a tangible form.

Trend analyst Faith Popcorn solicits opinions from her Web site visitors on the latest trends for marketing to women. What a great way to keep your finger on the pulse of public opinion. Ask for it.

HOT TIP!

START A TREND BANK.

Gather others' opinions to generate ideas. Their fresh views will help broaden your own ideas and angles. If you have a Web site, ask for visitors' comments on subjects related to whatever you are promoting. You can conduct your own polls, support your findings with statistics and research, and then use that information in your next press release. You will be able to find out fast what potential or existing customers love or see as lacking. You might consider rewarding them for their thoughts with a contest. People adore winning prizes.

Publicity distinguishes you from your competition

Founder of the Shabby Chic stores and line of furnishings, retailer Rachel Ashwell says, "Because I am on TV, people ask for my autograph at the flea market." Whenever your name appears in print, or someone sees or hears you on TV or the radio, people believe you are either famous already or will be soon. You have one thing that your competition doesn't—public awareness. When your customers are ready to buy, they are more likely to buy from you. They *perceive* that you are a notch above the people who have not yet made it to the media.

Publicity gives potential clients a chance to trust you

Some people need a testing period before they'll approach you for business. Consider publicity a referral service. Audiences trust the media they listen to, watch, or read regularly. Before customers call you, or check out your Web site, or ask you for a packet of information, they can discover a bit about who you are through an interview they've seen, read, or heard. Though they may have heard about you or be familiar with your work, they get a look at you up close and personal—from a safe distance. The media lets people who are considering doing business with you remain anonymous until they're ready to hire you.

Reading an article on the Internet or in print, hearing you on the radio, or seeing you on TV often prompts people to take action. But it may not happen the first or even fifth time a potential customer notices you. A marketing rule of thumb is that your potential clients or buyers often need to get seven "impressions" before they'll buy. This means they need to see, hear, or read about you consistently in the media seven times before they register that they need what you have.

Potential buyers and clients are waiting to find you. Give them the incentive to connect with you by making it easy. Put your name out in the public domain every chance you get. Once you reach the "seven times" mark, notice how many responses you receive.

Publicity helps you be perceived as an expert

Once you get media exposure, you start to be perceived as someone who knows what you are talking about. I was on a panel discussion about book promotion that aired on C-SPAN (at strange hours of the night) nationwide. Who watches C-SPAN anyway? A lot more people than insomniacs and shut-ins. You would probably be as surprised as I was when people from all over the country began calling and e-mailing me to inquire about my services. Among them was my old college heartthrob, Mike McCoy, who wrote to congratulate me on how "successful" I was. People assume you know what you are talking about if you are on TV.

When I publicized Larry Magid's *The Little PC Book*, in 1993, many radio stations didn't want to do an interview that had anything to do with computers. It is a different world now. At that time twelve-year-old Polly Klaas had just been kidnapped from her home in Petaluma, California. Hers was a national story that gained attention for its poignancy and strangeness. One day Larry was driving in his car when he heard about Polly on the radio. He realized that this kind of incident could happen to his own children and he began to cry. Through his tears he wondered what he could do to help. He came up with the idea to put the kidnapper's picture (drawing or rendering from the description) on a special Internet site along with a picture of the missing child. His example was immediately adopted by others and has since expanded into a nationwide system for helping to find missing children and their abductors.

Larry was written up in *Time* magazine as "a high-tech hero." Because the story tapped into parents' fear for the well-being of their children, I was able to book Larry on dozens of radio and TV shows to talk about child safety on the Internet. Of course, every time he was being interviewed, his book was mentioned, which helped move it to the best-seller list.

Larry then offered to write a safety brochure for the National Center for Missing and Exploited Children, for which he later won the Ten-Year Anniversary Award for his work in helping develop a system for finding missing children via on-line services. Anytime there was a call for an expert on child safety, producers called me to book Larry. As his expertise blossomed, so did his recognition. His reputation shifted from just high-tech or computer expert to the leading authority on Internet safety for children and teens.

Publicity raises your professional profile exponentially

Walter Winchell said social position is "more a matter of press than prestige." Those of you not born into prestige can have it through media coverage. That said, many prominent professional organizations and associations require you to have gained media publicity to join. They want to be assured a certain stature of individual before admitting you to their exclusive club. Think of it like this: Doctors who want to receive increased recognition in their fields must publish their findings in medical journals. University professors need to write textbooks and publish articles to gain tenure. In order to be held in high esteem you need to show that you are an active public figure. Publicity affords you that status.

Publicity makes it possible to get grants

My brother, Joshua Horowitz, found it nearly impossible to get his first grant. At the time, he was a struggling musician with a small word-of-mouth following. Once he got his first grant, he was able to get substantial press for his research to preserve rare klezmer music throughout the world. With the publicity he received, he found that it was simpler to get additional grants. To date he has received over forty grants worth more than $150,000 and has become quite an expert in both grant writing and getting press for his Austrian-based klezmer group, Budowitz.

The publicity he received throughout Europe, a glowing review from the *Wall Street Journal,* not only gave him the credibility and clout to get more prestigious grants, but also got him invited to play for thousands at major concert halls, including the Berlin Philharmonie. He has now been invited to give lectures, workshops, concerts, and media interviews on an ongoing basis because he is regarded as an international creative figure.

Publicity gives you personal prestige

Joan Logghe has been dubbed the "Poet Laureate of New Mexico" by the press. Winner of a coveted National Endowment for the Arts grant, Logghe is celebrated in her community. Joan says, "I think the main thing publicity has given me is credibility. I know what kind of job I can do, my family knows, but since I don't have papers, an MFA, or a pedigree, this has made my work manifest in the world." One article called her "poet mom" for her exquisite balance of work and home.

Joan already has "personal" prestige. That is something that can never be measured in talk shows or articles. Her life and work are a blend of richness that she shares with the poignancy of a Diva Terra—mixture of opera star and earth mother.

Publicity galvanizes public support for your community or cause

Carmen McKay, president of Corporate Comedy, an organization that brings humor to corporate events and trade shows, tells this story.

> After attending your workshop, I became inspired to try something creative to get press. Since I am in the industrial entertainment field,

I decided to send a press release for National Fun at Work Day on April 6. I took those fake peanut cans with paper snakes that jump out and filled them with candy and the press release that linked my business with the fun holiday.

First, the *San Jose Business Journal* did a big feature story on me. The next month I developed a project to put homeless women on-stage to tell their stories. The event, sponsored by my own company, supported my vision of using humor to transform communities as well as corporations.

Four hundred people attended the one-evening event, which raised $20,000 for a local homeless shelter. The connections and reputation I created from the event keep on growing. The shelter nominated me for a philanthropic award in San Jose for the project, which I won. My picture and an article will be in the *San Jose Business Journal* again. The shelter plans to send the video of the event to Oprah for the "Angels" feature of her show.

The biggest rewards are in the heart, of course. The women involved in the show have moved on to jobs and homes. It was a transformative experience for them. The shelter's organizing executives found new life for their vision, and their entire organization experienced a new vitality.

I have attracted some funding and am producing the show again soon, professionally this time. I get e-mails from strangers on the East Coast asking me if it will go on the road. Articles about the show were written up in several offbeat magazines that I keep hearing about. People from shelters in other cities have asked me to give them the model so they can produce shows like this for fund-raising.

Publicity for causes gains you goodwill within your community and can make changes that you could never possibly predict.

HOT TIP!

SUPPORT A CHARITY WHOSE VISION SUPPORTS YOUR OWN, OR CREATE AN EVENT TO BRING AWARENESS TO YOUR FAVORITE CAUSE.

Publicity opens up all sorts of opportunities

My agent, Patti Breitman, says that most of the time she finds her clients—they don't find her. This doesn't mean she doesn't get hundreds of unsolicited calls and manuscripts every year. It means that she finds whom she wants to work with and lets them know she's willing to represent them. When I first met Patti, she politely but firmly said she wasn't taking on any new clients. That was the end of that . . . for the moment.

A number of months later I was invited to speak to the Authors Guild in San Francisco about how to create a wildly successful book, without selling your soul. Right after my talk Patti approached me and said she loved my philosophy of generosity combined with practicality. She told me that she was interested in seeing the book I'd mentioned I was working on (still merely an embryonic inkling), which gave me the incentive to write the proposal. That is the story of how she became my agent and how it came to be that you are reading this book.

Publicity begets publicity

Once you have been a radio, TV, or Internet "chat" guest, it is much easier to convince other producers to host you as a guest. Why? I call it the "believability factor." Once one producer sees that another producer has given you the green light, he believes you are "show worthy" or "mediagenic." The media world is really like a small town where everyone knows everyone else's business. Producers are in the business of talking. And they talk to one another just as fluidly as they talk on the air. Once you've been a great guest on one show, you have the credentials to get on another show.

As you become a more seasoned on-air guest, producers will invite you to their shows as a regular and you will have a venue to expound on your informational virtues. And if you are really, really great, you may be offered your own show. If you are golden-tongued and you appear professional in your manner and attire, you can gain the attention of seminar sponsors or meeting planners and be offered speaking engagements at conferences, corporations, organizations, and universities.

In print people "hear" your voice on paper, which results in publicity of a different kind. When I needed relationship experts for an article I was writing for *Bride's* magazine on the topic "Are You Moral Misfits?

When Love and Honor Clash," where did I look? In articles that already quoted psychologists and relationship therapists. I noticed who had written books, and who hadn't, whom I'd heard of before, and who had been quoted or invited on radio and TV shows. In other words I searched for men and women who had a proven track record and impressive credentials, and who had already said some fascinating things. I called them to get their opinions for my article. Producers and reporters will do the same when it comes to you.

Publicity can diminish stereotypes by disseminating accurate information

Anyone who feels they, their profession, their gender, or their race has been wronged in some way is entitled to send out information to contradict the prevailing stereotype. I recall reading an article about Broadway singing star Audra McDonald thinking that she was a remarkable woman, accomplished, driven, and relentlessly cheerful. Relentlessly cheerful to me meant that something was desperately wrong. Nobody can sustain such pep without some dip in moods.

Everything I'd read about Audra had me liking her except this excessive zest. I confess that I was both saddened and on some level relieved to read that she had tried to commit suicide. She's human! Thank God. Not only did she prove my theory that relentless cheer has its downside, but she dispelled my belief that her life was a lighthearted lark, and that everything came easily as she galloped toward perfection, winning Tonys, marrying for true love, and following a career trajectory toward the heavens.

Publicity will encourage you to get real

"Some people wanted to get rich or famous, but my friends and I wanted to get real. We wanted to get deep," said writer Anne Lamott of her college days. Embarking on a marketing and publicity plan will allow you to get deep, to get real, if you will allow it.

Doing publicity says that you are willing and able to face public scrutiny. That you have the confidence and ability to withstand the judgment of others no matter how harsh. You have guts. Publicity encourages a willingness to do whatever it takes. Whatever you are open to learning will find you, if you let it.

Publicity can help you have fun

In her book, *Publicity Stunt,* literary agent Candice Fuhrman tells of the wild and extravagant lengths people have gone to to publicize their whatever. This book goes back into history to take a look at how people have positioned themselves or their products in the public eye. Look for your own wild and wacky ways to move along your publicity path. "Experience is not what happens to you; it is what you do with what happens to you," noted Aldous Huxley. Whether you are promoting a product or person, protesting an injustice, or supporting an idealistic idea or cause, learn not to take yourself so seriously and have a little fun with your experiences.

~ ~ ~ ~

PART II

Begin a Publicity Campaign

CHAPTER 2

Develop a Marketing and Publicity Plan

Before you begin to write your press materials, you will want to assess your desires and motivation for doing a marketing and publicity campaign. For those of you doing a onetime event this process will be fast and straightforward. For others who are promoting a product or service that is intrinsic to your business, book, presence, or cause, more thought and consideration are necessary.

The first thing is to set your objectives. You need to know what outcome you want from your publicity. You don't just want to get publicity for its own sake. Publicity takes on a life of its own, so you want to make sure you are shaping the plan accordingly. That way when you get more publicity, you will know how to structure your key messages and will have the outline of a plan. Following the eleven steps below will give you a map to arrive at your destination, the procedures to plan a safe trip, and a handle on keeping potential snafus at bay.

Evaluate your desires, motivation, and time

Step 1. Determine the results you want from your publicity efforts, then rank them in order of importance.

Why are you marketing yourself, your services, your project, or your business in the first place? Once you know your desires and priorities, you can focus your plan accordingly. Architects & Heroes, a hair salon and art gallery in San Francisco, used many of the articles written about them in prominent beauty magazines to enhance their prestige and develop national recognition.

They attractively displayed clippings from articles written about them at the front desk and in the dressing rooms, where all the existing and potential clients could see them. When the owner decided to sell his business, he presented the extensive press to investors in order to increase the value of his company. The prestige, famous clients, and clientele attracted from all over the country translated into the perception of higher worth. In addition the nationwide media attention I got for them showed that they were a leader in their field, which was then reflected in the selling price.

Invitation

Publicity can give you all kinds of things you may never have even imagined. It opens the door for you to make important connections, expand your business, become a valued resource, and much more. Think about which of the advantages in this chapter are important to you. I invite you to list them in the order of importance and to post that list nearby for when you are ready to begin your campaign. Deciding what is most cherished to you will help you focus on what it is that you really want.

Number the following in order of importance:
____Be perceived as an expert.
____Raise my professional profile.
____Distinguish me from my competition.
____Acquire professional prestige.
____Acquire personal prestige.
____Gain credibility.
____Sell more products.
____Get more clients or customers.
____Find ideas for products, books, or services.
____Galvanize support for my community or cause.

____Get grants, funding, donors.

____Open up new opportunities.

____Create a consciousness shift.

____Diminish stereotypes.

____Encourage me to get more real.

____Help me have more fun.

My top five reasons for doing publicity:

1. _____

2. _____

3. _____

4. _____

5. _____

Step 2. Recognize your (self-) management style.

When textile artist and accomplished aikido practitioner Andrea Siegel sat down to write her book *Open and Clothed,* she realized that she had internalized all the worst values and traits of her bosses. She set herself up on an impossible writing schedule of eight hours a day with a half-hour lunch. For two weeks she browbeat herself by allowing only scant bathroom breaks and a meager lunch hour.

"I was miserable," she says. "I asked myself what would make me happy. At first I didn't even know. Then I heard one request. A two-hour lunch. With enormous fear I began taking a two-hour lunch and my productivity soared. I'd eat for maybe fifteen minutes, take time out to go to a thrift store, and score a Chanel shirt for fourteen dollars. I wrote a three hundred page book in nine months and had a great time doing it."

⌒ *Invitation* ⌒

Ask yourself these four questions:

1. What kind of schedule would make me happy?
2. Am I being reasonable?
3. Would I ask the same of a person I was managing?
4. Is this is a schedule I can adhere to for a sustained period of time?

Step 3. Understand your working style.

When I worked with one of my very favorite clients, Larry Magid, we'd brainstorm every day for news angles. Then I'd pick up the phone and make calls so he could be interviewed at a moment's notice. Today he is the national CBS News computer expert and is on call twenty-four hours a day—which makes his life very interesting. Larry loves the spontaneous interchange and the freshness of news and knowledge commingling in the moment. It is natural for him to "wing" it. In fact, he feels hindered if he overprepares. This is a part of his personality that he's honed over several decades. He also knows his subject so deeply that he can address an issue he's researched and contemplated with ease. The key is to set up your plan in accordance with your working habits rather than to try to fit your working habits into your plan.

~ *Invitation* ~

Get a handle on your working style by asking yourself a few questions:

1. Do I learn best at the last minute, spontaneously, or do I need time to think and prepare?
2. Am I the kind of person who likes to see big, fast results to know something is working, or am I satisfied when something small but significant happens?
3. Do I prefer to work intensely for a short time instead of more leisurely for a long while?
4. Do I jump up and take action when the inspiration strikes me, or do I like to stay with a well-ordered plan?
5. Do I thrive when I am on call, ready for anything at a moment's notice, or do I want a schedule filled in advance?

Step 4. Set your priorities.

Consider how much time per day, week, month, you are willing to commit. Have you thought about taking time off work to focus solely on publicity for an intense spurt of time? If you take publicity as a practice, you can deepen your experience by a daily regimen.

It is important to commit to a program that you can sustain. Even if you make calls or practice speaking your message 15 minutes a day, you can make significant progress. Fifteen minutes a day is 2½ hours a week, 10 hours a month, 120 hours a year—the equivalent of 3 months.

Painter Paul Gauguin gave the advice, "Go on working freely and furiously, and you will make progress." Whether it is for fifteen minutes a day or five hours, it is important to make the space for the free and furious times so you don't miss the true opportunities.

∼ *Invitation* ∼

To determine your time frame take a look at what kind of person you are:

1. Are you a "do a little something daily" kind of person?
2. Do you want a flurry of activity full force 24/7 for a designated period of time and then a resumption of your regular life?
3. Are you an in-betweener who wants to go slow and steady, like a pot of baked beans, cooking for hours so all the flavors can get absorbed?

Step 5. Decide the length of your campaign.

You will want to set a limit on how long you are willing to work on your campaign—several months, years, periodically at set intervals, or consistent and ongoing.

For example, if you are promoting a book, your campaign will last a minimum of three to six months. You will want to begin about six to eight months before the book's publication date.

If you are planning an event for a cause, your campaign might last only one month. But there are other things to consider. You will need to begin it at least three months before the event because of competition for radio public service announcements (PSAs). If you want to get coverage in local magazines, their lead time is also about three months.

For a product or service with no pending event or release date you might decide to develop an ongoing campaign that coincides with newsworthy topics over the course of a year. Consider the changing of the seasons and the holidays as "deadlines" to publicize something significant about whatever you are marketing.

Step 6. Name the regions you want to target.
  Local: Your town, city, and surrounding areas.
  Regional: Your state or other states.
  National: The entire country.
  International: The world.

If your local or hometown papers are your intended market, then there is more latitude as to what makes "news." Smaller newspapers and radio stations will accept items that more prestigious companies would toss in the trash. I suggest that even if you are presenting your new store opening as an event someone should care about, it is still up to you to figure out what impact it will have on the people and community you are serving. In most small business papers there is a place for announcing promotion, new hires, awards, or some other movement within a company that the community might find of interest. Likewise, if your company posted record profits for your industry, or you received significant funding, you might get mentioned.

Is your company offering some new service or program that impacts the population at large? Do you have a new product release or a new version of an existing product that changes the face of your industry? If so, then a national or an international scope may be more viable for you than simply local or regional interest.

Step 7. Know your core audience.
  Consumers—the population at large. Consumers consist of people who may or may not be familiar with your industry or business, but who would be the end buyers interested in purchasing your products or using your service.

  For example: If you are selling a toy, you would want to reach publications and shows that appeal to parents. If you are a consultant for executives, you would want to reach CEOs and other C-level (CFO, CIO, COO) executives. Consider the publications and shows these people would read and attend.

  Trade—your specific industry. People "in the trade" consist of your competitors and people who work within your specific type of business.

  Define your core audience by specific industries, interests, and needs and you will be well received. Think through your market before you begin dashing off your materials in a helter-skelter fashion. Knowing your audience will be critical to determining who you send your information to and how well they will respond.

~ *Invitation* ~

Whose lives would be improved by using your product or service?
1. Who *needs* your product or service now?
2. Why can't they get your knowledge or product elsewhere?
3. What do you do best?
4. What proof do you have that clearly shows there is a market for what you have?
5. What statistics can you use to back up the above assumptions and support your findings?

Step 8. Narrow your niches.

Take a serious assessment of the marketplace, then narrow your niches. I know that many of you will want to include all the major markets—the top fifty newspapers, the top shows, the top this, and the top that.

I'd suggest that you start with your local press and build from there before you do any kind of mass mailing to the big guys. Unless you have a newsbreaking story that can't wait, preparation will save you lots of money on Tums, and everyone around you will be thankful for it and praise you for your foresight.

Andrea Siegel has foresight. When she finished her second book, she headed to the library, read Bacon's and Ulrich's (databases for media contacts), and made a list of 168 editors and journalists she wanted to review or feature her book. Since her major target market was in New York City, she narrowed her niche to fashion editors in women's and fashion publications in her hometown of Manhattan. She then simplified her campaign by hand-delivering her books and press packets personally to everyone. Her mom even volunteered to chauffeur her around to speed up the process. She saved herself time, money, and aggravation by spending the time to thoughtfully plan her true audience.

Step 9. Select the media you want to include.

- Print: Newspapers, magazines, alternative weeklies, newsletters.

- Radio: Local, national, syndicated, news, talk, (Morning Zoo).

- TV: Local, cable, national.

- Internet: Chats, newsletters, listserves, on-line radio and TV "shows" (streaming video).

Circle all or one, or any combination, depending on your desires and abilities you will later determine in chapter 3.

Step 10. Choose the right method to contact the media you want.

Managing a database can be a mighty task given that most contain many thousands of contacts and dozens of categories and types of publications. Even choosing a database can be overwhelming. You can use a skilled publicist to help you tailor a database to your specific needs. Many publicists specialize in particular niche markets, so when you buy one of their databases, you are more likely to get one that is up to date. You have a number of options. You can

- *Buy a complete database.*

    A database lists the names, titles, phone and fax numbers, and addresses, as well as other vital information on, editors and producers of publications and shows. The information is laid out on a disk or CD-ROM in a format that translates to commonly used programs that help you manage all the contacts. Realize that the size of these databases is more than monolithic. We're talking over 20,000 contacts in over 60 categories. You track and manage your calls.

- *Buy a partial database.*

    Purchase only the database information or list that matches the market you want to reach.

- *Use a newswire service.*

    A newswire service faxes or e-mails your press release to producers and editors at publications and TV and radio shows who subscribe to their service. They also post your press release on their Web site.

- *Subscribe to a newswire service.*

    You pay a subscription fee and receive daily e-mail postings from journalists with requests for experts and information on stories they're developing.

    (More about this in chapter 14.)

- *Take out an ad in* Radio-TV Interview Report *or* The Yearbook of Experts, Authorities and Spokespersons.

    You pay for ad insertions in these publications (the number of times your ad appears), which are sent out a number of times per year to editors, producers, and speaking coordinators, who can then contact you if they're interested.

- *Take out an ad in Guestfinder.com.*

    You pay for an ad that is posted on the Guestfinder.com Web site. Editors, producers, and speaking coordinators contact you if they're interested.

- *Hire an on-line publicist.*

    An on-line publicist will write, fax, and/or e-mail your press release to a selected list of contacts much like a newswire service does. Some will handle a small, very focused list and make follow-up calls. Others do not follow up with calls unless you pay additional fees.

- *Work with an experienced publicist.*

    An experienced publicist will develop the appropriate market, create your press release, and send it out to a targeted list for you with or without follow-up calls. Reputable publicists have relationships with the media who want and accept their calls. They will usually charge you a monthly retainer ranging from $1,000 to $10,000, with a three- to six-month minimum. Others base their fees according to "campaign," e.g., a city-by-city tour or a radio-only campaign.

- *Employ a combination of the above suggestions.*

    (See Resources for the companies and people who provide these products and services.)

If you want to send your press materials to only a small mailing list, you can create your own personal database by collecting the names of editors at newspapers and magazines and of producers at radio and TV stations, or buy a hard-copy book of contacts. Better yet you can play it smart by going to a media agency in your local area that has already collected a solid list for your city and the surrounding towns. Many chambers of commerce publish these lists for a reasonable fee as well.

Step 11. Identify the type of press you want.

- Features:

    Features are full-length articles on one subject. They may include one or many experts to substantiate or illuminate a topic.

- Columns:

    Columns are short daily, weekly, or monthly articles written by established journalists. Newspapers and magazines have regular columnists who cover a certain topic or "beat": health, finance, dating, work and life balance. Columnists have a style and slant all their own and have clear interests they cover.

- Syndicates:

    Syndicates are the companies who license the "property" or articles and make them available to the publications interested in paying for regularly running material. Many columns are syndicated, or sold to other publications from the original one.

- Serious commentary or scholarly reviews:

    Commentary and reviews are heavily researched or highly opinionated articles found mainly in intellectual or academic journals. They cover timely topics, thought-provoking pieces considering both sides of an issue, or pieces geared specifically toward their audiences' interests.

- Roundups:

    Roundups are articles that review a number of products or services for one type of thing, say, women-friendly aikido classes, the best cup of coffee for under two dollars, the most romantic Valentine's Day presents that aren't chocolate. Roundups are especially popular around holidays and special events.

- Product or book reviews:

  Reviews focus on the advantages and disadvantages of a product or book. They summarize the features and benefits by explaining their own personal experience or that of others to support their findings. Based on their conclusions they slant their information to influence you to either buy or stay away from the product or book.

While you may prefer a feature article over a teeny little mention at the back of some scholarly journal, keep in mind that many small mentions add up. And you'd be surprised to find out how many people find that eensy bit of information tucked in between major news, especially if you are lucky enough to be picked up by a syndication service.

～ *Invitation* ～

Contemplate the consequences of getting "placed" in the publicity outlets you seek:

1. If you have a serious subject, will you be offended if the press presents it in a humorous or light way?
2. Will it enhance or harm your image?
3. Carefully consider the presentation, style, and subject matter the press person covers *before* you send in your materials.

～ *Invitation* ～

Summarize by referring back to the steps and transferring your answers from the invitations in this chapter to this and the following pages. You'll be able to see the total pattern of your style and the kind of plan that works best with your personality, motivation level, and schedule.

The results I want are

1. _____
2. _____
3. _____

4. _____

5. _____

I'm the kind of boss who

1. Sets a daily schedule of_____hours.
2. Sets a weekly schedule of_____hours.
3. Sets a monthly schedule of_____hours.
4. Sets a yearly schedule of_____hours.
5. Sets a onetime flurry of_____for_____ days.
6. Sets a seasonal/holiday schedule of_____seasons/holidays per year.

I like to

1. ❑ Prepare. ❑ Act last minute. ❑ Act spontaneously.
2. ❑ See small and significant results. ❑ See fast results.
3. ❑ Work intensely for a short time. ❑ Work leisurely longer.
4. ❑ Stay with a well-ordered plan. ❑ Work when the inspiration strikes.
5. ❑ Thrive on a schedule planned in advance. ❑ Thrive on last-minute opportunities.

The length of my campaign will be

❑ 1 month.
❑ 3 months.
❑ 6 months.
❑ 9 months.
❑ 1 year.

The regions I want to target are

Cities	States	Countries
_____	_____	_____
_____	_____	_____
_____	_____	_____
_____	_____	_____
_____	_____	_____
_____	_____	_____
_____	_____	_____

Cities	States	Countries
_____	_____	_____
_____	_____	_____

The top ten publications, shows, and Web sites I plan to contact are

Print	Radio	TV	Internet
_____	_____	_____	_____
_____	_____	_____	_____
_____	_____	_____	_____
_____	_____	_____	_____
_____	_____	_____	_____
_____	_____	_____	_____
_____	_____	_____	_____
_____	_____	_____	_____
_____	_____	_____	_____
_____	_____	_____	_____

The type of press I want is
❑ Features.
❑ Columns.
❑ Syndicates.
❑ Serious commentary or scholarly reviews.
❑ Roundups.
❑ Product or book reviews.

Since all of your decisions will be as individual as the products you are promoting, much depends on your personal dedication to making your product or project a success. Once you have established your reason for doing publicity, the market and the media you want to include, the type of press you want, and the time and effort you are willing to commit, you can set the foundation to build a powerful package on paper. Which is what we'll do next.

CHAPTER 3

Set the Foundation for Your Plan

There is something I can't wait until chapter 16 to tell you. I think you need to know it now. Virtually every spiritual master teaches this one thing. It is an essential practice that they believe is a crux to mastering yourself. And you don't need to be a spiritual seeker, or even a believer in anything, to put it to use, though I hope you believe in something that brings you a certain peace. The one thing is this: *Know your intention.*

Before you begin launching a campaign of any size, for one specific event or for a long-term marketing plan, it is important to know what you want: the vision, the feeling, the quantity. When designing an empowering personal marketing and publicity plan, your intention will be the underlying force that supports your foundation. Intentions precede actions. So before you even lift a little finger, sit yourself down in a comfortable place for contemplation and writing. Find a quiet corner where you can process your thoughts and write in a journal or on your computer.

Follow the five steps to creating an intention

Step 1. State the result you want.

What action do you want to happen from your intention? It should be something that is both quantifiable and has a practical application.

Do you want investors to give you $5 million for your start-up? Do you want a committee to vote you into office for a one-year term? Do you want your team to win an account? Use numbers. Be concrete. The more exact you are—the clearer your intention—the better results you will have.

Step 2. Name the intention.

Naming things makes your ideas solid. It anchors them to a place in time. Do you want more business, recognition, sales, clients, money, happiness, harmony?

Step 3. Develop the form the intention will take.

Plan the way you will present your information. What is the situation? Are you going to write a press release and send it out? Are you giving a public talk, being interviewed on the radio or TV or in print? Are you asking an investor for money? Are you planning a presentation to a client? It doesn't matter. What matters is being clear about the way you see yourself presenting your material to your audience.

Step 4. Decide on the style of presentation.

Map out the manner in which you will present your material to your audience. What are you trying to do? Entertain, inspire, teach, persuade, provoke? Or a combination of any of these? Have your goal in mind before you begin. This will determine your manner, tone, content.

Step 5. Get clear on your deeper hope.

Be clear on the deeper hope that you wish to realize. This is an encapsulation of your higher intention, your heartfelt reason for doing what you are doing. It includes the experience you want people to have when they interact with you and what you are offering.

Example for someone organizing a blood drive

1. *State the result you want.*

"I want to receive two hundred pints of healthy blood by the end of a four-day drive set for September 8, 2003. I want this blood drive to supply our county hospital with enough blood to save the lives of any residents who need it over a one-year period."

2. *Name the intention.*

"To save lives and improve the health of the residents of West-field, New York."

3. *Develop the form the intention will take.*

"I will send a press release [see chapter 4] in hard-copy form to local radio and TV stations and community affairs departments and e-mail it to health editors at all the local newspapers."

4. *Decide on the style of presentation.*

"The press release will be informative and entertaining."

5. *Get clear on your deeper hope.*

"I want to bring awareness to the residents of the community of Westfield, New York, so they will volunteer to give blood regularly to the blood bank. As a result the hospital will always have a fresh blood supply to assist anyone who is ill at any time."

Marry your intention to time

My great writing teacher, poet Joan Logghe, used this expression and I became enamored with it. It means set a timetable to make your intentions a tangible reality.

When I tell students in my classes to set a timetable to their intentions, a look of panic spreads on their faces that says, "Do I really have to *do* this?" I tell them that their timetable isn't set in stone. All it takes to keep us alive is one breath at a time. Your timetable is a fluid ocean, not a hard, immovable rock.

⌐ *Invitation* ⌐

Send Yourself a Letter of Intention.

In one of my favorite childhood books, *Harold and the Purple Crayon,* Harold drew whatever it was he needed to embark on his journey. All he needed to start was a window so he could get out of his bedroom. He drew that. And his adventures began out in the big wide world as he created at the end of his crayon whatever he imagined. Your intentions are the drawings for whatever it is you need to begin your own adventure.

In my classes we do this invitation as a way of putting the process of creating an intention into solid form. Please read the instructions through once before beginning.

1. Follow the five steps to creating an intention by writing down each step fast without thinking and without taking your hand off the page. If you find yourself slowing down or halting, write: "What I really want to say is . . ." or, "What I really don't want to say is . . ." or even, "I feel silly writing . . ." The point is to keep on writing no matter what, until you are done. Then you can go back and review what you have written.

2. Refine and edit this until it represents exactly what you want in this moment. (Remember, you can change it next week.)

3. Infuse it with the emotion you want as you are writing. Get that feeling in your whole body. Pour it through your fingers onto the page.

4. Marry your intention to time. Set a date to accomplish your intention.

5. Put your finished letter in an envelope.

6. Seal the envelope with a kiss or a star or some kind of sticker that represents part of the intention or the feeling you want to evoke.

7. Mail it to yourself.

8. Open it and post it someplace where you can see it and reread it to help you stay on track. It will serve as a reminder to you, a sort of love letter to yourself of your own deepest intentions.

The act of sending your letter of intention is a form of letting go. It is just as important not to be attached to an outcome you envision as it is to set an intention for your hopes. Who knows what form your intention will come in?

Receiving is a hard thing for many of us, but it is not so hard to write, mail, and open a letter.

Start now

Many people ask me when they should start a publicity campaign. The time to start is now. Now means as soon as you have the idea for a product, business plan, project, or book. Let me clarify. The creative process should remain pure if that is right for whatever you are developing. For artists who need to gestate and futz around with their hands in clay or an eye to a camera, you are focused on the beauty of what you are creating in this moment. At some point you will begin to think about the people you will reach with your offering and you may keep them in mind as you continue your project.

But what if you are beginning a commercial venture from the start? You will think about what you want to communicate, share, or sell, and who you want to do that with, at the same time as, or slightly after, the inception of the idea. Marketing and publicity become inseparable from your project, a welcome new little brother or sister to your creative process.

When you are developing your art, product, presence, or cause, let it unwind in its natural time and space. Once that process of creativity is complete, it is time to begin to incorporate a publicity plan into your project. Unless you don't intend to share your "work" with anyone, someone somewhere will want to view, buy, interact in some way with you, your product, or your service. Including those you want to reach in your overall master blueprint will bring a rich dimension into your offering. I suggest you start right now.

~ ~ ~ ~

PART III

Write Your Press Materials

CHAPTER 4

Build a Powerful Publicity Kit

Even as long ago as the 1980s, then *Wall Street Journal* executive editor Frederick Taylor admitted that up to 90 percent of his daily news originated in self-interested press releases. This is one of the most reputable papers in the United States. They receive hundreds of press releases every day from individuals like you and marketing consultants like me, who want to be written about for whatever they do, are, or sell. And when the public reads the articles that have been created with that information, they perceive it as reliable and respectable. Often the perception is that this information is "the truth."

"A lie can circle the globe in the time it takes truth to put on its shoes," Mark Twain noted. Take care in anything you put to paper. It is important to craft your materials carefully and thoughtfully whether you are writing a memo or marketing to the media. Once you begin to disseminate "the facts" about your business, book, presence, project, product, or cause, you put in motion a publicity wheel that can take you to unexpected places. We all know how fast news travels—both to our dismay and pleasure. I am going to focus on how to keep your news positive.

Socrates had some good advice on this topic: "The way to gain a good reputation is to endeavor to be what you desire to appear." In this chapter I will show you how to be your best on paper.

You need only a few things to start. The six essentials to have ready before you consider contacting the press are:

1. Press release.

2. Biography.

3. Pitch letter.

4. Ten questions.

5. Tip sheet.

6. Photo.

All the other materials I'll describe are optional and are suited to different situations that may or may not pertain to you right now. You'll want to know about them for the future, and you can consider writing them as part of an ongoing campaign to continue growing your publicity.

What goes into your press kit? Send as little as possible at first. If your information is relevant, you may be asked for more. This reason alone is good enough to have the appropriate materials prepared. Once you begin a dialogue with an editor or a producer, you can offer your other information.

If you have to scramble and throw something together under pressure, you won't be perceived as professional and the quality of your materials could suffer. Remember, when members of the media need something, they want to have it in their hands ASAP.

Guidelines are as follows:

- Print publications:

    Send your press release and tip sheet. When it's appropriate, send a xeroxed color copy of your photo(s). If an editor is interested, he'll request a photo or slide. For magazines you might include a list of your tip sheet titles and feature articles on your bounceback (see page 92) in the event an editor wants more information.

- Radio shows:

    Radio pitch letters are often faxed. Only fax one to two pages maximum. If you are sending your pitch letter hard copy, include your quote or "rave" page (see page 102) if you think it will close the deal. Have your ten questions and one-paragraph bio ready to fax.

- TV shows:

    Send your press release along with a product if you have one. If your raves are outstanding, you can include those as well. If you have an article about you from a *well-known* publication that will add to your credibility, include it. Be sure to highlight the parts that quote or focus on you so the producers can find and read them easily.

- Internet:

    (See chapter 14 for how to format your materials for a chat room.)

These are guidelines, not rules. Use your good judgment. If something is absolutely relevant, then by all means include it.

Press release

The first way to convey your news-making story is through a press release. A press release is a one-page explanation that shows the news media why you, your product, or your business deserve media coverage pronto. It is your challenge to create a compelling reason for readers, listeners, viewers, to be interested in what you have to offer *now*. Your "message" is the gist of what you want to share. Your "hook" is the grit that message is carried upon. Consider a hook the megaphone to get attention. It is a collar-gripping statement that must be compelling enough to make your press release stand out from the hundreds of others that crowd editors' and producers' desks every day.

Press releases are formulaic. Use the format below to write your press release. Journalists and producers are used to receiving materials with this formula, so don't deviate from it. You are welcome to be as creative as you like in the content. See page 42 for an example of one I wrote for a book by Karen Wood.

(1) The standard format:

    Flush left put the words "For Immediate Release." Underneath those words write the title of the event or book, or a catchy phrase that explains what you're promoting. (For Karen's we used the title of her book.)

② Contact information:

Flush right put the contact name (the person the press will be calling) and phone number. An e-mail address is optional. (Since she doesn't have a publicist or an assistant, Karen is the contact person.)

③ The headline:

Don't bury the lead. Once you have created a hook, then write a compelling, informative headline summarizing your hook in one sentence. Including the benefit to the public in the headline will make your idea more appealing to the media. This can be implied or explicit. Your first sentence is also designed to capture attention at first glance. Reporters and producers won't read past your headline if it doesn't make them cry, "Fascinating!" (Karen wanted to write the headline in a style suited to the *Wall Street Journal*. Her angle is geared toward a business audience. She wanted her statement to be shocking. Her specific audience is failing overachievers.)

④ The proof that supports your headline:

One to two paragraphs backing up your claim is sufficient. (Recent statistics show the timeliness of this problem. We personalized it to the people who identify themselves as the best and brightest.)

⑤ and ⑥ The six questions you must answer:

The next paragraph or two answers the questions who? what? when? where (physical address or whereabouts)? why? and how? in a succinct and interesting fashion. The paragraph after that can contain quotes, anecdotes, or historical data about your subject. These are straightforward facts that support your angle or hook. (Karen answered the questions raised in the headline. She explains who she is [who?] and what happened to her career [what?] that she wants to share with others so they don't make the same mistake. This phenomenon is happening to millions of others like her in the workplace today [when?] in corporate America [where?]. She was taught to focus on her own success [why?] and to work hard to get ahead [how?].)

⑦ Your expertise:

Included in the who, what, when, where, why, and how is biographical information that highlights your expertise or the credibility of your company. (We listed Karen's personal and professional experience in the corporate world and why she is an expert on this topic.)

⑧ Your critical information:

Include all the practical information necessary about your product, business, or service (prices, addresses, phone and fax numbers) so the media has accurate information that permits them to run an article effortlessly and swiftly. (We included the ways Karen's book can be purchased and all other pertinent information so the media could contact her or find out more information.)

HOT TIP!

PUT IT ALL ON ONE DOUBLE-SPACED PAGE.
Limit yourself to 350 words and you will encourage yourself to be concise and to the point.

HOT TIP!

PERSONALIZE WHENEVER POSSIBLE.
If you're familiar with a journalist's work, attach a short note that tells him what you like about his style and the subject he's covering and why your topic fits in.

The following is a sample press release:

Enlightened Concepts Publishing & Communications

① For Immediate Release: ② Contact: Karen Wood
Don't Sabotage Your Success!   510.469.9697
Make Office Politics Work

③ **Everything You Learned in School about How to Succeed
(in the Real World) Was Wrong!
The Plight of the Failing Overachiever**

④ *Silicon Valley, California.*—According to the Bureau of Labor
Statistics, 936 companies laid off more workers this past September than any month since they began keeping statistics. Thousands of others were overlooked for a promotion they may have been well qualified to receive. You have a big chance of being one of them—especially if you are one of the best and brightest. Why?

⑤ *You probably don't know it's your job to make your boss successful. Period.* In school and in the workplace we were taught to focus single-mindedly on performance and getting the grade. Rather than becoming the key to success, for many, overachievers especially, this notion has locked in their failure.

⑥ Karen Wood, Management Consultant for IBM, thought she had a secure career. On the fast track up the corporate ladder at multibillion-dollar corporations, she consistently cut costs and exceeded expectations. But instead of being promoted, she was fired from her six-figure job. What went wrong? "I focused on doing the best possible job I could while I watched mediocre performers get the promotions I thought I deserved," she said. "I should have focused on the most important thing—to make my boss successful—but I didn't know it." Neither do millions of others like her. Relationships are the foundation for everything you want to create in your career, stresses Wood.

⑦ In her new book, ***Don't Sabotage Your Success! Make Office Politics Work*** ($14.00, Enlightened Concepts Publishing), Wood provides surprising insights into how most smart people sabotage their chances at success and happiness. Based on her own personal workplace experience and case studies of other overachievers, she points out ways to "unlearn" common behaviors that have a devastating impact on your professional relationships. She gives practical tips to create strong and lasting bonds among superiors, subordinates, and peers to ensure your place as a valued employee, and reveals secrets to securing the promotion you deserve. As a frequent seminar leader, Wood's practical advice has already helped hundreds of business people succeed in the jobs they have or find careers suited to their skills.

⑧ ***Don't Sabotage Your Success!*** (ISBN 0-9702143-0-8), 179 pages, February 2001, is available in bookstores or by sending $14.00, plus $3.49 shipping and handling for the first book, $0.99 for each additional book, to Enlightened Concepts Publishing, P.O. Box 1017, Oakland, CA 94604-1017. To order with credit card, call 1-800-266-5564. **Download press kits at: http//www.karenwood.com.**

Enlightened Concepts Publishing & Communications
PO Box 1017 Oakland, CA 94604 510-469-9697

E-mail press release

When you e-mail, send only one or two paragraphs highlighting the main points from your press release to test interest. Put your catchy headline in the subject line. Do not under any circumstance send an attached file. You will be considered unprofessional and ignorant. With such a gaffe some journalists will ban you from their in-box forever. Short and to the point is key. See pages 44 and 45 for examples.

The following are two sample short e-mail press releases:

```
Date: Tue, 6 Mar 2001 10:27:11-0800
To: Bay Area Journalists
From: susan@publicitysecrets.com
Subject: Discover unsung entrepreneurs in the Bay Area
```

Susan Harrow's Learning Annex class is a hotbed for unscooped stories.

You're invited to attend Sell Yourself Without Selling Your Soul: Secrets to Becoming a Media Sensation as her guest on Wednesday, October 18, 6:30–9:30 p.m., in downtown San Francisco.

The class attracts fascinating undiscovered people looking for media attention as well as famous and established entrepreneurs.

A look at some attendees from past classes:

• The man who created the happy massager.
• A woman who gives parties for dogs.
• A man called Dr. Clue, who creates treasure hunts for the young and old.
• A ceramicist who began making huge, wild nonfunctional teapots and Mexican-style altars after being diagnosed with breast cancer.

NO RISK: We introduce ourselves with a 30-second pitch in the first half hour of the class. If you're not interested in anyone after that point, you can leave.

TIMESAVER: If you are interested in someone, you can meet at the break at the end of the first hour to set an appointment.

HIGHLIGHT: Harrow gives a theatrical demonstration of the three faces of fame (snotty, serious, sexy) to show you how your body talks louder than your words.

RSVP via e-mail or call 510.419.0330 for exact location.

Best,
Susan

Date: Tue, 6 Mar 2001 10:27:11-0800
To: Bay Area Journalists
From: susan@publicitysecrets.com
Subject: Discover unsung entrepreneurs in the Bay Area

Susan Harrow's Learning Annex class is a hotbed for unscooped stories.

You're invited to attend Sell Yourself Without Selling Your Soul: Secrets to Becoming a Media Sensation as her guest on Wednesday, October 18, 6:30-9:30 p.m., in downtown San Francisco.

The class attracts fascinating undiscovered people looking for media attention as well as famous and established entrepreneurs.

A look at some attendees from past classes:

• The man who created the happy massager.
• A woman who gives parties for dogs.
• A man called Dr. Clue, who creates treasure hunts for the young and old.
• An ex-Catholic, founder of Q-Spirit, who wrote the book "Coming Out Spiritually" for gays and lesbians.
• An entrepreneur who started astrology.com—the most popular astrological site on the Net.
• An authentic urban cowboy.
• A stripper from the finer "gentlemanly clubs" who gives a class in how to defrock for your lover.
• A ceramicist who began making huge, wild nonfunctional teapots and Mexican-style altars after being diagnosed with breast cancer.

NO RISK: We introduce ourselves with a 30-second pitch in the first half hour of the class. If you're not interested in anyone after that point, you can leave.

TIMESAVER: If you are interested in someone, you can meet at the break at the end of the first hour to set an appointment.

HIGHLIGHT: Harrow gives a theatrical demonstration of the three faces of fame (snotty, serious, sexy) to show you how your body talks louder than your words.

You'll get two or more benefits out of attending:

1. Potential new story contacts and leads.
2. The opportunity to interview/write about me and my class.
3. Get quoted in my upcoming book (publicity and recognition for you—a career boost).
4. Be interviewed for my upcoming publicity book.

RSVP via e-mail or call 510.419.0330 for exact location.

I look forward to seeing you there.

Best,
Susan

Course description follows.

A JOURNALIST'S ADVICE—SEND LESS NOT MORE

Journalist Zillie Bahar says, "I wonder about huge packets which are expensive to produce. We journalists don't have time to read them. You should get all your information on one page. And don't try to be sneaky about what you are doing. Be frank that you are promoting something. Why else would you be contacting us?"

Many prominent media people receive over 100 press releases a day! So while creating a memorable presentation might include an apt trinket, Zillie advises, "Try not to overwhelm people with freebies. It makes people who are serious about journalism cringe. It may even backfire if you inundate them with stuff. If you are including something, keep it simple and relevant."

SEND FOOD OR A KEEPER GIFT

Another journalist-turned-publicist told me a secret. Journalists appreciate food and unusual things. She included special coffee and macadamia nuts for a press release about vintage Hawaiian shirts. The coffee and nuts made sense, since those two delicious comestibles pertained to the subject matter. Make sure whatever you send matches the product or service you're promoting. The food keeps their mind on your material as they happily ingest, though the memory of you will last only as long as the morsel. Whereas, if you send a keeper gift, they'll often display that memorable item on their desks or pin it on a bulletin board—an excellent reminder of you.

Apply the three secrets to creating a hot book to write your press release

What do producers and editors love? For you to take a strong stand; to tempt them with something that rubs them the wrong way; to tease them with the strange, weird, bizarre; to titillate them with the counterintuitive. Create a hook that will rivet them to your page by doing one of three things:

1. Debunk a myth.

Make an assertion. Take something that is generally believed by the public and disprove it. Any kind of prevalent thought, like boys are better in math than girls, will do. For musician Stephen Halpern, I wrote a press release called "The Mozart Mistake" to prove that the Mozart effect, or the theory that listening to Mozart makes you smarter, is sadly untrue. Halpern took the research to task for being based on an invalid, statistically unsound test of only thirty-two students.

2. Create controversy.

People love what they hate. David Talbot, editor in chief and founder of Salon.com, one of the most respected and successful on-line magazines, says, "The best dinner parties are those where people disagree with each other. If everyone is just nodding their heads in harmony all night long, it is pretty dull. Unless you have a vivid voice, a controversial voice, often the reader isn't going to stick with you."

Controversy creates an instant debate. There is one word that you can use that will turn an ordinary statement into one buzzing with friction. That one word is "but." The word "not" helps set up the "but" that follows. Two examples: "When it comes to creating criminals, it is *not* parenting that matters *but* the environment a child grows up in." "It is *not* eating too much *but* dieting that makes you fat."

3. Ask a gripping question for which you have the answer.

You first identify a problem, then state why you are the answer to that problem. Ask yourself, "What will people lose if they don't listen to me? What will it cost them financially, emotionally, physically, spiritually?" Can you quantify their loss in a specific way? Two examples: "Help! What can you do if your doctor is killing you? Six strategies to save your life." "How do you find soul in the workplace if your job is hell? Carol Adrienne tells the 80 percent of Americans who report that they are unhappy with their jobs how they can cope."

HOT TIP!

GIVE YOUR SUBJECT EMOTIONAL ZING.

There is one potent part that's often missing from a press release—emotional resonance. Make your subject call up a shock of feeling. If whatever you are promoting has elements that will stir up strong positive and negative feelings about a subject, you have a better chance of being heard through all the noise of those competing for media attention.

Below are some examples to assist you in thinking up your own hot hook or angle:

- A new development about your product, business, or organization that would benefit others in a significant way.

- Why you are different from your competitors and why that matters.

- An upcoming contest, fund-raiser, event, or award. Something you have done or are doing to help the community.

- A controversial or surprising discovery.

- An amusing or humorous bit of information that delights and entertains.

- Something outrageous or (nearly) unbelievable.

- Something weird, quirky, or strange.

- Statistics, surveys, research, or polls that elucidate something significant.

- A direct connection to a holiday, anniversary, celebration, or historical event.

- A correlation between whatever it is you offer and a current trend, a trend started by you or your business, or a backlash against a trend.

- A tie-in with your product, business, or personality to a breaking story or timely news topic or event.

Invitation

To help further position yourself as unique consider the following:
1. Spend time taking inventory of everything your competitor has, does, or is.
2. Take notice of the gaps in their experience, product, or service. What have they not covered?
3. What can be elaborated upon? What do you give in your own way that no one else can?

HOT TIP!

TELL A GREAT STORY.

What is the quickest way to get in the news or make your own? The secret is so old and so obvious, you may have missed it. According to reporter Dennis Stauffer, in his book *MediaSmart: How to Handle a Reporter,* it is this: Tell a great story. "A news story is supposed to be true, but otherwise the criteria for what makes a good story are the same as in fiction. We look for strong characters (newsmakers), good dialogue (sound bites/quotations), and something novel and dramatic to tell (scandal/disaster/victory). We strive to somehow touch our audience by relating things in personal terms, and we try to present it in a way that will attract and hold someone's attention."

THE FIVE BIGGEST MISTAKES MOST PEOPLE MAKE WRITING PRESS RELEASES

1. A dull headline.

The headline is the most important part of your copy. Remember the teacher who made you write a topic sentence in grade school? The topic sentence told boldly what the rest of the paragraph was about. The headline has got to be your topic sentence for the entire release. And it must do one more thing. Arrest the editor or producer. If it doesn't, it ends up in that already overflowing circular file. Your headline answers the question, "Why should anyone care?"

2. A boring second paragraph.

When I review news releases for my clients, I am always on snooze patrol. Will it pass the nap test? The paragraph after the headline must sustain the interest of the editor or producer. If he has read this far, keep the momentum going with your key facts and the gist of your story. Be brief, gripping, and to the point. Do you know what editors and producers are looking for from you? Information that they can use today. Don't disappoint. Make them say, "Wow, my audience can't possibly live another minute without knowing about this story."

3. Focusing on what you are trying to sell.

A press release isn't an ad for your product, service, or self. It is news. Either link your release to a current news story or make your own news. Remember that saying by radio personality Scoop Nisker? "If you don't like the news, go out and make some of your own." Granted you have to mention you, your product, or service. Surround it in news and you have got the attention of the media.

4. Writing exclusively with narrative.

Yawn. You don't want editors to get even a hint that you may be beginning your autobiography. Enliven your narrative with dialogue. That way they know there is someone real involved in this thing. Oh, and also write it as if it's casual Friday rather than a formal affair. At least once use a witty or informative quote that shows how you have helped someone, or plan to. If you can work them in, use short quotes in two or three places. Concrete results are best.

5. Making it too long.

If you can't say it in one page, you have a problem. Publicist Leslie Rossman has publicized books for so long, she says jokingly that she can't write anything longer than one page. "And I have publicized some pretty heavy people," she says. (Terence McKenna and the Dalai Lama, to name two.) "So it takes some thinking to boil down sophisticated ideas into a few key points." Writing a press release is a great exercise for extracting the essence out of what you have to sell. For all of you who have labored over your tome, go back and do the Cliff's Notes version. Don't worry, if a journalist or producer wants more, he won't hesitate to ask you.

Make your release snappy, short, exciting, newsworthy, and quotable and the media will rush to call you. Go to it!

Bio

A Biography (Bio) of you, your service, product, or business in a short paragraph should include your most outstanding and important accomplishments. Begin with a memorable first sentence. Continue with the other essential information you want your readers to know. Then include this in the press release. Most of the time journalists won't take the time to read a full-page bio. You can prepare a half- or full-page bio on a separate page in the event they ask, but don't send it unless requested. (See the expanded biography on page 53.) Producers and hosts have even less time. The radio biography on page 53 and outlined next serves as a condensed version of a longer biography and is in enlarged print so that producers can read it easily on the air. (Note: A TV bio will usually be only one or two lines stating your expertise.)

Here are the three things your bio must do:

1. Establish your credibility.

Name anything that qualifies you to speak on your topic: an advanced degree, a prestigious title, an exceptional award. (I included the fact that Carol earned a Ph.D., which gives her instant credibility as an intellectual or academic thinker.)

2. State what it is you're promoting.

List the name of your product, book, company. Mention anything that adds to your stature as an expert in relation to what you're offering.

(The words "the *New York Times* best-seller" have a more powerful impact than just "best-seller," which has become a loosely used term. Carol has written *two* best-selling books, both of which are mentioned by name.)

3. Quantify your expertise.

Report any statistic or number, or something that can be measured, to back up your original claim as an expert. (The last element that clinches Carol as an expert is that she has helped *thousands* of people find their life purpose.)

HOT TIP!

ALWAYS USE THE WORD "YOU" IN YOUR BIO TO SHOW HOW WHAT YOU DO HELPS OTHERS.

If it seems awkward in the context of your business, substitute "people."

HOT TIP!

WRITE EACH PARAGRAPH AS IF IT WERE A SELF-CONTAINED TEN-SECOND MESSAGE.

Each paragraph has to be a mighty communicator of your points.

The following are two sample bios, one for radio and an expanded bio for general use.

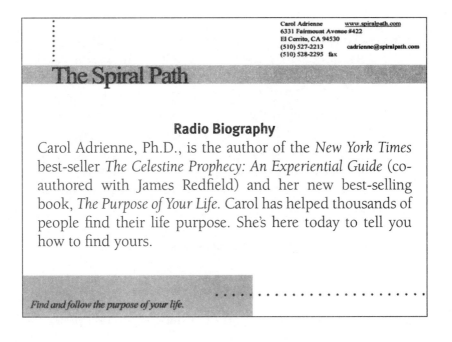

Carol Adrienne   www.spiralpath.com
6331 Fairmount Avenue #422
El Cerrito, CA 94530
(510) 527-2213   cadrienne@spiralpath.com
(510) 528-2295 fax

The Spiral Path

Radio Biography

Carol Adrienne, Ph.D., is the author of the *New York Times* best-seller *The Celestine Prophecy: An Experiential Guide* (co-authored with James Redfield) and her new best-selling book, *The Purpose of Your Life.* Carol has helped thousands of people find their life purpose. She's here today to tell you how to find yours.

Find and follow the purpose of your life.

SUSAN   HARROW

MARKETING STRATEGIST - PRESENTATION & MEDIA COACH

Expanded Biography

Susan Harrow was born to a gypsy mother who read people's futures on their faces. She inherited her mother's gift for seeing what is most important in a person. Her father was a marionette maker who taught Susan to go through life with no strings attached.

She uses her own life, which explodes with contradictions, to help others make sense of theirs for the media.

She has lived the life of a celibate monk, a wild woman, a vegetarian, a carnivore, an au pair in Paris, an English teacher, a tennis pro, a jewelry designer, a sales rep, a publicist, a media coach and marketing strategist, and is constantly discovering new roles to try.

She was almost sold into slavery to a bedouin sheik in Israel for ten camels and a mule, chased by elephants in Africa, was loved by the leader of the Anarchist Party in Italy, narrowly escaped drowning while rafting down the Zambezi River in class-five rapids, was recruited by the CIA but decided she didn't want to leap tall buildings in Bolivia in a single bound, and so she elected to teach English at Mission High School in San Francisco, instead. On her first day of teaching she saved a student from being knifed in the hallway, and miraculously escaped her tenure there without any visible flesh wounds.

Which all made the perils of publicity seem sweet.

For the past thirteen years, Susan Harrow has run a media-coaching and marketing firm that specializes in promoting executives, authors, speakers, entrepreneurs, and dot-coms whose projects have a lot of heart or art.

Her clients include PlanetRx, iVillage, Random House, Celestial Arts, Peachpit Press/Addison-Wesley, Gibbs-Smith, Bill Graham Presents, the North Face, and best-selling authors Carol Adrienne and Larry Magid, among others. She also consulted with Pacific Bell Directory, the Yellow Pages, throughout California for over nine years.

Susan Harrow is the publicist for several best-selling books and has given a number of previously unknown clients much more than their fifteen minutes of fame.

4200 Park Boulevard PMB 333 S ~ Oakland ~ CA 94602
telephone 510.419.0330 *email* susan@publicitysecrets.com *website* www.publicitysecrets.com

Pitch letter

A pitch letter is typically sent to TV and radio producers. Its purpose is to position you as *the* expert to solve a pressing problem. It explains why you, your service, or your product is the answer to an important issue that affects the lives of a specific group of people. In other words, it explains why the public should listen to you and why they should care. The format varies slightly depending on your content, but the typical format is as follows:

① The first paragraph includes a snappy lead that introduces your subject by stating a problem.

② The second paragraph gives details about the expert. It can include mini-testimonials, or short quotes from clients, or media contact comments. You may also quote yourself or others in your company. Make sure these quotes actually say something significant about solving the problem.

③ The third paragraph is a bold statement or gives the nitty-gritty details about your product or service, the price if applicable, and the advantages of using it.

④ Next, concise bullet points outline what it is that you are prepared to discuss. Inherent in these points is the solution to problems you've identified. More topical and news-oriented issues, those with a time deadline, take priority because they are more urgent. (Note: Urgency has both advantages and disadvantages. It has a quicker response time because of the timeliness, but a shorter shelf life for the same reason. "Evergreen" topics, or those that can be used at any time, don't have the same immediacy, but can often be used as "fillers" when a producer or editor is short on material.)

⑤ This paragraph highlights your experience and gives solid evidence of your expertise.

⑥ The final line states how you are available for an interview. In this case "phoner" indicates that Karen is only giving interviews by phone and will not travel to be interviewed "in studio." Using a closing line such as "I'll call you next week to arrange a mutually convenient time for a 'phoner' interview," creates a sense of urgency. If you choose to use that line, mark your calendar to call.

Leave a phone number where you can be reached easily. And check your messages often. Radio and TV producers work on very tight deadlines, and replying to a message soon after it was sent can mean the difference between getting booked on a show or not.

⑦ Put 911 in big block letters on your pitch letter.

If you are prepared to be awakened in the wee hours of the morning or the werewolf hours of the night, put "911 interviews available" in bold caps and in prominent view. This means whenever there is a cancellation or guest no-show, you will fill in. It's a great way to become indispensable to producers and to get increased airplay. P.S. You can also specify the hours you will be available if you don't want your phone to ring all night. Be sure to indicate your time zone.

⑧ Always put your pitch letter on stationery which includes multiple ways to order your products, contact you, and/or use your services.

The following are two sample pitch letters:

Enlightened Concepts Publishing & Communications

Dear Producer:

① **Why are millions of overachievers failing miserably in the workplace?**

They didn't know their job was to make their boss successful. Period. As a result, superperformers are often the very people who are fired, are perceived as poor team players, or are overlooked for promotion. This devastating "fail factor," as IBM Management Consultant Karen Wood calls it, can sabotage your career—unless you know how to change it.

② Karen Wood, Management Consultant for IBM, thought she had a secure career. On the fast track up the corporate ladder at multibillion-dollar corporations, she consistently cut costs and exceeded expectations. But instead of being promoted, she was fired from a six-figure job. What went wrong? "I focused on doing the best possible job I could while I watched mediocre performers get the promotions I thought I deserved," she said. "I should have focused on the most important thing—to make my boss successful, but I didn't know it." Neither do millions of others like her.

③ In her new book, ***Don't Sabotage Your Success: Make Office Politics Work*** ($14.00, Enlightened Concepts Publishing), Wood demonstrates with real-life examples how excellent work doesn't automatically equal a successful career. She provides surprising insights into how most smart people unwittingly sabotage their success and happiness—and the solutions to stop.

④ Warm and engaging, Wood can discuss

- Strategies to become your boss's loyal, trusted ally.

- The one fatal flaw guaranteed to sabotage your career.

- The reasons why you must master office politics if you are to succeed.

- Why you cannot escape office politics no matter how small your company.

- Why overachievers are more likely to fail in the workplace.

- Easy ways to "unlearn" common behaviors that can have a devastating impact on workplace relationships.

- The four red flags that let you know your job may be in danger.

- Secrets to having more power and influence in meetings.

⑤ As a highly rated seminar leader, Wood's practical advice has already helped hundreds of business people succeed in the jobs they have or find careers suited to their skills.

⑥ I'll call you next week to arrange a mutually convenient time for a phoner interview.

Best Regards,
Karen Wood

⑦ **911 INTERVIEWS AVAILABLE! Call anytime 7:30 a.m.–7:30 p.m. PST**

⑧   *Enlightened Concepts Publishing & Communications*
      PO Box 1017 Oakland, CA 94604 510-469-9697

PEACHPIT PRESS

Dear Producer:

① Whatsamatter, you got something to hide?

Even if you don't, someone somewhere may be interested in your data profile. Whether it's the U.S. government trying to pass legislation to put a computer chip in every American's phone, or a business that can buy a competitor's data from a bank or government clerk for a few hundred dollars, safeguarding electronic information has become a hot topic for any individual who wants to protect his personal security. Cybersnooping is now a fact of life. And personal information about you or any other individual is just a phone call away.

② In his new book, *The Computer Privacy Handbook: A Practical Guide to E-mail Encryption, Data Protection, and PGP Privacy Software*, author, scientist, and technology expert André Bacard explores the issues surrounding electronic surveillance in today's society.

③ Reading like a high-tech thriller, this book is destined to become a classic for people everywhere who are concerned about their shrinking rights to privacy.

④ Entertaining, informative, and a pioneer for a citizen's right to privacy, Bacard can discuss

- 👁 Computer snooping—how privileged information is compromised.
- 👁 The pros and cons of a cash-free environment—how using "plastic" can result in a consumer privacy meltdown.
- 👁 The Clipper Chip initiative controversy—the government's role in the privacy invasion/Big Brother in the bedroom or boardroom.
- 👁 Your social security number—strategies for keeping it safe.
- 👁 Pretty Good Privacy (PGP), computer encryption—how to protect your e-mail from snoops.

⑤ A guest on hundreds of radio talk shows, André Bacard was judged one of the best public speakers in America by the International Platform Association. Bacard writes about technology and society for numerous publications and is author of *Hunger for Power: Who Rules the World and How.*

⑥ André Bacard is now available for print and radio interviews. I'll contact you to arrange a mutually convenient time for an interview.

Best Regards,
Susan Harrow

∅ 415.861.2420/Harrow Communications, for Peachpit Press

⑦ 911 Interviews available! Call anytime.

⑧   1249 Eighth Street, Berkeley, CA 94710
510 524 2178
Fax 510 524 2221

Ten questions

Typically questions are used for a radio interview. Most producers and hosts are grateful that you have done this work for them, as they are burdened with assimilating an astronomical load of information before their shows. One client who didn't prepare questions was a bit miffed when the host asked the one question she'd prepared and then said, "Well, that is all the questions I have for you." Thankfully he was a quick thinker and said, "Well, then, why don't you ask me about . . ." The interview proceeded smoothly once he fed her the questions. On the other hand, most journalists will be insulted that you have prepared their questions for them. Tut tut. Better to be prepared than to be left slack-mouthed wishing upon a star. Don't send questions to a journalist before asking permission.

How do you develop the right questions? I work with my clients by interviewing them on the subject they wish to market. After I have a firm idea of the key points of their presentation, I develop the questions to fit those answers. The questions serve as a guide, or an anchor upon which you float your information. As you become more experienced, you will be able to answer any question with the information you wish to convey. I suggest that at first you practice answering the questions in the order in which you'd like them to be asked. Then practice them in random order. After you get comfortable doing that, practice answering questions that are only loosely linked to your questions.

Questions help make the journalist's or radio or TV producer's job easier. He may not have had time to research whatever it is you are promoting. Many have not read even one line of your press materials. Creating questions for them helps them prepare to interview you more professionally.

HOT TIP!

INCLUDE YOUR BIO AT THE TOP OF THE PAGE.
Make it easy for producers to introduce you correctly by keeping the information you want them to read accessible.

HOT TIP!

PREFACE YOUR QUESTIONS WITH BACKGROUND INFORMATION.

If producers choose to read them verbatim on the air, it sounds as if they are as knowledgeable about your subject as you are, and you are disseminating the information you want revealed. See the example below that I wrote for Sedona Training Associates. The actual questions are in bold.

HOT TIP!

INCLUDE YOUR 800 NUMBER OR WEB ADDRESS (URL) ON THE QUESTION SHEET SO THE HOST CAN ANNOUNCE IT FREQUENTLY.

The following is a ten questions sample:

Transforming Minds, Transforming Lives - Worldwide

Sedona
Training Associates

Sedona AZ 86336 USA
tel 520-282-3522
fax 520-203-0602
release@sedona.com
www.sedona.com

Ten Questions
The Sedona Method/Hale Dwoskin, President

Hale Dwoskin is the CEO of Sedona Training Associates. In the last twenty-six years he has trained thousands of individuals and companies worldwide in the Sedona Method. Hale developed a series of Free-

dom Now audiotapes that helps people become happy, healthy, and
wealthy. He's here today to show you how you can become one of those
people.

1. The Sedona Method is endorsed by Harvard University because it's simple and gets fast results. You say it's not a religion, lifestyle, or spiritual path. **Explain to us what the method is and how it works.**

2. Many people fear the word "change." It's almost synonymous with "pain." **What is the one thing that our audience needs to do to allow change to happen easily?**

3. Many people in our audience have tried to eliminate stress or to stop smoking or drinking and have failed. **What's the biggest mistake they make and why don't they succeed? How can they succeed?**

4. Everybody gets into a fight with somebody. Your boss, your partner. You've worked with executives and employees at AT&T, Merrill Lynch, TWA, and the Marriott. **How can we bounce back from these conflicts at work or at home?**

5. Food! Who hasn't tried to lose weight? **What's a simple thing we can do to enjoy our food without feeling guilty?**

6. **Explain what you mean by "Nature's secret escape valve."**

7. All of us feel guilty about something. **How do we change guilt from an IOU for punishment into an IOU for pleasure?**

8. **You said that there are surprising ways we're feeding the very things we hate about ourselves. What are they?**

9. **Can you tell us the difference between suppressing, expressing, and releasing unwanted problems and patterns in our lives?**

10. **What's the one thing that our audience can do today to start feeling better?**

   Call 1.888.282.5656
   to order your FREE audiotape
   or the series today.

Tip sheet

I want to share a secret with you. This may prove controversial. . . . Many publicists think otherwise, but I believe that the tip sheet is the most important piece in your press kit because there is no ego in it. There is no ostensible "I" promoting the information. A tip sheet is pure knowledge.

A tip sheet, often called "ten top tips," is a list of five to fifteen points that highlight your expertise while providing solutions to personal or professional problems. It begins with one or more short paragraphs followed by numbered tips.

Examples:
- Ten Ways to Reclaim Your Power as a Speaker (see page 65).

- Ten Steps to Securing a Raise or a Promotion.

- "Cyberspace Civility: Nine E-mail Dos and Don'ts Every Business Person Should Know." (see page 69).

- Five methods to Choose a Wine That Suits Your Personality or Mood.

Tip sheet format:

1. Clever title:
   Gains the reader's attention instantly.

2. Introductory paragraph:
   Explains what you will cover.

3. Useful tips:

Outline informative and entertaining data gathered from your expertise that benefits others. Include anecdotes, quotes, statistics, stories, and facts that support your findings.

Put the tip sheet on your stationery so all of your contact information is available. (Note: For a shortened, one-page version, omit the introduction and make your points in a few sentences as on page 72).

HOT TIP!

MAKE A STATEMENT WITH YOUR STYLE.

If you already have a recognizable style or voice, use it. Editors prefer substance with style over flat facts. Notice how I've written Lee Glickstein and Dana May Casperson's tip sheets in their unique style and voice. Discovering your voice is an exciting aspect of promoting yourself.

HOT TIP!

USE EXAMPLES OF THE KIND OF CLIENTS OR CUSTOMERS YOU PREFER.

Here is how to develop a tip sheet so it will bring you the business you want without having to blare it. In other words, the right people will be attracted to what you have to give. Use examples that include the kinds of clients or experiences you want. I remember one of my jewelry-designer friends telling me about a particular pitfall when selling a line of earrings. She had one type of dangly thingamajig readily available in red and yellow, both of which the buyer ordered. She then asked the buyer, "Would you like to buy them in purple also?" The buyer responded, "I don't know; show me the purple." She realized that the buyer couldn't make the visual leap to imagining the earrings in purple. This buyer is not alone. Many people, no matter what their profession, don't see how you can help them unless you state it explicitly. Odd as it may seem, it must pertain to them or their business exactly for them to understand you are a match with what they need.

HOT TIP!

NUDGE THAT FUNNY BONE.

Humor makes a piece more attractive to journalists. They want to entertain their audience even if the subject is serious. (The tip sheet I wrote for manners maven Dana May Casperson's publicist on page 69 is in keeping with Casperson's humor and sense of fun about what is proper.)

HOT TIP!

STAMP YOUR STYLE ON EVERYTHING.

The really valuable "how to" or tip sheet pieces incorporate your advice, personality, opinions, philosophy, style, and standards. If you have compiled just a list of how to do something (ho-hum), your clients could go to your competitor for the same skinny. Link your advice directly to your audience's needs using your unmistakable style and they'll pound a path to your door.

The following are three sample tip sheets:

SUSAN HARROW

MARKETING STRATEGIST ~ PRESENTATION & MEDIA COACH

Ten Ways to Reclaim Your Power as a Speaker

Traditionally, speaking has been thought of as a performance. A way to wow people with all the excellent qualities of the speaker. Lee Glickstein, creator of Speaking Circles, coaches speaking as relationship ahead of showmanship. He believes that good speakers communicate for connection. He says that "the best technique is no technique." For those people with stage fright this process has been the answer to the prayers they've been too nervous too pray. Here is Lee's advice:

1. Open your talk with receptivity instead of seeking to create an effect.

"Start from stop." Take at least one full breath after the applause ends, as you look into the eyes of a few members of your audience and receive their support, before speaking. Allow yourself to feel the surge of your opening line. Then speak it conversationally.

2. Open with a personal story or anecdote of a failure you've turned into a strength.

Conventional wisdom is for speakers to open with a joke. Glickstein believes that jokes often set a superficial tone that may create discomfort and distrust. The personal story is your own material and serves the purpose of getting everybody on the same page, which is often the intention, but not the result, of telling a joke. And whether or not your story has natural humor in it, the personal touch allows your audience to empathize with you and silently acknowledge perceived failure in their own lives. Likewise, they relate to you when you explain how that failure has contributed to developing a strength.

3. Receive one person's support at a time.

You do this by slowing down and looking gently into the eyes of your listeners, holding the gaze of one at a time to establish rapport. Engage each person with 100 percent of your focus. You do not need to contact 100 percent of the people. You create a community that connects everyone when you connect with a few of them deeply. In this way you move toward your audience and honor them rather than distancing yourself or trying to impress them. When you listen to the audience, they listen to you and the energy keeps building.

4. Opt for "anxious authenticity" or "vibrant vulnerability" instead of masking your anxiety.

It's not the crime, it's the cover-up that's a problem. When there is an incongruity between the way you feel and the way you act, your audience instinctively knows and regards it negatively.

Accept your nervousness, even acknowledge it. Perhaps turn it into a story. People appreciate honesty above arrogance, nonchalance, or feigned confidence. Bringing your vulnerabilities to the forefront allows you to receive support from the audience. By being yourself you give your listeners permission to be themselves.

5. Treat your audience as if they were already your friends.

Your audience wants the best for you. They are investing their time and would rather see you succeed than fail. When you view them as a sea of friendly faces, they see themselves reflected back as they are.

6. Abandon the idea that you must be perfect.

Perfection is not being real. And if you put yourself up on a pedestal, someone will want to knock you off. Being real is connecting with people on the same level, no matter what your "title" or "expertise." Being real means living your message, embodying and modeling your topic or subject. Your presence speaks louder than your words.

7. Act natural rather than cultivate a style.

"Style" is simply the natural ability to be yourself without pretense. Pipe down for more attention. Often speakers think that when they increase their volume or intensity, they are more powerful or interesting. Just the opposite is true. Slowing down, becoming more magnetic (rather than dynamic), draws people toward you. Think of children at a puppet show, waiting and watching for the characters' next moves. They sit in rapt attention, patient and willing.

8. Pause often even when you know what you want to say next.

"White space is your friend," says Jeff Rubin, a Speaking Circle practitioner and business newsletter designer. In speaking, white space is silence. Pauses, or natural silence, allows for less clutter and more focus. When you allow silence, your audience can take in your ideas more readily. And you allow inspiration the opportunity to join you. Silence often speaks more loudly than words.

9. When you draw a blank, draw a blank of openness rather than one of fear.

If you find yourself suddenly at a loss of what to say, first give yourself a chance to tolerate the unknown. It could mean that your talk was headed in a direction that wasn't working well, or felt canned. The "void" gives you a chance to creatively connect with the audience. Don't be afraid to ask them, "What do you need now?" or, "Where was I?" Audiences love to help.

10. Learn to accept the wisdom of not knowing.

This doesn't mean not preparing for a talk or using notes. It does mean making room for the unexpected thought, story, emotion, new concept, or humorous idea. When you make a decision to be open, new notions or creative directions often appear. And when they do, a synergy happens that involves everyone. This is a surprise element that couldn't have occurred with overplanning.

Adapted from Lee Glickstein's book *Be Heard Now! Tap into Your Inner Speaker and Communicate with Ease.* He developed Speaking Circles to dissolve his own stage fright and has led over 3,000 workshops and helped many thousands speak and be heard without fear. Call 415.381.8044 for information on Circles in your area.

e-mail: *lee@glickstein.com*
http://www.leeglickstein.com

4200 Park Boulevard PMB 333 S ~ Oakland ~ CA 94602
telephone 510.419.0330   *email* susan@publicitysecrets.com
website www.publicitysecrets.com

"Manners open doors that power & money cannot."

DANA MAY CASPERSON

Post Office Box 3637
Santa Rosa, California 95402

707. 579.4367
fax 707. 579.1998
danamay@authoritea.com
www.mannersplace.com

① Cyberspace Civility
Nine e-mail dos and don'ts
every business person should know

② E-mail has become the Lonely Hearts Club of Cyberspace. All this chat room coziness has zapped into the business world at fiber-optic speed. The trouble is, until now, there have been no rules of proper e-mail etiquette to follow, and everyone has been left to their own devices. This has led to slackness and chaos. Historically, manners and rules of etiquette were adopted from the ethics of common courtesy and common sense. I have tried to apply these to the Age of Communication so we may all become better digital dilettantes.

③
1. Is it proper to send jokes through e-mail?
I'll admit, I enjoy a hearty chuckle every now and then. But this constant barrage of Dilberty witticisms and reams of one-liners leave me somewhat brain-dead. It's becoming the work equivalent of daytime TV. I say enough's enough. Joke senders should special-code these ubiquitous tee-hees and not expect cute replies and gracious chortles in return.

2. Is it kosher to transmit love letters by e-mail?
Transmissions by nature are almost always unwanted. Everyone knows what happened to the CEO when he accidentally broadcast his voice mail message to his "group," which j.... ....

to be the entire company. Catch a clue. The written word can circle the globe and wind a noose around your neck if you're not careful. If you want to rendezvous, do it in the flesh, for God's sake.

3. How should you respond to unexpected and unwanted personal messages?

The whole push-button immediacy of the medium encourages rash behavior. It's just too easy to type and send. E-mail fosters a kind of boundarylessness that threatens the downfall of society as we know it. If you really want to get chummy, old-fashioned face-to-face contact is best. Otherwise, any maudlin goings-on must be chalked up to the curious phenomenon that I call "e-blurt" or *bla-tant, lax, unpromted, and rash transmissions*. If you reply rather curtly (or not at all) to an e-blurt, well, you're just putting the firm parameters back where they belong.

4. Must you use strict manuscript formats when writing memos, etc.?

E-mail messages should conform to the same style you would have used in a snail-mail correspondence. Don't chintz on proper spacing, and watch your spelling. If you don't have Spell Swell or the equivalent, write your letter in your word-processing program first, so you can take your time and get it right. My e-mail program doesn't have a spell-checking program, and if you're like me, when you're typing, you may be oblivious to the actual page and bam! before you know it, you've sent something really important and misspelled "rapport" or "prioritize." Now, good speller though you may be, here you are for all to judge, not only a poor speller, but slovenly, not an attention-to-detail type player; oh my!

5. Does every e-mail message require a timely response?

Check the darn things first thing in the morning and reply to urgent requests pronto. If someone went to any trouble to put their message together, then, by all means, respondez-vous. The standard lag time generally expected is twenty-four hours. One-word answers will suffice, and by all means limit your questions.

If they have just added you to some chain letter or are passing around tidbits of gossip or jokes, don't waste your time. It just encourages this kind of thing.

6. Is it okay to include little smiling faces and other cutesy expressions in your message?

I say ban them altogether! I think we've all seen enough smiley faces and "Have a nice days" to last us through the next blue moon. As the mother says to her little child, "Say it in words!" I say the same to you.

7. If someone leaves you a voice message, can you respond via e-mail?

If the required response is not urgent, yes. If you really don't want to actually talk to the person, finagle your way through the company's internal voice mail system and leave a message on their voice mail. Remember, you get some leeway with e-mail, as the expected turnaround time for response is twenty-four hours, while for voice messages it's three hours. This is the beauty of e-mail. People are tired of bells and buzzers and beeps. Instead of the jangling of phones all the time, they'll hear the pleasant pitter-patter of little keyboards.

8. Is it proper etiquette to include self-promotion in your signature file?

The first rule of etiquette is never blow your own horn; if you're doing everything up to snuff, your right actions will speak for themselves. Subtle and pithy are the watchwords for your sig files. Some people include favorite quotes that capture a sense of their personality. This is acceptable as long as it's short. No matter your business or occupation, if you want to communicate something else about who you are and what you represent, choose your words carefully, and keep it brief. We are already spending far too much time reading minuscule mots from anyone who has nothing to say about anything. And that includes Christmas letters. I can't tell you the number of Christmas letters I received on e-mail. Not even a nice card and holiday stamp. Did they actually expect me to read those dollops? This whole e-mail revolution has gone way too far. We have to get our wits about us and return to the writing of hard copies. I say stand up to the techie nerdites who are controlling the very fabric of our lives. Do something radical; write a letter today!

9. Is it okay to argue on-line?

Some of you will absolutely bristle at what I'm about to say, but I think arguing on-line is the only way to argue. Perfectly acceptable. In a face-to-face duel, you're likely to lose your temper and say things you don't mean. And you know how tongue-tied you get when under attack. No, I say, compose your message with well-chosen words. Let the sotto voci be flung about Cyberspace at will. You will be out of firing range. And if you really need to chill, turn the whole mess off and go take a hot tub.

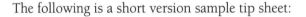

Keynotes   Corporate Training   Breakout Sessions

The following is a short version sample tip sheet:

SUSAN HARROW

MARKETING STRATEGIST ~ PRESENTATION & MEDIA COACH

Ten Ways You Can Become a Superstar Speaker

1. Create instant rapport with your host and audience.

Engage your audience by telling a story that everyone can relate to. You can use the words "Imagine with me . . ." to begin your journey together.

2. Make frequent neutral (no agenda) eye contact.

By not judging them or expecting anything from your audience (including approval), you allow an exchange of energy that encourages openness.

3. Vary your facial expressions to match your enthusiasm.
People tend to be more expressive with children. Practice your talk to a real or imagined audience of tots and you'll find your face will follow your feelings naturally.

4. Develop a relaxed comfort with your own body.
Ahhh, if this was as easy as it sounds—and it can be. Begin by tensing up your whole body and holding your muscles in a contracted position for ten seconds, then release. You'll be able to release a lot of anxiety that has built up in your muscles. Squeeze, release, squeeze, release.

5. Have a clear, fascinating focus and direction of your talk.
If you practice creating a one-line theme for your entire talk, you can more easily adhere to your intended topic.

6. Make sure the content is right for the audience.
Make sure that your subject matter consists of information that is relevant and worthwhile to the people who will receive it.

7. Use appropriate humor appropriately.
Humor that relates to your topic directly, that people can respond to quickly, and that doesn't offend tends to be the most effective.

8. Involve your audience emotionally.
Give your audience something to laugh or cry about. They'll remember you and your stories better that way.

9. Allow for silence to create impact.
Silence is your friend. It allows the audience to absorb the meaning of your words. And it creates greater impact when you want to make a point.

10. Work with your fear of failure in every speaking scenario.
We all fear rejection and failure. Being aware of it and comfortable enough to mention it will help ease its existence. But don't make

that the focus of your talk. Your audience expects you to deliver on your expertise.

11. Extra! Match your tone to the words you are saying.
When you're enthusiastic about the points you are relaying, let it show. Your audience will be glad to join in your enjoyment.

4200 Park Boulevard PMB 333 S ~ Oakland ~ CA 94602
telephone 510.419.0330   *email* susan@publicitysecrets.com   *website* www.publicitysecrets.com

Photo

Your photograph is the visual representation of who you are. It should match the image, words, feeling, and message you want to convey. You want to be original without being outlandish (unless that is what you want). And your pose should show that you are comfortable, credible, approachable, inviting, and friendly.

A head shot is essential to start, as the media generally request this first. You can include one of your full body if it helps express your medium (proper business person, painter, dancer, computer software designer) or shows you in action doing your craft. Props are appropriate if they help explain what you do visually, without being distracting.

At your session you may want to bring a number of outfits that show the different aspects of your profession or life. By having a number of different pictures ready you will maintain your freshness as you begin to appear in a variety of print media.

HOT TIP!

BURN IN ONE IMAGE.

Instead of varying your image you may want to burn a single image into the national psyche. Or burn in the image with one outfit or style like talk show host Larry King, known for his suspenders.

There is an erotic photograph of painter Francis Bacon with sides of meat hanging around him (one of his trademark themes). For many years it was the only picture Bacon would allow to be published.

HOT TIP!

CONNECT TO YOUR AUDIENCE DURING YOUR PHOTO SHOOT.

Karen Kingston, feng shui and space-clearing expert, told me that she used a special technique so people would be attracted to her photograph. During the session she imagined all the people she wanted to connect with all over the world. Her intention came across in her expression. People often write to her to tell her they feel like they know her.

It is wise to have both color and black-and-white 5" × 7" prints, since magazines and many newspapers now offer color. Since some magazines prefer slides or transparencies (for products or art objects), these are something to consider as well. Make sure you tell your photographer that you want your photos in digital format so you can also make them available as JPG files or GIF images on your Web site.

Before you send out your photograph to the media, put your name and contact information, along with a credit of the photographer's name, on the back with a label. Since photographs are expensive, I always include a self-addressed stamped envelope (SASE) to ensure their return.

Product photo or sample

If you have invented or made something that is easy to send, by all means, include it.

You can personalize a folder by gluing your logo, product drawing or photo, book jacket cover, even your business card, on the face of the folder. Always include your contact information on every piece of material. In busy offices, papers can easily get separated. You wouldn't want to lose out on an opportunity for a little omission that could easily be handled.

For photographer Nina Glaser's press kit we included high-quality black-and-white copies instead of expensive prints. Once an editor was sold on the story, we sent the slides for reproduction. We also included an artistically designed brochure that added to her professional image. When you get a print run of postcards or brochures, get extra so you can use them for marketing purposes. Consider getting postcards printed if you are marketing something that is highly visual.

Fact sheet

Fact sheets provide data that a reporter would otherwise have to search for himself. Ideally, you want to give reporters the data or statistics they will need to do an article on the subject you're proposing, and sound intelligent (without having to extensively research the subject themselves). By providing important unbiased information, you establish yourself as a reliable source. (Of course there is no such thing as "unbiased" facts. The very facts you choose represent some angle you are suggesting.) While journalists might trash a press release, they tend to save the information that may come in handy at a later date, for an impending timely topic. Remember to include all of your contact information so you can be properly credited—and so you can be called for additional information if necessary. Update your fact sheet as you gather new information.

I've included two very different fact sheets here to give you a sense of possibility as there isn't one standard format. The first one represents a business to business (B2B) fact sheet. This might be sent to trade publications or consumer magazines (general public). Suzanne Jackson, who wrote this one, says that she often writes highly targeted custom fact sheets. "I find every fact sheet needs to be tailored to the effort, and oftentimes, to the publication itself." Consider tailoring yours.

The other fact sheet was written by Ann Keeler Evans for her company, A Rite to Remember. Notice how Ann weaves in the advantages of using her service with the statistics she's chosen to support her point of view.

HOT TIP!

DON'T KNOCK ANYONE WHEN MAKING YOUR POINT.
When you put someone down, you are the one who will look bad. You can inspire controversy and be intentionally incendiary without knocking anyone. Or by humorously (good-naturedly) poking fun at your offending opposite.

The following are two examples of fact sheets:

11232 Cedar Hill Rd
Gordonsville, VA 22942

FACT SHEET FOR MEDIA:

PAYNET: Revolutionizing Commercial Lending's Credit Process

"We are committed to creating information services that help our partners make better, more profitable decisions."
—Bill Phelan, President of PAYNET

The Issue

As its most basic, credit is the likelihood or predictability that someone will pay his or her bills. Every business, in order to survive, must know that its customers will pay for services rendered in a timely manner. This is so important that most businesses have credit departments whose main purpose is to make decisions about a customer's ability to pay its bills. With better information credit personnel can make better decisions, helping improve company profitability.

Information on consumers is collected by companies, such as Experian, Equifax, and TransUnion, which provide accurate data about customers' credit history. However, to date, credit data on businesses has been lacking and incomplete. Payment history experience has traditionally been verified by manually calling references provided by the applicant or by the limited information provided by third party credit-reporting agency. The current process is costly, tips off competitors about a pending transaction, and provides an incomplete credit picture of the applicant.

The PAYNET Solution

PAYNET is a repository of term payment history information on publicly—and privately—held businesses. The service is made up of commercial lenders who—in return for contributing information—gain access to a universe of proprietary credit and payment history information. The database is composed of historical and current lease and loan credit experiences aggregated across contributors. This highly relevant data enables lenders to make better-informed credit decisions.

Thanks to the power of PAYNET, lenders can quickly assess their applicant's financial capabilities through data on how the applicant paid similar obligations in the past. The PAYNET Alliance's cost-effective payment information services provide subscribers with such benefits as:

- Increased approvals

- Lower credit losses and delinquencies

- Better information for deal pricing

- Streamlined credit process

PAYNET (The Payment Information Network)

PAYNET's pilot program launched in 2nd Quarter 2001. PAYNET has organized a group of major commercial finance companies to contribute their customer payment experiences into the PAYNET credit repository. In exchange, the contributors gain exclusive access to the entire pool of payment history information, an unparalleled resource of credit information. This cooperative approach, pioneered by PAYNET, revolutionizes the commercial information services industry by providing a comprehensive, relevant source of data enabling lenders to make better-informed credit decisions. The payment history data is downloaded monthly directly from the lending company via a seamless interface to their systems. The data is transmitted through secure transfer and run through a data accuracy test by PAYNET's proprietary technology, ensuring the data is usable, relevant, and accurate.

Important Note: PAYNET ensures all data is secure. The data collected will never be used or sold for marketing purposes.

Market Potential

The commercial credit market is estimated to be $1 billion in annual revenues according to industry sources, with more than 40 million credit applications annually. Commercial lending to businesses is estimated to total $1.35 trillion in annual volume in 2000 with historical annual growth of 7.3 percent in the last decade.

The equipment leasing industry, a sub-segment of the commercial lending market, generated more than $220 billion in new volume and more than 10 million lease applications in 2000 alone. This market is forecast to grow 14 percent to more than $240 billion in originations in 2001.

About PAYNET, The Company

PAYNET manages the Payment Information Network for the commercial equipment finance industry, an industry that represents more than $550 billion in Net Assets. This network produces the nation's largest on-line, proprietary database of lease and loan payment history information used for credit decision purposes.

The Payment Information Network currently has many leading commercial lenders as members, representing a substantial portion of the net assets in the industry. PAYNET uses its proprietary technology and the power of shared data to increase profitability, to improve operational efficiency, and to reduce credit losses for commercial finance companies.

Partners with PAYNET include the Equipment Leasing Association, consulting firms, and major lease accounting and software providers. Industry leaders and respected consultants compose PAYNET's Board.

Founded in 1999, the company is headquartered in Skokie, Illinois.

Contact information:
Bill Phelan, PayNet, Inc.
847-324-3400, x12
bphelan@paynetonline.com
www.paynetonline.com

contact   Suzanne Jackson
phone   540-832-0583
fax   540-832-0586
e-mail   sj@CornerstoneDelivers.com
website www.CornerstoneDelivers.com

A Rite to Remember
Principal: Ann Keeler Evans, M.Div.

Live your life with gratitude, passion, and intention! At A Rite to Remember, founder Ann Keller Evans, M.Div., works with you to create ceremonies and rituals to mark important events in your life. Celebrate relationships, families, lifestyle and livelihood, weddings, baby blessings, coming of age(s), homes, the seasons, and your community. Rev. Evans can help you put sense and the sacred back into the passages of life in this complex and confusing world. Allow ritual to help you lead the life you desire!

Ceremonies Celebrating Your Life

Ann Keeler Evans, M.Div.

5337 College Ave., Suite 116
Oakland, California 94618
phone & fax ~ 510-339-7561

Fact: Ritual can enhance your life. It provides a time, a place, and a reason to clarify your goals within the context of your beliefs and values. Well-crafted ceremony conveys your deepest meanings and invites those you care about to stay involved in your life and supportive of your dreams. Rev. Evans knows ritual and understands how it works. She provides a structure and a format to plan and celebrate your life.

Fact: Only three in ten Americans attend religious services regularly. Yet, more than half believe religion can answer the problems of today. A Rite to Remember helps communities celebrate age-old rituals and make meaning around our changing world. Even those with strong religious affiliations today find solace and support in disciplines and traditions from around the world. Rev. Evans's ecumenical background and training provide everyone possibilities for reflection and change.

Fact: Most people no longer have a family priest. This can result in intimate events being cold and impersonal. You deserve to be seen and known by the person celebrating your life. Rev. Evans's warm personal touch invites you to enter into the process and enjoy your ritual moment, from an exploratory meeting, through questionnaires and drafts, past rehearsals, and at your special event.

Fact: Life is difficult when you're separated from family and friends. Celebrations call your loved ones together and help cement your bonds. You deserve the support of your community. They deserve to know how to support you and how to be a community to one another. At A Rite to Remember, Rev. Evans helps your loved ones recognize their role in your relationship and in one another's lives.

Fact: Weddings are much more than legal actions or ancient religious traditions. They are celebrations of your hearts' and souls' connections. On your wedding day, focus on what matters most and what is real! When the spiritual aspect is emphasized and attended to, marriages have a much higher chance of success. Eighty-five percent of couples successfully reuniting after separation have prayed together. A Rite to Remember helps you celebrate what is true and meaningful rather than what the law demands or the doctrines prescribe.

Resources:
Rev. Evans's first book is *Promises to Keep: Crafting Your Wedding Ceremony.* She is currently at work on a book of rituals for women

and one on creating intimate and meaningful memorial services. Having graduated with a Masters of Divinity from Union Theological Seminary, Rev. Evans augmented her studies with courses and workshops in a variety of disciplines and traditions.

Contact Information:
See A Rite to Remember's Web page at *www.ritetoremember.com* or contact Ann directly at *ann@ritetoremember* or 510-339-7561.

Public service announcements (PSAs)

Most radio stations and some TV stations have public service announcement (PSA) departments that air information about events sponsored by the community or nonprofit organizations. The format is straightforward and informational:

① The words "For Immediate Release."

② The date the PSA was written.

③ The "kill date": The day to stop airing the ad because the event is over.

④ Contact name, phone number, and e-mail address (optional).

⑤ Statement of purpose for the event: What the fund-raising is for or whom the event benefits.

⑥ Statement that declares that this is a PSA.

⑦ Fifteen-, twenty-, and forty-five-second ads to be spoken by the announcer. The producer/director will use whatever version is appropriate for the time slot.

⑧ Date, time, and location of the event.

⑨ Description of the activities that will take place at the event. Include the cost and a telephone number for information and registration (if applicable).

Send in your information in the format shown. Use all capital letters and state the airtime (time it yourself with a watch to make sure you adhere to the time stated). If it is for TV, send in a visual prop (banner, toy, art) that the host can show while reading the announcement. Put this on your stationery with your contact information.

Since these announcements or postings are free, there is a lot of competition for airtime. Send in your PSA at least six weeks in advance. Eight to ten weeks is optimum. The station chooses to air PSAs both on a first-come, first-served basis and according to what they deem worthwhile for the public. The PSA director decides on the worthiness of the cause and then fits the PSA into the schedule whenever possible. See below for a sample PSA.

S U S A N   H A R R O W

MARKETING STRATEGIST ~ PRESENTATION & MEDIA COACH

④ Contact: Susan Harrow
510.419.0330

① **FOR IMMEDIATE RELEASE**
② **MAY 1, 2001**
③ **KILL DATE: JUNE 27, 2001**

⑤ THE RETAIL STORE HEAVENLY ANGELS SPONSORS AN ANGEL STREET FAIR FUND-RAISER TO SUPPORT CASA (COURT-APPOINTED SPECIAL ADVOCATES), A NATIONAL NONPROFIT ORGANIZATION FOUNDED TO TAKE ABUSED CHILDREN FROM THEIR HOMES AND MOVE THEM THROUGH THE COURT SYSTEM TO SAFETY.

⑥ PUBLIC SERVICE ANNOUNCEMENT/COMMUNITY CALENDAR

⑦ 15 SECONDS:
HEAVENLY ANGELS RETAIL STORE SPONSORS AN ANGEL STREET FAIR TO SUPPORT CASA (COURT-APPOINTED SPECIAL ADVOCATES) ON ⑧ SATURDAY, JUNE 27, FROM 11 A.M. TO 5 P.M., AT HEAVENLY ANGELS, 2100 SINGLETON AVENUE, IN DENVER. ⑨ A DAY OF MUSIC, FOOD, FACE PAINTING, GAMES, FOR

ALL. ADMISSION IS FREE. FOR INFORMATION CALL XXX-XXX-XXXX.

⑦ 20 SECONDS:

HEAVENLY ANGELS RETAIL STORE SPONSORS AN ANGEL STREET FAIR TO SUPPORT CASA (COURT-APPOINTED SPECIAL ADVOCATES) ON ⑧ SATURDAY, JUNE 27, FROM 11 A.M. TO 5 P.M., AT HEAVENLY ANGELS, 2100 SINGLETON AVENUE, IN DENVER. ⑨ A DAY OF MUSIC, FOOD, FACE PAINTING, DUNK TANK, CARNIVAL GAMES, COTTON CANDY, AND A RAFFLE FOR UNUSUAL PRIZES PROMISES EXCITEMENT FOR ALL. ADMISSION IS FREE. FOR INFORMATION CALL XXX-XXX-XXXX.

⑦ 45 SECONDS:

HEAVENLY ANGELS RETAIL STORE SPONSORS AN ANGEL STREET FAIR CARNIVAL TO SUPPORT CASA (COURT-APPOINTED SPECIAL ADVOCATES). ALL PROFITS GO TO CREATE ART PROGRAMS FOR ABUSED CHILDREN. ON ⑧ SATURDAY, JUNE 27, FROM 11 A.M. TO 5 P.M., AT THE HEAVENLY ANGELS STORE, 2100 SINGLETON AVENUE, IN DENVER. ⑨ A DAY OF MUSIC, FOOD, FACE PAINTING, DUNK TANK, CARNI-VAL GAMES, COTTON CANDY, A FINE ART AUCTION, AND A RAFFLE FOR UNUSUAL PRIZES PROMISES EXCITEMENT FOR ALL. WIN A *TOUCHED BY AN ANGEL* OR *DR. QUINN, MEDICINE WOMAN* SIGNED TV SCRIPT OR A STAY AT THE SECRET GARDEN MANSION BED AND BREAKFAST INN. HEAR LIVE DJ'S SPIN YOUR FAVORITE RECORDS. BE ENTERTAINED BY CHILD-PERFORMED PLAYS. LET YOURSELF BE REGALED BY STORYTELLING. ADMISSION IS FREE. FOR INFORMA-TION CALL XXX-XXX-XXXX.

4200 Park Boulevard PMB 333 S ~ Oakland ~ CA 94602
telephone 510.419.0330   *email* susan@publicitysecrets.com   *website* www.publicitysecrets.com

Calendar of events

This is the print equivalent of a PSA and appears in your local newspaper as a community listing. Newspapers also choose the events considered most worthwhile for their readership. Your local newspaper prints a free listing of community goings-on at least once a week. Most require that you send in your information three to four weeks before the event. Take a look in your paper to see the length and style that fits its format. Like the PSA, these placements are competitive.

Articles about you

Articles about you tell the people who receive your press materials that you are already a viable bet. Journalists and producers assume they're in good company if one of their colleagues has taken it upon himself to scrawl about the illustrious you. Even more impressive of course is if the publication is prestigious. The more you are in demand, the more attractive you become. Include these articles as credibility builders. Once you have gotten a number of them, you can excerpt the best parts and put them all on one page with the masthead (the title's distinctive type and/or design) of the publication.

One woman wishes she had taken the date off her 1991 story in *Inc.* magazine. She continues to use the glowing feature article about her talents in the press kit she sends to potential clients and the media, but wonders if it wouldn't have more impact if it was current. Think about how you are going to use your articles in the future *before* you reproduce them. Especially when you pay for professional glossy reprints. Ask yourself if the articles are time sensitive versus "evergreen." You can then use your judgment to decide if it is better to have an article with or without the date.

The alternative to the princely price you will pay for reprints takes a sculptor's hand, an artist's eye, and the patience of a saint to cut and paste the masthead, artwork, or logo of the publication with the body of the article. I tend to have octopus fingers and inevitably get a non-erasable smudge in the most important part of the piece. Middle ground: I have paid copy shop people to do it for me. You choose.

Feature articles

A feature article is a story that can be used "as is" in a newspaper or magazine. It is written in the style of an objective observer. Since these are written by experienced journalists, freelance writers, and publicists and have many formats, one example is provided as a guide. (It is one I wrote for an art exhibit at a cutting edge—no pun intended—hair salon and art gallery.) If you are targeting your materials for a particular publication, send for their guidelines so you can tailor them appropriately.

Feature Article
Contact: Susan Harrow, 510.419.0330

Ma Jaya Painting Exhibition
FACES OF THE MOTHER

She calls herself a Jewish Hindu woman who loves Christ. Ma Jaya, affectionately known as Ma, which in the Indian tradition means holy woman, turns the seriousness of spirituality on its ear. Following in the tradition of puckish masters such as the Dalai Lama and Sogyal Rinpoche, Ma uses humor and directness to elucidate the nature of living and dying.

Before she took an Indian name and swathed herself in saris and bangles, she was a housewife from Brooklyn who sold wholesale goods out of her garage. At home one day, while attempting to lose weight by breathing in full lotus position ("Don't worry, it didn't work," she says), Jesus appeared to her carrying the Cross. Still locked in the position, Ma scrambled up her staircase on her knees and hid under the sheets with her husband and dogs. "It wasn't a vision," she says in her nasally feisty voice. "He was there." The third time he visited, they had an all-night chat in the bathroom, and Ma began the process of discovery that today has grown a following so large, she founded the eighty-four-acre Kashi Ashram in Roseland, Florida, that houses temples for Hinduism, Buddhism, Judaism, and Christianity.

If all this sounds impossibly dramatic, it is. But beneath the still strong Brooklyn accent and clanking bracelets ("What'd you expect, some quiet little holy woman?") there is a seriousness of intent that is unmistakable. Tall, with ink-black curls, and having gained a black belt in tae kwon do, Ma presents her own style of vision. Every morning she plays team Rollerblade hockey with teenagers and adults. At fifty-three, her face appears ageless and youthful as she tirelessly devotes herself to service.

As always with spiritual masters their message is clear and simple, yet profoundly difficult. Ma begins with a simple touch. She believes that kissing people's brows and hugging them gives a stronger, more important message than "preaching about God." She isn't afraid to kiss and cradle the people with life-threatening diseases whose physical bodies are often gaunt and ravaged with sores. She calls being present to share a person's death an incredible privilege. "No matter how much I do it, I continue to love it. It's sad and beautiful and frees one from pain," she says.

Once every three months Ma visits San Francisco, giving a *darshan,* or spiritual service, at the Center for Living, and then travels to numerous hospital beds throughout the city. Her work extends not only to people with HIV and AIDS, but to abused children and the elderly. "It's all about service," she says. "What else is there?"

One of few major women speakers at the Parliament of World Religions last year in Chicago, Ma spoke out loudly and persistently about the plight of people with AIDS. The president of the Parliament tried to quiet her, to no avail. "AIDS is not a pretty thing," she says. "It would have spoiled the moment. But it was necessary to bring it to everyone's attention." She has begged the Pope to hug one adult person with AIDS. "It would change the world if he did. People would follow his example of compassion."

Full of personality, Ma's exhibition at Architects & Heroes' Fillmore location titled **FACES OF THE MOTHER** exudes the same boldness of spirit that she embodies in her daily service. With passionate colors swirled, dabbed, thrust onto canvas, the work almost jumps out at viewers. There is a largeness of spirit, an invitation to act and embrace the unpredictability of life.

An internationally acclaimed artist, she has exhibited in Rome and Paris, using the proceeds from her acrylic paintings on canvas to support the River Fund, a volunteer-based foundation she began to help people in need. River Fund volunteers and provides donations of food, gifts, and money to support hospices, food programs, care facilities, and AIDS service organizations. Ma began to paint in 1983 as an expression of her devotion to God. There is no separation between prayer and painting for her. She takes the forms, visions, and ideas she has in meditation and, making liberal use of paint, transfers them directly onto canvas. The result is work that captures a sense of the moment. Ma's art, reflective of her personality, is like a slap of awakening, delightfully lived. "The act of painting a sacred image becomes like a prayer being said over and over again. If everyone could love the mother, there would be no wars. *That's* how my art is received."

Ma Jaya will be in San Francisco for her opening reception and fund-raiser on Friday, April 22, from 7–9 p.m., at Architects & Heroes, located at 2239 Fillmore Street, next to the Clay Theater. At that time, she will be available to answer questions about her art, which is deeply connected to her spiritual work.

207 Powell Street, Suite 400, San Francisco, California 94102 (415)391-8833
2239 Fillmore Street, San Francisco, California 94115 (415)921-8383
18 Hysan Avenue, Causeway Bay, Hong Kong 852-881-1808

Question and answer (Q&A) sheet

Publicist Anita Halton of Anita Halton Associates always requests that her clients do a Q&A sheet for two reasons: It helps them begin to ferret out their most important points; and publications often use these more lengthy answers in a finished piece without having to take the time and effort to interview the people who wrote them. Since the information is often taken verbatim, it also ensures that you get quoted accurately. There is a thoughtful Q&A sheet below by publicist Kath Delaney for her client Shambhala Publications author and Buddhist meditation teacher Sharon Salzberg.

The following is a sample question and answer sheet:

SHAMBHALA PUBLICATIONS, INC.

Horticultural Hall 300 Massachusetts Avenue Boston Massachusetts 02115

FREQUENTLY ASKED QUESTIONS & ANSWERS
SHARON SALZBERG

Q. For the beginner, briefly describe Buddhism's practices and principles.

A. The practices of Buddhism are based on the development of wisdom and compassion. It is believed that each of us as human beings has the capacity to understand ourselves more fully, to care more deeply for ourselves and for others. The practices of Buddhism help us to unfold this capacity.

Q. What is the best way to learn about Buddhism?

A. The very best way to learn about Buddhism is to learn about yourself, your own mind. This is done through meditation practice. You can look for centers or groups in or near your community for help with guidance. We even have a correspondence course in meditation at the Insight Meditation Center for those who cannot find the resources close to home for support in meditation practice. And, of course, there are books that help explain the spirit with which to pursue practice, which is an essential ingredient.

Q. How many sects or schools of Buddhism are there? What basic tenets do they all agree on?

A. There are many different schools of Buddhism, roughly divided into three traditions of Theravada, Mahayana, and Vajrayana. All schools are united in their fundamental respect for the Four Noble Truths—that is, the acknowledgment of the suffering found in life, that the causes of suffering can be discerned, that suffering can be alleviated, and that there is a practical path that can be utilized toward this end. The methodologies come down to developing mindfulness in order to see the nature of life more clearly (e.g., the relationship between the body and the mind) and to be free of habitual, mechanical reactions that cause us unhappiness; and to developing loving-kindness to replace the specific habit of fear in our minds and in our relationships.

Q. What can Buddhism offer contemporary Americans?

A. Buddhism offers an opportunity to look within ourselves for a sense of abundance, depth, and connection to life, rather than being caught in endless consumption and addictive behaviors. It also presents a chance to slow down a bit, experience life more fully through the power of mindfulness. In addition, Buddhism gives us a chance to develop sincere self-respect, rather than habitual self-judgment.

Q. What was most inspiring for you as a Westerner encountering Buddhist teachings?

A. The emphasis on forging my own understanding of reality, which I found incredibly empowering . . . not believing anyone else's version of the truth, even the Buddha's, but using the tools of greater awareness to see things more clearly for myself. Buddhism's emphasis on love and compassion as the primary motivations also touched me deeply . . . and the importance of developing these qualities for oneself.

Q. Isn't having loving-kindness toward someone who has hurt you just giving in and justifying their abuse?

A. For many reasons, in our time love seems to have become associated with a sense of weakness, almost a foggy sentimentality that has no power or clarity. This is a terrible degeneration. I think it is quite possible to recognize the importance of both justice and compassion in our lives. In Buddhist terminology, justice would be wisdom: seeing clearly, seeing things as they truly are, acting from that clear seeing. Loving-kindness or compassion toward someone who has hurt us means that we might understand their conditioning that gave them the inclination to behave in that way; or we might recognize how much pain they are in; or we might recognize how much pain we are in from obsessing over the hurt. In any case, we can experience the freedom of not casting someone permanently into the role of the "other," the "enemy." This does not mean we develop amnesia, or get stupid, or allow ourselves to be abused again and again. It means that our motivation for seeking change is not so driven by forces, like hatred, that diminish our clear seeing and limit our options.

Q. Is there anyone for whom you would *not* recommend meditation?

A. I think it is important to differentiate between doing some daily meditation practice and entering a silent, intensive retreat to learn meditation. If you're emerging from a recent terrible trauma, or you have a long-seated deep psychological problem, it might not be so helpful to put yourself in a situation, such as a retreat, where you're cut off from your normal support system. Virtually anyone can do a daily meditation practice and benefit from it if they have an understanding of the crucial role of balance in meditation. The forms can be quite flexible to suit someone's needs: If someone can't do sitting practice, they might do walking meditation; if they can't walk and are in a wheelchair, they might do wheeling meditation. If you feel uncertain about your experience or are uneasy, it is good to seek out a teacher.

Q. What do you mean by compassion, mindfulness, and loving-kindness? Do they mean more than is apparent to the Western reader?

A. These words, as is the case with many words, are used quite specifically in the Buddhist tradition. Language takes on layers of meaning in Buddhism because of centuries of practical and direct exploration of the nature of the mind and of life. Loving-kindness is a state of heartfelt inclusiveness toward all aspects of ourselves and ultimately toward all of life. Exploring loving-kindness challenges our assumptions about aloneness, loss, and our deserving of true happiness.

Compassion is the trembling or quivering of the heart in response to pain or suffering. It is not a thought or a sentimental feeling but rather is a movement of the heart. Yet, it is not the same as feeling shattered or having our hearts break in the face of pain. Exploring compassion challenges our assumptions about suffering, and our need to turn away.

Telephone: (617) 424-0030 · Fax: (617) 236-1563

Bounceback

Think boomerang. A bounceback is based on the direct-marketing concept that people who are really interested in your project will prove their commitment by taking action. Ever notice how on those sweepstakes you have to lick, stick, peel, or scratch something in order to receive you millions?

The bounceback is a one-page interest barometer. It gauges the true commitment of the recipient. Instead of including your product, sample, or book, you list what is available and let the person decide what they would like to receive. You might want to create a bounceback that is even more specific than the one on page 93. For example, it could include the opportunity to receive photographs of the product or yourself.

The following is a sample bounceback:

MEDIA BOUNCEBACK

Please complete and
return to:

Your name:
Your address:
Your phone:
fax:
e-mail:

Date:_____

From:

_____
name and title

_____
publication

_____
phone, fax, e-mail

_____
address

_____
city, state, zip

Please send the following material. I am seriously considering
reviewing (name of your product or service)

_____
BOOK

_____
photos (slides, glossies—color or b&w)

_____
additional material

_____
_____
_____

Compilation or "roundup" pieces

Gathering a number of experts' advice together for a full article is a viable way to position yourself among your more prestigious peers. This serves double duty by being seen as well informed, by association, and by giving you occasion to call people of stature in your field. You are sharing the spotlight with big names and providing a more selfless way to give away your knowledge.

Opinion letters

Called "op-ed" pieces by journalists because they are typically in newspapers and magazines *opposite the editorial* page. They give the reader a chance to respond positively or negatively to articles that have appeared in the publication. They take on an almost lawyerly quality trying to convince you that their "argument" has the most merit. In a broader sense an opinion piece often takes its lead from the front-page news story, the holiday season, or a significant trend. Your "letter" is more like a short article than a casual note to a friend.

HOT TIP!

VOTE YEA OR NAY.

The letters that appeal to editors are strongly for or against the points raised in the piece. Support your reasons with persuasive arguments, facts, statistics, other expert opinions, and topics that are timely.

Letters to the editor

Newspapers and magazines both run letters to the editor. Newspapers print them on or near the editorial page. Magazines provide space right after the editor's letter. Newspapers give readers a chance to participate by sharing their opinions about articles published or issues of concern to them within their community or the world at large. Magazines focus on comments on specific articles written by their staff or freelancers.

The opportunity to contribute a letter to the editor for a magazine doesn't last long. You must read the publication regularly and act immediately by sending off a response via e-mail or snail mail. The tone of a letter to the editor usually takes four forms:

1. Voicing strong disagreement.

2. Voicing strong agreement.

3. Pointing out an inaccuracy in the content.

4. Giving additional information about the subject that would have given the article a more fair or less subjective slant.

While TV or radio call-in shows will broadcast only your first name and city, newspapers and magazines publish the writer's full name, city, state, organization or business name, and (sometimes) e-mail address. (*Fast Company* magazine generously includes your title, too.) You can get your key messages out and then give all the people who resonate with your opinions a chance to contact you. Great alliances of all kinds can be created.

Here is the format to follow (see the example on page 96):

① Even if you know the name of the editor, it is customary to begin your letter with "To the Editor."

② When you are responding to a previously published article in the magazine, you will want to make it clear which one you are responding to and why. Be sure to include the title and date.

③ Sum up your "argument" in the first few sentences.

④ Make your case with one strong point or with backup evidence. (Statistics or facts.) Susan makes her case with a single point.

⑤ Beneath your signature, state your name, title, organization or business name, city and state, and e-mail address if you'd like that printed. Most publications require that you include a phone number, but won't print it.

Keep your letter short—around 250 to 350 words—so the editor won't be tempted to do what he is hired to do: edit.

HOT TIP!

DON'T LEAVE IT UP TO THE EDITOR TO INCLUDE YOUR TITLE.
You can incorporate your title (along with heightening your credibility factor) into the body of your letter.

HOT TIP!

COMPLIMENT THE MAGAZINE.
(Editors love that!) And give some inside knowledge, perhaps with a touch of attitude, about your own industry.

The following is a sample letter to the editor:

Women Do It Right

① To the Editor:

② Thanks for revealing new—yet also very old—ways of mentoring ("Women's Ways of Mentoring," September 1998). My most recent mentor liked to call herself a "femtor." She had this incredible ability both to nurture me and to teach me the ropes as I began my professional-speaking business and my life as an author.

③ More important, she taught me that as you grow, you can outgrow your mentor. A mentor who was there to help you through a particular stage of your development might not be the best-equipped person to guide you through the next stage.

④ That is why I have come to believe that we don't need just mentors, we need MOMs (mentors of the moment).

Susan RoAne

⑤ Author, *How to Work a Room: The Ultimate Guide to Savvy Socializing in Person and Online* (Quill, 2000), New York, New York

susan@susanroane.com

(*Fast Company* magazine, issue no. 19, November 1998, p. 36.)

Susan RoAne really practices what she preaches. In almost every book on publicity I have read, her name pops up. In the above letter she covered an issue important to her, as well as "worked in" her profession and the title of one of her books. "That letter earned me my first private would-be-author coaching client," she says. "My mentoring thoughts were based on that chapter from *The Secrets of Savvy Networking*." Notice how she managed to work in the title of another book into this quote? A short letter to the editor sells your products and services to the publication's subscriber base—thousands or millions of people who are your prospective buyers.

Your mission in writing a letter to the editor is to express your opinion while also mentioning the valuable service you provide to your community. When you are amused or excited by an article, you can express your emotion while connecting it to yourself, your business, book, product, or cause. Weave in why the article mattered to you and how you can be of service within your "community." By your community I mean your peers, professionals in your field, customers, whoever you are looking to attract.

If you have already gotten publicity by being mentioned in an article, you can accomplish several things at once by writing a letter to the editor. You can thank the writer publicly by penning a thank-you letter for the acknowledgment in the article—and make an additional point that wasn't included in it. By so doing, you are adding value to the article and making yourself visible again in the next issue. When (unhappily) someone misquotes you, or puts incorrect information about you, in an article, immediately send a polite, to the point, correction. Never reiterate the original inaccurate or damaging information, since that will reinforce it. State just the correction along with the message you want the public to read.

But what if an article was written about your profession or business and included many of your competitors, but you were overlooked? Don't despair, repair. While your competitor is absorbing the golden beams of prosperity and frantically answering phone calls, you can take a seat in the sunshine with your favorite pen and inscribe a reply to let readers know you are alive. This is a grand time to show just how you are different from the people, businesses, or organizations profiled. Tell what you can do that they can't, within the context of the original article.

Personal experience pieces

People are attracted to truth. No one else can write about your feelings, perceptions, and experiences but you. A friend of mine specializes in personal essays. Her pieces are gripping accounts of the travails of motherhood. When everyone else was penning pieces about child molestation, she wrote about pinching. Her take on the subject was subtle and thoughtful because it dealt with an in-between kind of personal invasion that many women experience. First published in the on-line magazine Salon.com, it was later picked up by *Glamour* magazine (see below for the full story). If you have something to say that makes you red in the face, burns a hole in your psyche, or tugs at you like an insistent toddler, I'd encourage you to write about it.

The following is a sample personal experience piece:

"No Boy Do That!"
By Hope Simon

My father-in-law is a pincher. He pinches his wife, his aunt, assorted lady friends, and he pinches me. Been pinching me for years. Never on the butt, always on the arm or on the waist. He'll come up from behind and take a big thumbful of whatever I've got there and just tweak it. It's not an easy pinch, it hurts, and it's always reeked of something just a little too intimate, with a twist of anger thrown in. But in the nine years I've known him, I've never said one word, not one "ouch" or one "quit it." I just grimace and squirm away.

I'll spare you the story about being raised a nice girl. We all were. Taught to laugh things off, brush someone away without offending them, walk past the catcalls, and endure the poking. Nice girls know how to do that, enduring the intrusion while remaining beautiful and desirable at the same time. It's an art really, and the more you're able to integrate it into the way things are, the less sensitive you'll be to the intrusion, even to the point of not recognizing it, even if it is a fierce pinch to the flesh that rides your middle. And although I'd grown plenty in thirty-seven years and learned to take care of myself and tell the truth more often than not, I still couldn't tell this fine Christian man to stop pinching me. I didn't want to hurt his feelings because I knew it was a pinch in the name of some kind of love and I felt obligated to it.

Little did I know that liberation from pinching wouldn't come from the latest self-help book or from a flame-throwing Discover Your Inner Power guru charging me $300 for a weekend of shouting. No. Liberation came from my two-year-old daughter, Jessie, loving scoundrel that she is.

I'd always hoped that if I had a daughter, I'd be able to show her how to take care of herself in the world and that she'd be strong and forthright. I wanted her to have the self-esteem that I lacked. She wouldn't take shit from other people, she'd feel entitled to speak her mind, and she wouldn't let anyone touch her without permission.

But I realized early on in her life that I wasn't doing the greatest job of showing her the way. The first time I noticed the gap between what I wanted for her and what I was actually teaching her was when she was four months old and I brought her to the exercise class I'd been going to before she was born. The baby-sitter seemed competent enough, and the other mothers assured me that their kids loved her. Still, I'd pick Jessie up after the sweaty hour was over only to find unsteady toddlers running around with sharp pencils, hopping and flopping around my innocent babe, who lay peacefully in her portable car seat, binky plugged in her mouth. I was horrified and sure that some harm would come to Jessie, but I couldn't bring myself to say anything to the baby-sitter because I was embarrassed that I would seem, well, neurotic.

Even later when I saw the baby-sitter plant a few full-on mouth kisses to my daughter, I concealed my shock and said nothing. Aside from the fact that she smoked and didn't wash before handling the kids, you never kiss little babies on the mouth. Still, I never said a word to her because I simply couldn't manage to say, "Uh, please don't kiss my kid on the lips." I didn't want to seem like one of those overprotective yuppie mothers who hover over their kids like maniacs. I'd go home night after night from this class and torment myself.

So when my in-laws visited last week, I had already endured at least three pinches from my father-in-law and I wasn't even close to erupting. My anger lay way below the surface and I was only aware of a dull dread as I counted the days until their departure. I felt conflicted. I've always been motivated to maintain a warm and loving relationship with my in-laws, yet these pinches flew in the face of that. Had the pinches come from my own father, he would've heard from me a long time ago. And although my father-in-law is "family," he's not blood, and a kind of formality and need to remain in his favor kept me from telling him to stop.

It was an overcast morning and we were getting ready to go visit the US something or other, a ship once owned by Elvis that my father-in-law was pretty excited about. Jessie was naked and in my mother-in-law's arms when Grandpa came sidling over to give her a tweak on the butt. I saw it. Then I heard Jessie yell with all her two-year-old might, "No boy do that! My butt! My body! No boy do that!" I just froze. "Oh my god," I thought to myself, "did you hear what that girl said? That was my kid who said that and I cannot fucking believe what I just heard." I mean, it slipped out of her mouth like honey, like it was just the most natural thing in the world, like it's the kind of thing you say to someone who pinches your butt. I stood there in awe of this person whom I'd brought into the world, amazed and grateful that even after watching her own mother stuff it, she still had the edge on, that she instinctively knew how to take care of herself. I woke right up.

Later that day at the park I told her that what she'd said to Grandpa was really cool and she looked at me in confusion like, "What's the big deal, Mom?" and ran off to the swings.

Several days later and after much buoying by friends, I asked my father-in-law in for a talk. I asked him if he realized that he pinches people, and he said he did. "Well, I don't like it," I said. "I never have. It hurts and I've never known how to tell you." "Gee, I'm sorry," he said uncomfortably. "I always thought it was a kind of sweet thing, you know, friendly. I never meant any harm." I went on to explain that as women we grow up taking all sorts of sweet, well-meaning things from men that are meant to flatter us, but that actually demean us. I told him that pinching was no longer acceptable for me. And while I liked it when he held or cuddled Jessie, pinching was out of the question.

I don't know if my father-in-law grasped the full impact of what I was saying. He may have walked away thinking that my upsetness was something personal to me, not understanding that this was a gender issue—that it was political and that maybe he ought to think twice before pinching someone. He did say that he'd stop pinching us and to brick him if he ever did it again, and as he said that, things felt more clear between us.

It was Jessie who made it all possible. I know I have things to teach her about the world and how we ought to live in it, but instead of assuming that I've got all the answers, I want to pay more attention to what she instinctively seems to know. I want to yell more, too, and scream, "Ouch!" if someone pinches me and I want to stop worrying about other people's feelings and take better care of my own. As Jessie has shown me, there's a kind of clarity and liberation in having the courage to trust yourself and speak up. You can always be forgiven if you've tread too hard, but it's much harder to forgive yourself for remaining silent.

Client list

If your client list is impressive, include it in your press kit. If it consists of Aunt Clara's next-door neighbor you worked with out of the goodness of your heart, keep it to yourself. One publicist I know breaks hers out in categories: corporate clients, authors, film directors, entrepreneurs. Use your own good judgment when reflecting your true experience.

Quote page

Your quote or "rave" page lists testimonials excerpted from various publications that have included you. They can be from feature articles written about whatever it is you are promoting, media reviews from reliable or notable journalists, other experts in your field, or authorities that are well known and easily recognizable by name.

The following is a sample quote or rave page:

PEACHPIT PRESS

Rave Reviews for Larry Magid

Larry King—who has had him on several shows—called Larry "a hell of a guy."

Time magazine (November 1, 1993) called Magid and his colleagues "high-tech heroes" for the work they are doing to help find Polly Klaas, the twelve-year-old who was abducted at knifepoint from her home in Petaluma.

NPR's *All Things Considered* host Robert Siegel said, "Larry Magid introduced me to the World Wide Web with great clarity and insight."

The Little PC Book: A Gentle Introduction to Personal Computers described by the *Wall Street Journal's* Walt Mossberg as "the class of its field."

"At last . . . an exceptionally clear and simple book for the computer novice."—Britt Hume, the *Washington Post* (for *The Little PC Book*).

"Coupled with coupons for free time for all three services, *Cruising Online: Larry Magid's Guide to the New Digital Highways* is the most comprehensive and user-friendly source of information on the online world."
—Kenzi Sugihara, vice president and publisher of Random House Electronic Publishing.

"There was a time when my criterion for computer books was whether or not reading the book gave me a headache. I now know more about computers, but do I know too much to judge a book for beginners? Not this one. I learned a lot!

"*The Little PC Book* offers marvelous illustrations, graphs, cartoons, and discusses every aspect of computer use I can think of, including hardware and software. [*The Little PC Book*] provides a comprehensive and comprehensible explanation of DOS and Windows, and of what can be done and what cannot be done on PC."   —Digby Diehl

1249 Eighth Street, Berkeley, CA 94710
510 524 2178
Fax 510 524 2221

Quiz

A quiz gets your audience involved in your offering. People love to take quizzes to find out more about themselves and the world. Quizzes are also ready for publication as is, so editors love them, too. Develop yours from facts and other information that is surprising, little known, or reveals some hidden truth.

The following quiz is from speaker and communications expert Kare Anderson with some information about how people interact with each other and their environment.

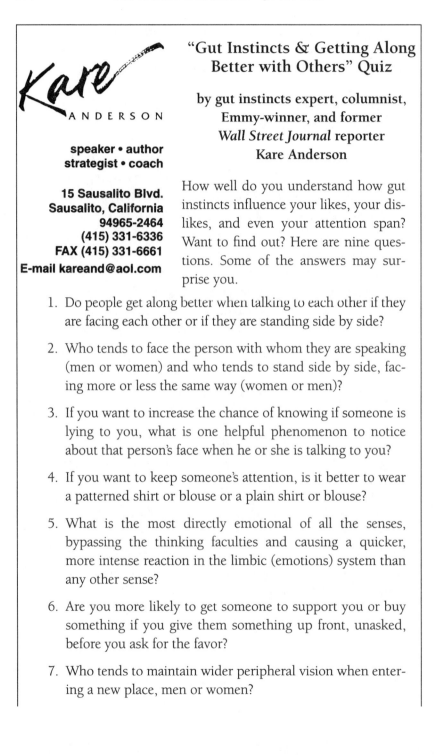

"Gut Instincts & Getting Along Better with Others" Quiz

by gut instincts expert, columnist,
Emmy-winner, and former
Wall Street Journal reporter
Kare Anderson

ANDERSON

**speaker • author
strategist • coach**

**15 Sausalito Blvd.
Sausalito, California
94965-2464
(415) 331-6336
FAX (415) 331-6661
E-mail kareand@aol.com**

How well do you understand how gut instincts influence your likes, your dislikes, and even your attention span? Want to find out? Here are nine questions. Some of the answers may surprise you.

1. Do people get along better when talking to each other if they are facing each other or if they are standing side by side?

2. Who tends to face the person with whom they are speaking (men or women) and who tends to stand side by side, facing more or less the same way (women or men)?

3. If you want to increase the chance of knowing if someone is lying to you, what is one helpful phenomenon to notice about that person's face when he or she is talking to you?

4. If you want to keep someone's attention, is it better to wear a patterned shirt or blouse or a plain shirt or blouse?

5. What is the most directly emotional of all the senses, bypassing the thinking faculties and causing a quicker, more intense reaction in the limbic (emotions) system than any other sense?

6. Are you more likely to get someone to support you or buy something if you give them something up front, unasked, before you ask for the favor?

7. Who tends to maintain wider peripheral vision when entering a new place, men or women?

8. Who tends to be more specific in their descriptions, adults or children?

9. Of the previous eight questions, which is the one people are most likely to ask for the answer to first, and if reading the questions in a group, are most likely to comment on first?

Answers to "Get Instincts & Getting Along Better with Others" Quiz

by Kare Anderson

1. People get along better when they "sidle" stand or sit side by side rather than when they face each other.

2. Men are more likely to sidle than women.

3. Note the timing and duration of the first "reactive" expression on someone's face when you think that person is not telling you the truth. When lying, most people can put an innocent expression on their faces, yet few (except pathological liars) will have the right timing or duration of that expression. If you ignore the expression itself and, instead, consider whether the timing and duration of the expression seem natural, you'll greatly increase your chances of knowing if that person is lying.

4. Wearing a plain, unpatterned shirt or blouse will increase the chances that the listener will hear you longer. A patterned top or ornate jewelry or loud tie will break up the listener's attention span sooner, and that person is more likely to go on more "mental vacations" sooner.

5. Smell is the most directly emotional of the senses. The right natural scent can refresh or relax you and others in your home or work site. Vanilla, apple, and chocolate are the scents Americans most like.

6. Yes, up to fourteen times more likely to get their support or a purchase. This gut instinct is often called the "reciprocity reflex."

7. Women. That is why store owners who serve men will increase their sales if they have prominent, eye-level signage over large displays where men will see the signage soon after entering the store.

8. Children are more vividly specific, hitting their prime around fourth grade and then beginning to speak in generalities, more like adults. Yet the specific detail proves the general conclusion: Specifics are more memorable and more credible.

9. Question number 3. It seems that we have an inordinate interest in lying.

~~~~

Kare Anderson is a "Say It Better" speaker, author, national columnist, Emmy winner, and former *Wall Street Journal* reporter. Get a free subscription to Kare's "Say It Better" monthly on-line bulletin, now read by over 17,000 people, by signing the guest book at her Web site at *www.sayitbetter.com*.

The Compelling Communications Group
Meg Wheeler, Outreach Coordinator
15 Sausalito Blvd., Sausalito, California 94965-2464
415/331-6336 ~ Fax 415/331-6661
kareand@aol.com ~ www.sayitbetter.com

Now that you've finished writing all your press materials, review this checklist to ensure your success

Before you send them out, check your materials to make sure you have accomplished all of the following seven steps:

❑ **Have you angled different press pieces for each of your niche markets or audience?**

For the Sedona Training Associates ten audiotape series, I wrote up three separate pitch letters and press releases with different headlines and essentially the same body copy. I angled one for the business market, one for the women's market, and one for the New Age market—their three top niches.

❑ **Is the tone of your writing objective and focused on newsworthiness?**

Any kind of hype, praise, or superlative makes journalists' and producers' stomachs turn. I remember journalist Pete Hamill once saying that he never uses the word "tragedy" in his pieces. If he thinks his story is tragic, then he includes all the details that show it to be so and lets his readers decide on what emotion to feel. Choose the details that show proven results.

❑ **Have you checked for any kind of error?**

Most computer programs now have both spell check and grammar check available. While these tools are handy, they are no replacement for the human eye. Have at least three people review it for mistakes.

I have heard told that one of the sweetest things a person can hear is their own name. We all know how important this is, so triple-check the name of the person to whom you address your correspondence. The very first publicist I worked for told me the story of a friend of hers who applied for a job as a journalist at the *San Francisco Chronicle*. The friend sent in her "thank you for the interview" note and misspelled the word "Chronicle." The editors were rather heartbroken because this woman had excellent credentials and they debated for a long time before they declined to hire her. But none of them could fathom giving a job to a journalist who couldn't even get the name of the newspaper for which she wanted to work correct. What kind of accuracy could they count on for her stories?

❏ **Will you be available to be interviewed after you have sent out your press kits?**
Getting press can happen in less time than it takes for a leaf to fall, or more time than a yearly hibernation. You will want to be easily reachable soon after you have sent out your precious information. Typical lead times for each of the different media varies. For magazines three to six months is usual, but many airline magazines' editorial schedules are planned over a year in advance.

Newspapers like at least one to three weeks; however, I remember sending information into a major newspaper a month in advance of an event and still encountered a problem. When I called to follow up a week later, I was informed that their mail service was backed up by three weeks! Beware, even if their mailroom isn't behind on delivery, many journalists' desks look like their own tiny mailroom or a small bomb shelter. For radio and TV send your materials out two to three weeks before you'd like to be called. Major TV shows have a longer lead time and many (like *Oprah*) go on hiatus in summer.

If your information is newsworthy, you could get a call five minutes after your press kit is received. Keep your pager on and your cell phone charged, and don't go on vacation to the South Seas.

❏ **Did you set a time frame?**
Continue the process of marrying your intentions to time. Set yourself up on a daily, weekly, or monthly routine that you can adhere to.

❏ **Are you ready to send out your press kit?**
Segment your database by deciding who will receive hard copy, fax, or e-mail. You might want to try a small burst first before sending everything out at once to see what kind of interest you receive.

❏ **Do you know who is going to place follow-up calls?**
Are you going to call or e-mail or will you just allow whatever is going to happen, to happen? More and more journalists and produc-

ers won't take your call unless they know you. This makes it ever more important for your materials to stand strong on their own and to captivate interest with a headline backed up by your compelling facts or anecdotes. When you call, what you say in those fifteen to twenty seconds will determine whether you get a call back or not.

———

What you will find if you have done an excellent job of writing your materials is that many publications will print them as is! One of my press releases was printed almost verbatim in the *New York Times,* and they included a photo. Some journalists or editors may take your ideas and just translate them into their language and style.

Still others will pick up the phone and call you for an interview. Producers will invite you to be a guest on their shows and use your questions, making them sound like they're talking off-the-cuff. Many are masters at this, and if you give them the guidelines, they'll often take your lead. Others will have nothing to do with your materials when it comes to fashioning their show. They have a strong idea of a direction they want to go in, so you will honor their lead by following them, while still getting your message out in a way that makes you (and your mother) proud.

PART IV

Create a Campaign
That Suits Your Style

CHAPTER 5

Find Your Pacing and Style

An empowering personal marketing and publicity plan is one that suits your personality style while going slightly beyond your self-described comfort zone. Comfort often has to do with how much we're willing to accept—from and for ourselves. I am no expert in self-acceptance, but I can tell you how to practice radical acts of self-acceptance little by little. The more you can be sweet to yourself, the more empowered your plan will be.

Recognize your pacing

Fast and furious

Beat spokesperson Jack Kerouac wrote *On the Road* in three weeks. He liked to work in fast and furious sessions. Are you the kind of person who prefers to do things in great bursts of energy? Do you gravitate to doing things swiftly and intensely? If so, you will want to carry out your plan quickly. Block out time in larger chunks so you can write, send out, and do your media interviews in such a way that you can see your progress instantly.

Slow and steady

Now, if you are the kind of person who does things in a methodical manner, following steps in order of their importance, you might want to give yourself a time frame that respects that style.

Combination fast and steady

My client Debbie Gisonni is a blend of both. She's an experienced speaker who has the ability to be spontaneous with words and likes to set a strong foundational plan. She called me well in advance of her book publication date (a miracle in itself) stating that she wanted to get her whole program in order. First, we developed her angles and niches, wrote and edited all her press materials. Then we did media coaching. After that, we worked on the content of her Web site and developed her workshops—all several months before the launch of her book. In addition, she had developed a five-year plan complete with all the products she planned to license. Wow.

We developed not only a general press release, but also tip sheets for each angle or niche market she wanted to cover and subject topics for three separate workshops/seminars. We then tailored everything to fit her Web site format.

Whatever type of person you tend to be, the following questions and examples will help you in defining the length, breadth, and focal points of your personal marketing and publicity plan so you can maximize your strengths and minimize the rest:

Find the right publicity speedometer for your personality type

Are you a diver or a dipper?

The Diver

There is a saying by some wise soul that "if at first you don't succeed, then skydiving isn't for you." The poet Billy Collins talks about poetry in terms of two types of cooks. The first one cleans as he goes, wiping off the board after chopping. The second makes a mess and cleans up later. He says he prefers to write and finish a poem like the second cook, in a burst of energy and enthusiasm of the moment so the heart of it comes out all at once. In these moments of fresh creativity he doesn't want to invite the collaboration of the other more critical parts of himself into the process.

When you devise a publicity campaign, take into consideration if you are the kind of cook who cleans as he goes or finishes the entire meal in the spirit of the artist. When you plunge forward fast, you keep all the different sides of yourself at bay for the moment. You can then reflect after your first flurry and revise and further define your plan. Find out what is working and what is not.

The Dipper

If you are a dipper, start your publicity campaign slowly and let it simmer like a good soup. You might want to keep to standard recipes you are sure of for a while and perhaps try one thing new for an appetizer. This would be the cook's equivalent of contacting the smaller venues and your local media first. Call people you know who can arrange for you to speak to the organizations they chair. Get in touch with the professional groups you are a member of and speak on a panel or write up a short piece in the area of your expertise. Once you start to get a feel for the process, you can expand your circle of influence. Think of yourself as an understudy to the wonderfully roguish Julia Child, who said, "Life itself is the proper binge," and try your crème anglaise on the family first before you enter it into the National Culinary Academy contest.

Are you a risk seeker or averse to risk?

One of my clients, Kelli Fox, a vice president at iVillage, always says, "If in doubt, don't." It is important to honor your limits, and nudge yourself a bit beyond them. Many of my clients have said to me that I hold their hand and kick them in the butt (well, perhaps they say "ass") at the same time. You can envision me doing this with you if it helps. To keep yourself in motion, pick and choose the kinds of things you are willing to do, taking your temperature along the way. I advise checking in with yourself often while remembering what Erica Jong said, "And the trouble is, if you don't risk anything, you risk even more."

On the other end of the spectrum, if you are the kind of person who thrills at the unknown, then, hey, here is your chance to go hog-wild.

Call up Howard Stern so he can ask you your bra size (which he did to one of my clients) and revel in being in the hot seat.

Are you reluctant or hungry for publicity?

The Reluctant

In the book *Harry Potter and the Chamber of Secrets* the flashy wizard Gilderoy Lockart is the epitome of the glossy, slick publicity hound. He accused our hero Harry of trying to get publicity by flying a car back to the Hogwarts School for Witchcraft and Wizardry instead of taking the train with all the other students, which was so un-Harry-like. He proudly believes that he gave Harry the "bug," the "taste" for publicity, after he invited Harry to be in his photo shoot at his book signing, implying that the addictive nature of fame is as powerful as some magic potion or a wizard's sorcery. While glitz, sleaze, slick, or pushy persistence is reason to run from such people, there are those who are welcome beacons of light, those who take their place in that little golden circle as if they were born there.

The Hungry

Even if you are ravenous for fame and could eat a heaping plate of it right now, you can still maintain your dignity by taking a bite at a time, chewing carefully, and not talking with your mouth full. Some of you are very comfortable with the idea of a microphone being thrust into your face. For you it feels natural and right to be speaking your mind to millions of viewers or listeners, but please don't get grabby about it.

You know who you are. My dad's best friend, Dude, was a man like that. I even brought a tape recorder to the last Thanksgiving before he died so I could get some of those great stories on the family record. He started the Foundation for Macular Degeneration and was featured on 20/20 to bring awareness to this little-understood disease. Dude could even make disease a delightful topic of conversation.

Are you better behind the scenes or in the spotlight?

I became a publicist to help others get fame and fortune. I prefer to be behind the scenes, though I love interacting with people in person. I am a keen observer and can teach what I have learned, but I can tell others how to do it much better than I can do it myself, so I wouldn't choose the constant spotlight. An occasional little 100-watt bulb for me works just fine.

For those of you who are more reluctant about occupying the Broadway bill, assign the job of speaking with the press to someone who enjoys the task of spokesperson, or get practice and training.

HOT TIP!

BUDDY UP.

Ease into publicity slowly by becoming a dynamic duo. Ron Zoglin and Deborah Shouse, who wrote *Antiquing for Dummies,* have created a delightful rapport and repartee together. They share their knowledge in a way that is respectful of each other and spotlights their talent for talking about what each one is most passionate about. Shouse comments, "If one person gets stuck, the other is there as an instant parachute. Also miraculously, on the days that one is nervous, the other is somehow calm."

Are you solitary or social?

When I speak at writers' conferences, at least one participant asks the question the whole audience wants to know: "Do we really have to speak? Can't we just write?" You don't have to be a writer to feel this way. Some of you are more comfortable in the sanctity of your homes or offices or beach huts by the sea. You love your privacy and want to speak to others as the occasion rather than as the rule.

HOT TIP!

QUOTE YOUR OWN WISDOM.

If you really don't want to give interviews, then plan to quote yourself liberally in your press materials. You may even want to create an entire quote page of your wisdom to have ready when someone requests an interview. These selections need to be keenly honed to be effective. Excerpt a few of the best lines that describe what you are promoting clearly and vividly.

You can also do a thorough question and answer page (see page 89). Though refusing to give an interview isn't typical, this is a way to give a response that (hopefully) satisfies both of your needs.

If you are like my friend Colleen, who gets to know everyone in the whole restaurant on the way to her table, then "networking" is more a way of life than an event. You will want to get your materials in order and then get talking. Knowing your "style" will help you decide how to focus your time and energy. For you, radio and TV are the media of choice.

Are you a talker or a writer?

There are talkers and there are writers. Then there are people who are comfortable doing both. If either of the live media (TV or radio) makes you want to run for the nearest bathroom, then you might want to consider the slower pace of print. If you are a quick thinker on your feet, with a tongue to match, radio would be a good fit for you. If you are tongue-tied and would rather converse with a screen in between you and a breathing being, then the Internet might match your needs. In Cyberspace it helps to be a good writer who can write clearly in a unique voice.

TV is for people who project a natural comfort about themselves, and who can spout incredibly insightful thoughts in ten-second increments. With practice most people can master any medium to become at least believable and coherent. It depends on the kind of time and energy you are interested in investing.

I had one client who was an excellent lecturer and speaker, but put her in front of a camera or on the radio, and her expertise and ease just didn't translate. Even with media coaching she always looked and sounded awkward, like an elephant in a birdbath. She was an excellent writer and I recommended she concentrate on print. Of course it is wonderful to have a well-rounded campaign where you can easily handle each medium, but some folks just aren't made for that.

Invitation

Check off the boxes that apply to you to see more clearly what your plan will look like.

❏ Fast and furious	❏ Slow and steady
❏ Diver	❏ Dipper
❏ Risk seeker	❏ Averse to risk
❏ Hungry	❏ Reluctant
❏ In the spotlight	❏ Behind the scenes
❏ Social	❏ Solitary
❏ Talker	❏ Writer

Focus on radio, TV, and the Internet

Focus on local, regional, then national print and the Internet

If you find you're in between the two types, then a combination of all the media will work for you. Set a plan to focus on your strengths (the activities you prefer and know you can do quickly with joy), then put the rest in order of preference and importance.

Once you have identified the areas that are most comfortable for you, the next few chapters will help you identify and release your fears.

CHAPTER 6

Discover What's Holding You Back

Almost everyone has some fears about beginning a marketing and publicity plan. Some of those fears are well founded; others are largely inflated by our vivid imaginations. Mark Twain noted, "My life has been filled with terrible misfortunes, most of which never happened."

Those of you doing something innocuous and community-friendly like a blood drive or a bake sale won't have journalists nosing into your private parts—though they may try to weasel a well-guarded family recipe out of you. You will be focusing on getting interviews so your cookies will finance computers for your kids' schools.

But for those of you who are seeking to promote something you are attached to, something you hold dear to your heart, you are on an adventure of a lifetime.

I want to acknowledge first that all of your fears about moving from private person to public persona are legitimate. Hideous things do happen, but so do hilarious, exhilarating ones. The best way to prepare yourself for the unexpected is to prepare yourself for the unexpected.

The sheer volume of people you will be reaching encourages the possibility of some strange mishap slipping into your life. One of my most favorite stories is told by Jack Kornfield of Spirit Rock Meditation Center in Woodacre, California. I paraphrase it here:

A farmer's horse, the only one he owns, escapes from his pasture. The neighbor notices and says, "What bad luck. Now you have no horse and you will have to walk everywhere." The farmer says, "Maybe so, maybe not." The next day the horse returns with a pack of other horses. They graze in the aforementioned pasture. The neighbor peers over the fence and says, "Wow. Look at all those new horses and you didn't have to pay a thing for them! Great fortune." The farmer says, "Maybe so, maybe not."

The next day the farmer's son tries to break in one of the horses, gets thrown off, and breaks his leg. The neighbor says, "What a disaster! Your only son has a broken leg." The farmer says, "Maybe so, maybe not." The next day soldiers come through town to recruit all the young able-bodied men in the newly declared war. Since the farmer's son has a broken leg, they can't take him away. . . .

The story goes on and on like that. Fortune often looks like misfortune and vice versa. You just never know how something is going to turn out.

The story of the farmer is a lot like the Chinese saying, "For every flip side there is a flip side." I would like each of you to feel comfortable, to the degree that you can, about receiving recognition for yourself, your business, book, product, or cause. In this chapter I will sort out legitimate concerns from those that arise from fears promulgated in the culture at large. I will ask you to examine your beliefs to decipher what is really true for you. Lastly, I will attend to showing you how to set and respect your boundaries so you will never diminish your dignity.

Your private life will become public

Skeleton hunting is a journalist's finest craft. They are trained to put nose to ground when anything smells the slightest bit unsavory. Don't be surprised if they try to peer under your skirt or up a pant leg. It is their job to find a good angle to a story whether it puts you in a good light or not. Welcome to the joys of public scrutiny.

Most journalists aren't looking to dig up any dirt unless that is the nature of the story. They do, however, want to find the facts and support the evidence they may already have. This may involve researching your past.

What can you do if they want to interview your fifth-grade boyfriend, or worse, your mother? Control what you can control, and let go of the rest.

Solution: List of all the questions you are afraid to be asked

Make this list as personal and as terrifying as possible. You are the person that is most likely to reveal the secrets you want stashed in the attic of your memories. Practice with family, friends, or a media coach until you can answer each question without getting huffy, hysterical, or haughty. Rudolph Giuliani had a vulnerability report commissioned to analyze all of his weaknesses so he and his staff could strategize a plan to offset them with strengths.

His file was five inches thick! I am hoping that yours is a slim little novella that is not a titillating read. I believe the statement "Your greatest vulnerability is your greatest strength." You can delve into all the places you are tender and turn them into strong points (see chapter 9). Once you get used to being asked questions you fear, you will be able to maintain a neutral, benevolent demeanor. You can turn a potentially big-deal question into one that is "ho-hum" by deciding that you are not going to react to it. Answer it the same way you would if someone asked you how your day was going.

Solution: Prep your mother

But what if it is your mother the media hounds have sniffed out? We know your mother doesn't have the restraint or the presence of mind to hold her tongue when she knows some secret childhood gaffe would find a receptive ear. I don't hold any illusions about controlling my mother, and I wish all of you luck with yours. You can give her a list of stories that are off-limits and hope for the best. Of course, then you have delivered to her the perfect weapon with which to torture you, if she is the sort of mother who would do such a thing. Might I suggest that this is an ideal time to make peace with your mother if you have not done so already?

Solution: Prep your friends and colleagues

You can discreetly plant ideas about the subjects you would like them to focus on. Realize, though, that you have little control over what people say about you. Your actions and words have walked before you to announce the kind of person others think you are. There will be points, perhaps many of them, on which you disagree. When a journalist asks you to comment about what someone has said about you, that is the time to reframe the story as you perceived it. All the while not calling anyone a liar, of course.

Solution: Examine your public records

Anyone has easy access to information regarding your real-estate transactions, divorce, lawsuits, driving citations, credit reports, bankruptcy, police records. Take a look at your public records, in the event that something you might not want disclosed is readily available. Be the first to bring this up if it is relevant to the reporter's story. You can frame it as lightly unimportant or put it in its proper context.

Solution: Set your limits now

One of my clients turned down an invitation to become a client of her country's most prestigious public relations firm, which represents many elite public figures and stars. It is unlikely a high-powered public relations firm would call you up to ask to represent you, but she already had quite a bit of notoriety in the United States and in her native country. To be asked to become a client was considered a great honor.

Why did she decline their offer? "I don't want the dirt of my ancestors dug up," she told me. She is not the kind of person to make a public confession of her family hardships, so she made her choice. With a big PR firm promoting her it was inevitable that reporters from the largest and most sensational publications and shows would begin to unearth her past. At that level of stardom there would be little she could do to keep her private life out of public domain.

You have little need to worry about this until you are really famous or you have done something that sets a reporter to digging. If you have next to nothing to hide, then you have a much easier choice than this one client did. And while you can turn most stories into positive adventures, there is always a limit to what feels invasive to you. I am always surprised that people feel obligated to answer the questions posed to them. The first thing I work on with clients who have this fear is to put down on paper all the questions they don't want to be asked.

Thinking about your limits ahead of time (as you are reading these words) will save you much sadness in the future. Decide what you are willing and unwilling to discuss, then keep your promises to yourself.

⤳ *Invitation* ⤵

Write down all the questions you're afraid you'll be asked. Practice answering them.

You will get overwhelmed with business or people you can't handle

As my sweetie, Brett, would say, "Being overwhelmed with business is a good problem to have." But what if your psyche and phone system can't handle the number of calls you anticipate you will receive from good press?

Solution: Put your systems in place

You will be able to ease the overwhelming things that can happen when your good press results in a stuffed e-mail box and nonstop phone calls. Preparing even the simplest of things like explicit directions to your place of business can save you and your staff hours of time on the phone, computer, and in person. Set up your Web site to cover basic company information, bios, directions, frequently asked questions (FAQs).

Solution: Set up a screening device to help sort your calls

That may mean getting an additional voice mail system or auto attendant to screen calls. This simple screening equipment will help you distinguish the people who are serious about hiring you or buying a product, from those who want to compliment and connect with you, ask for free advice, or inquire about cost.

Solution: Create a newsletter

One woman who speaks on creativity created a paid-subscription hardcopy newsletter to answer all the questions her fans had about her subject.

Solution: Establish an 800 or 900 number

In addition this same woman set up an 800 number where those same fans could call anytime to hear her tell stories about her own adventures and give advice. This was enormously helpful in giving her the sense that she was satisfying the demand of the people interested in her, without taking on the impossible task of responding individually to thousands of people every month.

Due to the popularity of his Free Will horoscope column, which appears in over 118 publications worldwide, Rob Brezsny formed a 900 number so the readers (mostly women) who wanted more could hear him expound. Since he doesn't give one-on-one consultations, it is his way of being available to the thousands of people calling every day who want to know more about themselves and their sun signs.

Solution: Write a FAQ sheet

Cover the most common questions you are asked and post the information on your Web site. You can use your voice mail system to direct callers to your Web site to get their questions answered. You will be freed up to answer questions that pertain to the specific nature of a person seeking to do business with you.

These methods are effective ways to deal with overloaded phone lines and an avalanche of personal requests. They accomplish two things: satisfy an admirer's desire for personal contact and save a company's, your own, or your staff's sanity.

Having in place both phone and e-mail systems to automatically answer the most commonly asked questions can save you hours of precious time. Your voice mail system will become like a treasured employee. And your e-mail system can work for you instead of you working for it.

You believe that the media only want sex, smut, celebrity, glamour, and fluff

If you think that the media want lurid, loopy, scandalous gunk most people would rather sweep under a rug, you are, in part, right. The circulation and popularity of magazines like the *National Enquirer* and

People magazine bear this out. There is a thirst for the light, sassy, and scandalous, but, truly, that is not all.

Consider it natural that human beings are interested in how other people conduct their lives. In Europe, hanging out your window staring into the street to keep a bead on other people's goings-on is a favorite national pastime. Tongue wagging over coffee and cookies follows as a close second. But you don't need to cater to gossip lovers. Subjects that may not titillate still have merit.

Solution: Tempt the media with a scintillating story

Perennial crowd-pleasers are often based on archetypal stories. Three popular ones you can choose from are

1. Bad boy—or girl—makes good.

2. Rags to riches.

3. Overcoming the odds or triumphing over impossible adversity.

The media also love stories that cover unlikely or odd business successes, charities, children, animals, or anything weird. For some reason dogs always have a good chance of getting media coverage. Who doesn't love dogs?

If you happen to be able to throw the light of glamour or humor onto your subject, well, that is a plus. Whatever you are promoting, though, you don't have to be an ax murderer or a shamed sports star to get attention, you just need to be captivating.

You need nerve to approach the media—or your boss

Saying something nice about yourself is considered the equivalent of hara-kiri—unless you are a man. Then it is demanded of you. I am constantly amazed that my sweetheart, Brett, talks about his business accomplishments without a pinch of shame, as if he'd won some sort of prize for excellence. Men are trained and rewarded to communicate in this manner. Women are not. You don't need to have steel between your legs to say something nice about yourself, but it does take some practice. A way to ease into it is to talk about yourself through your results. You never even have to use the word "I." Here is how:

Speak through the eyes of another

A nonbragging tone of voice is everything. Women tend to try to make themselves small by minimizing their accomplishments so they won't be attacked or envied. To avoid anyone assigning you an epithet or turning an ugly shade of green, don't puff up or shrink down when you are talking. Speak neutrally, as if you were a colleague or friend and you wanted to spread good news about an exciting event or idea. I heard an interviewee on the radio the other day say, "If you can believe so and so, he said . . ." and then proceed to say a few delightful things about herself. They didn't sound grandiose or pretentious at all.

Here is how it might sound for you if you were talking to your boss about a new project idea based on a past one. "If you can believe John, he said that my report was the most thorough one he'd ever seen on the subject. . . ." John is almost there in the room, speaking your praises.

If you are thinking, "No way can I say that," try discussing your accomplishments with a few good friends until you get the hang of it. You can even ask them to repeat back what you have said. Often people hear the essence and feeling of your words more than their literal meaning, so you will be able to hear a number of hidden things that you are communicating. If you want to approach your boss but really can't, have a colleague do it informally. I know that to actually speak your accolades out loud may be the hardest part, so collect them in writing.

Solution: Keep an "incredible moi!" file

My friend Diana has a file she calls her "Atta Boy!" file. Whenever her boss compliments her on a job well done via e-mail or hard copy, she plunks it into this file. If your clients, colleagues, and/or employees have complimented you in any way, save these in a file marked "The Incredible Moi!" which sounds more elegant than "Atta Boy!"

Solution: Let the written word speak for you

If you give them the opportunity, people will come up with extraordinary ways of expressing their feelings toward you and your work. For public viewing I save all the informal compliments I have received, from handwritten thank-you notes, to official letters from the presidents of organizations to which I have spoken. In them are lines that can be lifted and put onto one packed page of raves. When it comes time to ask for a raise or a juicy project, or to prove you will be an excellent media guest, whip out that file. As you know from watching many court trials, written evidence is weighty proof. Let your paper do the talking.

Solution: Use voice mail or e-mail

I know many of you are not comfortable calling and talking off-the-cuff. So don't do it. If you have a bit of gumption but you are afraid you will sputter and spit out words and other unsavory droplets, use e-mail or voice mail. Call when you know that person will be out of the office. Write out your little spiel on a piece of prayer paper and have it handy. Practice saying it so it sounds conversational rather than a sanctimonious announcement to an omnipotent god. My dad always said of anyone high-and-mighty, "They put their pants legs on one at a time just like everyone else."

You will be considered a braggart

No one likes a braggart. We don't want you to be too perfect or fortunate lest we wish a thousand pestilences on your head.

Make sure you point out your faults (but not constantly) before someone beats you to it. We love you for all your ugly, harmful, and unredemptive qualities, because we can relate. Again, women naturally try to diminish their accomplishments, while maintaining rapport, by "equalizing" the power of the people in the group to whom they are communicating. According to Deborah Tannen, this tendency creates more community and encourages verbal sharing.

Men, however, can see this as putting yourself in a "one-down" position and giving them the advantage of being in a superior position. Best advice? Be sensitive to the group dynamics before you self-deprecate.

Solution: Tell about the benefits you have produced instead of how great you are

"You" is the most powerful word in marketing language, not "I." When telling others about yourself, your business, book, product, or cause, show how it applies to them. Instead of talking about yourself, talk in terms of results that other people have gotten from using your products of services. I know this is old advice. In sales language it is called benefits versus features, but I am not really talking about that. I am talking about your personal commitment to yourself.

Solution: Become dedicated to yourself

Are you 100 percent dedicated to doing what you do and to who you are? If not, then write down how you are not living up to your own standards and set a plan for changing them. For example, look to see if you have any integrity leaks, little holes where you let things slip by and then tell yourself, "Oh, that is not really so important anyway." This slow dribbling away at values you hold dear chews away your insides, sometimes with a nip, other times with a big bite. If this is not something you can do alone, hire a personal coach, join a mastermind alliance or success team, or enlist a friend that you meet with regularly who will help you stay on track.

I was so impressed when I called up textile artist and author Andrea Siegel to interview her for this book and she asked me, "Have you read my book?"

"No."

"Oh, you must! It is great! You can get it at Cody's."

Andrea had no shame and also no arrogance. She said this with conviction and without any self-conscious modesty. I asked her about it later. She said, "I truly do think my book is well worth reading. I am a person who deserves respect. I am proud of my work." It was as simple as that. If you feel ashamed in any way about what you are doing, it will come through. There is an art to talking about yourself and it has to do with telling the truth. It is hugely helpful to experiment with speaking about yourself plainly and directly.

Solution: Be a cheerleader for others

Nicole O'Rourke, global brand director for a multibillion-dollar health care company, got an assignment to work on one of the company's smaller brands. Seen as a "stepchild" to the bigger brands, it received little attention from the sales force or upper management. Yet because it wasn't as well-developed as some of the larger name brands, there was more room for innovation. In order to drive attention and energy to the business, Nicole began creating what she called "noise," reminding people her brand was like "The Little Engine That Could." She began her system of cheerleading by peppering upper management with voice mail and e-mail messages regarding the small successes of all the people she worked with.

In the form of updates she would be sure to give quick bursts of positive information. One week she would spotlight the success of an individual sales rep. The next week she'd mention a line or two about a great idea from their advertising agency. This helped keep her department, project, and staff constantly in the minds of senior management, giving the overall impression that exciting things were happening in her department all the time.

Another benefit: By carbon-copying the complimented person, Nicole's messages helped generate extra enthusiasm, camaraderie, and team spirit each time she sent them out.

Nicole knew that senior management didn't have the time to sit through hours of presentations about her department's accomplishments, but that they regularly checked their voice mail and e-mail. Her system of cheerleading gave the impression that her team was driving results and making great things happen. It was more than just an impression. The brand increased its revenues over 30 percent through the strong teamwork generated by her creative strategies.

No one will consider you a braggart if you are vigilant in touting others' achievements. No doubt someone will be cheerleading for you.

Solution: Give people ways to connect with you

At a Learning Annex panel one of my friends spoke about her experiences as a freelance writer. Afterward people from the audience rushed at her wanting to hear more, absorbing her intense energy. In a phone conversation later that day I said, "Gee, it is too bad you didn't have anything to sell or to give away." At first she balked at the idea and then said, "I get it. I should have given people a way to connect with me. That is what you are talking about."

The audience wanted to take away something of those great feelings she gave them. And by not offering something for free or selling something, she deprived them of that pleasure. The next time she talked, she offered to e-mail information she'd developed for a writing class, for free. Over fifty people e-mailed her!

The next time you feel self-conscious about selling something, try to view it in terms of enriching another person's life rather than lining your own pockets. I think you will find that with little effort it will do both.

Solution: Write about how great you are in the third person

When you write in the third person, it removes you from speaking directly about yourself and therefore exempts you from bragging. You can then freely give yourself the compliments others have assigned to you.

You don't want to beg for attention

I remember Zen teacher Bernie Glassman, founder of the Zen Peacemaker Order and other social service organizations, giving his students the assignment of begging on the streets of New York for three days. To understand the experience of the homeless they needed to beg not only for attention, but for money and food. Though most of us have not had to do this literally, it may call up some of the same feelings of shame and unworthiness when we think we're begging for attention.

Solution: Do everything with the attitude to help

You don't need to scrape the skin off your knees marching on beggar's bones to try and get others to notice you. Media people always need ideas for stories. When you approach them, do it with the intention of helping them out rather than groveling for a morsel of their time.

It may even be as simple as a phone call or a few lines of an idea you have for a story. Rather than making it into a big megillah, simplify. E-mail is made for this. The shorter the note, the sweeter it is. To Dave Murphy, the editor of the Career section for the *San Francisco Examiner,* I wrote, "What do you think of a piece on how to use sound bites in business?" I listed five points. His response: "Go for it." Because I read the section regularly, I knew that this topic would be appropriate for his readers. In no time at all you will find that when you change your attitude about yourself from groveler to helper, that is how people perceive you.

You think publicity is whoring

Over the years hundreds of people have admitted to me that this is their secret fear. I ask them if they feel like they are whoring themselves, why would they do publicity? The answer: They wouldn't.

In many of us there is a voice that says there is something dishonorable about wanting people to desire the gifts we have to give. I am still coming to terms with that.

Solution: Accept yourself as you are right now

It takes a radical act of self-acceptance to put yourself out into the media fray as you truly are. I heard a newscaster say that acting was the easy part of his job. He noted that the most difficult part was to be yourself while performing in public. I keep a postcard with a saying that I like taped to my computer. It says, "The truth always happens." And the truth is often found in unexpected ways.

Solution: Find the opening

As a media coach and marketing strategist I help my clients create an opening that truth can pass through, even when they can't see that opening for themselves. One such opening was created when Sepha Schiffman came to see me.

Sepha, a career counselor, was used to consulting with Fortune 500 companies at her high-level corporate job. Now that she worked for herself, she said, she cringed inside whenever she went to make a cold call. The thought of "selling" herself conjured up those images of plastering her picture on a highway billboard.

Instead of focusing on selling, we developed a profile of the type of client she wanted and included examples of how she had helped them achieve dramatic results in an article for the *San Francisco Examiner*. She got eleven clients from the piece. Those eleven people have referred two more. Writing one article led her to a full-time practice.

In addition a number of publications requested articles and a university asked her to teach a class. "A bit of an irony," Sepha says, is that "I was asked to do a short seminar on marketing counseling services for the Women's Therapy Center, as I was perceived as something of an 'expert' in self-promotion." One opening leads to another and another. I encourage you to check out what is really happening each time you feel like you are flipping up your skirt. Is that shame really yours to own?

You will be forced to endure the criticism of thousands of strangers

People feel entitled to comment on those in the public eye. Even if it is your first time "out." They don't know and they don't care. You will receive unwanted criticism by all kinds of people. It will come by phone, e-mail, fax, and in person. You can learn to let comments go right through without absorbing any of them. How?

Solution: Practice getting criticized

Have friends, children, anyone, start by criticizing your face and body—especially the parts that prickle you. Move on to any subject you are sensitive about. Then lastly have them focus on whatever you are promoting. After every other sensitive area has been probed, prodded, and pinched, you will find all the fingering has given you a good message in all the sore places.

Count on criticizers worming their way out of the woodwork to find you. E-mail makes it easy to send a snide remark without ever having to face any consequences. Dating expert Diane de Castro says, "E-mail is the worst thing for manners that has happened. You have to learn to let go fast of the kinds of things people think they have a right to say to you that they'd never say to your face."

Before e-mail, people had a chance to voice their opinions about subject matter and their subjects in the form of letters to the editor in newspapers and magazines. In this way they had to identify themselves as real people, denizens of an actual locale with proof they could pay their phone bills. It took a lot more guts in those days when you had to account for what you said. It also took more time. You had to lick, stamp, and get the thing to the post office, so if you had written anything rash, you had some time to think it over.

Solution: Remember the 50/50 rosebush rule

There is a saying that when you stick your head above the rosebush (speak out), fifty people will throw roses and fifty people will try to shoot your head off. The filmmaker Anthony Minghella (*The English Patient, The Talented Mr. Ripley*) said, "It is always very strange to me that people can either be so passionately for or against what I am doing, because I feel [like] the most equivocal person in the world." After the film *Truly, Madly, Deeply* showed in theaters, he read that he was on somebody's list of the ten best films of all time. He said he felt that "glow of pride." Then, the very next day on the BBC television show *Room 101,* where people could "consign the things they most hated to Room 101," he heard a guy saying, "the first thing I put in Room 101 was *Truly, Madly, Deeply*." Go figure!

Solution: Notice the three-sided fence

My friend Colleen and I were hiking in a lush flower-filled trail in Sonoma last weekend, stopping to (really) smell the flowers and catch up on our lives. I told her about a puzzling e-mail I'd received from a man criticizing me for a point that was totally unclear. She enthusiastically reported that editorials were her favorite part of magazines. "Isn't it fantastic that people's opinions can be so different and contrary? You always get these opposite points of view. There are always two sides to the fence, maybe more! I just love that there are so many kinds of people in the world. I am interested in all those mind-sets." What a great reminder of all that is strange and wonderful and wild about people. Thanks, Colleen.

Solution: Digest wounding words

Once your ideas are committed to paper, people feel entitled to voice their views on yours. Linda Weltner, author of *Family Puzzles: A Private Life Made Public,* a collection of her *Boston Globe* columns, said in a January 2000 *Writer's Digest* article, "You must be prepared to deal with readers who are angry, judgmental or simply opinionated. It is important to come to terms with your failings and shortcomings so that you don't feel defensive when others point them out to you—and they will. People come up to me as if they have every right to comment on the most intimate matters in my life and I appreciate their interest and concern. If this makes you feel uncomfortable, find another field."

I am not saying hearing criticism over and over will get easier with time. It can be hard to hear criticism no matter how unjust you feel it is. But it is a great learning experience to find all of your tender places discovered so quickly by others. Each time, you can use the opportunity to ask yourself what is true for you.

Any statement that has the ability to wound you is touching some unhealed place. This is your private practice. On your own you will take the time to digest and dissolve harmful words and "eliminate" them gracefully. Your public practice is to dodge and deflect the warrior words and remain standing without any gaping flesh wounds. The next time you are feeling attacked, stop, check in with yourself, and ask if there is any truth in the offending statements. If not, send them out of your mind, and move on.

You will be stalked or hounded by weirdos

It is true. It happens. A stranger may not be lurking in your hallway, but odd people do tend to make themselves known once you become a more accessible public figure. Keep in mind that though these singular events tend to feel invasive, the majority of responses you get are from friendly earthlings who want to reach out and touch someone. In almost every Learning Annex class I teach, there is at least one "loose cannon." I must admit, however, that this makes for great dinner-party conversation. I am not talking now about scary ski mask kinds of people, but those whose flavors might not be Life Savers cherry, lemon, or lime.

Wendi Rogers, informercial queen (remember the Sweet Simplicity hair removal system?) and a former host on HSN (Home Shopping Network) and Q2, received quite colorful responses from her spa and beauty shows. Perhaps the most delightfully twisted one was from a foot fetishist. This man would call in every week or so to Wendi's voice mail and request that Wendi do another pedicure on camera. He'd say something to the effect of, "You have such beautiful feet, why not show them off again?" Wendi would good-naturedly delete the message.

A bit less whimsical was the woman who wrote a bitter letter complaining that Wendi talked too much about being Jewish. "Why don't you just keep that to yourself? We don't care. We don't want to hear about your Jewishness." I recommend burning these types of letters, since they don't serve you in any positive way.

Most of these bothersome encounters are nothing more than innocuous intrusions. Your good humor and sense of perspective may be called upon often. I try to see the funny bone if possible in all of our awkward human interactions.

Solution: Brandish your umbrella

I remember hearing a parable about a young woman spiritual seeker riding in a rickshaw in India. The driver got increasingly bold with his advances, which quickly turned to attempted rape. All the while the woman was thinking she needed to act like the compassionate being she was taught to be during her spiritual practice. She finally evaded the driver and escaped. When she told her spiritual master about the incident, he said, "Oh, my dear. I hope you mustered all the compassion you could while hitting him hard on the head with your umbrella!"

Please don't hesitate to use that umbrella with strong force. If for any reason you feel threatened by someone, take action immediately. The rules of politeness don't enter in here. Do whatever it takes to protect your safety. Women are often too polite in the name of saving face. If you are concerned about this, read Gavin de Becker's book *The Gift of Fear: And Other Survival Signals That Protect Us from Violence* for strategies for staying safe. (He's a leading expert in predicting violent behavior.) Get ready now for any unwanted attention.

Solution: Handle obtrusive or intrusive people

Once your book is published, your business is profiled, the company you work for appears in the news, or other publicity opportunities have graced your life, many people will want things from you that you may not be willing to give. Some even think you *owe* them a positive personal response as a public figure. There may be times when you are not in the mood to deal with any kind of intrusion into your private life and prefer to remain anonymous. Also know that this is one of the consequences of becoming a household name.

Solution: Set your limits

Stephen King talked about times when admirers would interrupt him and his family as they dined quietly in a restaurant. He would politely ask them to leave them their private time. At being refused his autograph, more than a few who had initially approached him as his biggest fans snarled up into his biggest enemies. On the other hand, Frank Sinatra thanked autograph seekers as he signed their napkins or albums or what-have-yous, wherever he was. It is up to you to set your own limits.

Solution: Protect your time

Though an intrusion may not come in the same form as those who approached those famous folk, people will ask for your time and your advice, and seek personal attention. For example, a woman I didn't know e-mailed me and asked me to review and critique her Web site. Many people ask me for informational interviews and e-mail me asking for free consulting advice. I give away lots of free articles and ideas right on my Web site. While I am happy to share my knowledge and experience, I reserve my private time after work for friends and family.

After a National Speakers Association talk, a woman approached me and told me she'd like to "take me to tea to pick my brain." People actually say this! What an unappetizing thought. With the advice of Colleen Newlin, who is an expert in setting boundaries, I said, "Thank you very much for thinking of me. I reserve my private time after work for my friends. Thank you for your offer." I kept my answer short, sweet, and to the point.

Solution: Keep a cache of responses

Plan in advance how you will address the inevitable unwanted communication and you will feel easier in your skin. Keeping a cache of stock written responses for different types of intrusions will help you feel prepared on the e-mail and letter-writing front. Connie Hatch and Patti Breitman's book, *How to Say No without Feeling Guilty*, has some top-notch solutions to saying no. The one that works for unwanted or intrusive invitations is this: "Keep it short, sweet, and repeat."

Connie and Patti also recommend a technique called "invoking a policy." So by invoking a policy my response would have sounded like this: "Thank you very much for thinking of me. I have a policy that I reserve all my private time after work for my friends. Thank you for your offer." If the person presses you, simply repeat the statement again. Use a firm and polite tone and don't embellish your response. Most people don't mean to be intrusive. They just aren't aware of your time constraints. It is up to you to educate them graciously.

You will get overexposed

I suppose if there were ever a problem to be wished for, this would be it. As we popped black bean shrimp into our mouths in a Chinese restaurant, publicist Leslie Rossman told me she was surprised when she had this problem with the Dalai Lama. "Everyone thinks it should be easy to promote a big name like the Dalai Lama. But the feedback from the media was that he was no big news because he writes a new book every year." Leslie, persistent and creative as she is, protested, saying that the Dalai Lama actually *wrote* this book, while the others were written with the help of other people. Despite any initial murmurings or protests Leslie got major media coverage for him anyway, including *People,* the *New York Times,* the *New York Post,* the Associated Press, and *Newsweek,* which sent a crew to cover him in Dharamsala, India.

Solution: Reinvent yourself

"The biggest way to overcome overexposure is to point out why *now* is different from *before.* What is brand spanking new this time around? Be able to convey it quickly, acknowledging their concern but giving them the information they need to go to bat for your author, book, etc. Be prepared to listen, but overcome their objections with real ideas, facts, and knowledge of what your pitching," advises Leslie.

There is not much to worry about here, as you will constantly reinvent yourself so that the media and the public won't tire of your "youness."

You will believe your own hype

I know more than a few people too big for their britches. One woman and I were friends when one phone line was more than she could afford. And now after reaching a high level of success, callers have to go through the grilling of a couple of assistants to reach her in person. I work with people a lot more famous than I am or will ever be and so I have had the good fortune of learning some of their coping mechanisms for managing fame and a big name.

When one well-known man contacted me, I explained that I was nervous to begin working with him. I usually am not tongue-tied with my famous clients, but I had followed and admired his writing for years. (Okay, I had a crush on him never even having seen him.) Then

I met him. Crush increased. He set me at ease by saying, "I try not to believe my own hype. Some people see me as a guru. It is important to me that I don't buy into that." I already liked him a lot. His comment made me like him even more. It is important not to buy into your own hype.

The key: keep your goals in mind

When my agent reviewed this chapter, she said if she had read it before doing her publicity campaign for her book, it would have scared the bejesus out of her. If you feel that way at this moment, I encourage you to reread chapter 1 to remind you of everything that publicity can do for you.

I think it is wise to know what you are in for so you can prepare for the worst and the best. These are the facts—not for the bake sales and the blood drives but for a more long-term campaign for those of you who are serious about continuing your marketing and publicity efforts on an ongoing basis. I have structured this book so you can create a plan for a single event or for a lifelong adventure that is integrated into your personal and professional life. It is always up to you how deep you want to go. I am here to show you where the potholes exist and how to tunnel into the places that harbor the gold.

PART V

Prepare Yourself Verbally and Psychologically for Media Attention

CHAPTER 7

Use Sound Bites
Skillfully

Words are the ambassadors of our intentions. Whenever anyone calls to hire me as a media coach, I listen closely to the way they express themselves with words. More importantly, I listen to perceive who they are as a person. Do they respect my time, or do they ramble? What does their tone tell me about their genuine attitude? Do they know their subject? Can they communicate clearly and concisely?

Once you open your mouth to speak to anyone anywhere, you are auditioning. You are vying for their attention, for their time, for their commitment to you and whatever you have to promote.

There is a Zen story that illustrates how words are a powerful form of inciting action.

A big, tough samurai once went to see a little monk. "Monk," he said, in a voice accustomed to instant obedience, "teach me about heaven and hell!"

The monk looked up at this mighty warrior and replied with utter disdain, "Teach you about heaven and hell? I couldn't teach you about anything. You are dirty. You smell. Your blade is rusty. You are a disgrace, an embarrassment to the samurai class. Get out of my sight. I can't stand you."

The samurai was furious. He shook, got all red in the face, was speechless with rage. He pulled out his sword and raised it above him, preparing to slay the monk.

"That is hell," said the monk softly.

The samurai was overwhelmed. The compassion and surrender of this little man who had offered his life to give this teaching to show him hell! He slowly put down his sword, filled with gratitude, and suddenly peaceful.

"And that is heaven," said the monk softly.

The heavenly news is that with words you have the opportunity to express your vision to millions of people across the world. The hellish news is that you have less than ten seconds to do it. It takes some intensive practice to make meaning in such a short time. Under these circumstances it becomes critical to develop your sound bites for any occasion.

Choose the right words

What is a sound bite? "A minimum of sound to a maximum of sense," said Mark Twain, who was himself a master of sound bites. I have not heard it put any better. Twain also said, "The difference between the right word and almost the right word is the difference between lightning and a lightning bug." Sound bites are the lightning flashes of who you are and the message you want to get across. To say what you mean and mean what you say, develop your sound bites word for word. The process of developing your sound bites is about peeling away the unnecessary to arrive at the essential. But before you peel . . .

Create six dynamic sound bites

In order to speak your way to the hearts and minds of people, you should have about six sound bites or talking points. Sound bites are the essential things you want to convey. They are memory nuggets, or blurbable ideas designed to be easy for your audience to digest. You can incorporate these six juicy jewels into any conversation. They can consist of anecdotes, facts, statistics, stories, or something unlikely, unusual, controversial, shocking, funny, humorous, romantic, poignant, emotionally moving, or dramatic.

These six things will make your audience get their rear in gear to dash out to buy your product or service, choose you for a project or spokesperson, or pick up the phone right now to order whatever you are selling. More than that, these sound bites promise and deliver something worthwhile.

Invitation

Ask yourself three questions:

1. What are the most important things for my audience to know?
2. How or what do I want my audience to feel?
3. What do I want my audience to do?

After you answer these three questions, structure your sound bites to satisfy them. Next make your sound bites collapsible and expandable. Be able to deliver these six "stories" in as little as ten seconds or as much as two minutes each. This way you will be able to meet the audience's, producer's, host's, or journalist's time limits and still get your points across.

Acknowledge six of the most important things in stories and in life: beauty, poetry, music, timing, truth, and nuance

As a media coach I'm immersed in the squeezing down of concepts into a few pithy phrases that catch attention. Recently, I was talking to a client whose stories were already sifted into simplicity. That day I read a quote on the Internet that said, "Simplify things to their simplest form, but no simpler." She had. But the results were more like pulp than ripe fruit. I asked for the expanded versions so I could taste their full flavor and help her decide how they should be juiced down. I try to view these sound bites as a new form of language—haiku versus open verse, a Zen fountain versus a mountain stream, flowers in a window box versus a field of poppies ready to take you to a land deep in the opiated imagination. It is important to savor the lushness of nuance and the musical flow of language while shaving off unimportant details.

Eliminate "ifs," "ands," "wherefores," and "maybes"

Peter Jennings, anchor and senior editor of ABC TV's *World News Tonight*, says, "I would make for lousy sound bites. I tend to use a lot of inverted phrases and 'ifs,' 'ands,' 'wherefores,' and 'maybes' because that's rather the way I look at life. And so I find writing the evening news sometimes very challenging because I realize that what we're trying to give folks in the evening is black-and-white when so often I want to give them gray."

Though I am part of this plucking, sifting, pruning, and planting, this shaping into something palatable to the public, at times I mourn this process. Other times I delight in creating a hybrid when the stories are too full of weeds and have long overgrown their part of the garden. What I rebel against is when the blossom is already exquisite. Our language filtered through the media becomes an endangered species of sorts. I've tried to become a realist, to believe that there is a singular beauty to each version of a tale. It's an art to convey the essence of you and your work in as few words as possible. Hone your sound bites and leave in as much gray as you can without sacrificing clarity.

Make potent points

Keeping to your most potent points makes an interview move forward more smoothly. Jane Swigart, Ph.D, wrote her book *The Myth of the Perfect Mother* to help mothers parent without guilt. To convey the difficulty and complexity of motherhood, she came up with some key phrases like, "Being a mother is like asking half the population to do brain surgery without sending them to medical school." And, "There is a myth that women are divinely prepared for caregiving." Both phrases are short, to the point, and can be spoken in less than ten seconds.

Ira Glass, host of the National Public Radio (NPR) show *This American Life,* is a master at creating stories that touch us in a fundamental way. He says, "You will notice that every forty-five seconds or a minute someone will complete some thought . . . I don't know why that is, but that is the base rhythm of the way the news information shows on [national] pubic radio tend to work." Ira has actually timed quite a few shows and discovered that some sort of epiphany tends to happen in that forty-five-second to one-minute time frame. Designing your sound bites with this in mind will help keep your points potent.

Use this template for developing stellar stories

As a woman you have an advantage over most men. Why? Because you are more comfortable dealing with the *emotional* or feeling aspects of telling a story. Stories are most effective when they touch people emotionally. When you discuss your points, cover them in the following format to make the most of their emotional content:

① Explain the situation.

② Develop the action.

③ State the result.

④ Close with an epiphany.

The following story uses each of these elements.

Long ago when SARK was a starving artist, we sat on her bed eating chocolates and I read this story from her first book before it was published.

① When I was ten years old, one of my best friends was eighty, and his name was Mr. Boggs. He called me his "twirly friend." (Because I did a wheelie in his driveway.)

② Mr. Boggs taught me how to play checkers and gave me a microscope. Then he got sick and went into the hospital. Every day, I made him a card or a poem or did a drawing, and sent these to the hospital.

③ Mr. Boggs came home after a month in the hospital and said to me, "You saved my life. No one else called or wrote, and your mailings gave me the courage to live. Thank you."

④ I think it was then that I decided to devote my life to being creative.

When I finished reading, I had tears in my eyes. I realized that childhood stories make powerful storytelling tools, especially when connected to their present-day relevance. SARK's story took forty-five seconds to tell, yet it is packed with emotional importance. She included a "wrap-up" epiphany at the end that summarized her point and gave it additional impact.

HOT TIP!

CONNECT YOUR PAST (CHILDHOOD) EXPERIENCE TO YOUR PRESENT-DAY PROFESSION.

Tell a story that has a beginning, middle, and end

Robert Dickman, president of Firstvoice and media coach for corporate executives and Hollywood actors, explains that storytelling is at the core of communication. He says that there are three essential things everyone wants to know about you: who you are, where you have come from, and where you are going.

Besides those three elements your stories should have a beginning, a middle, and an end. Conflict, problems, and struggle make the story universal. In a great story there is an unexpected element, a sense of suspense where you don't know what is going to happen. "The key to creativity is the loss of control," Dickman asserts. "Trust your intuitive body and emotional sensations. If you are telling a story you are bored with, don't tell it."

To begin exploring your own stories, Dickman recommends getting into a hot bath with a recorder nearby. "There is something that happens in a hypnagogic state when you really relax. When you judge, you cut off the deeper richer part of the unconscious. A lot of the work we need to do is being done for us in the unconscious." As your muscles begin to relax, recall a story from your past. Envision yourself within the specific circumstances of your story. What does your story smell, touch, taste, and look like? If you can feel it, it is much easier for the audience to see it.

Once you have identified a story that is meaningful, ask yourself how it is connected to what you are currently promoting. Add that link to your story to tie it together. When you retell the story, tell it in the present tense as if it is happening now. That is one of the things that intensifies the experience of the person listening.

Convey a mesmerizing message in thirty seconds

You can create suspense and desire in your audience in less than a minute by telling a story. As the poet Muriel Rukeyser said, "The world is made not of atoms, but of stories." Stories are both profound learning tools and good fun. They can be a vehicle for moving the masses into action or for shifting a mood. To tell your mesmerizing message on TV or radio or in print it should contain three elements:

1. A human or heartwarming message (emotional).

2. Facts (mental).

3. Sensory images (kinesthetic).

Tell a story with a heartwarming message and you reach the people in your audience who respond to *feelings* (emotional).

Others in your audience need quantifiable data to stay interested (mental). For them, using statistics, facts, and things that can be proven makes a message take. Another part of your audience wants to be engaged through the senses (kinesthetic). They want to be involved in a concrete way, touching, smelling, seeing, hearing, tasting.

While you may not be able to send the scent of an apple pie through your TV set, you can evoke the sensory images that help your audience remember first opening the screen door, dropping their schoolbooks in the mudroom, following the warm smell of cinnamon to the kitchen counter, and Mom's promise of a slice of pie after it has cooled enough to be cut. Have your audience *do* something to keep them involved. Use all three elements to reach people on an emotional, a mental, and a kinesthetic level.

Be brief

When Johnny Carson first went to see Jay Leno in a nightclub, Carson told him he was funny, but not ready to be on the show. Leno asked why. Carson said his jokes were too far apart. At first Leno didn't know what he meant. But as he watched Carson's monologue, he noticed that he was doing fifteen to twenty jokes in the same space Leno was doing only five. Whether in late-night comedy, news-oriented programs, or daytime talk shows, the rhythm of TV is fast. You will have ten to twenty seconds to make a point before the camera cuts away to your interviewer, to another guest, or to B-roll (background still shots or taped action sequences). Use facts, anecdotes, short stories, and one-liners to express your main message. Here are examples of each:

Fact

In 1999 the Institute of Medicine estimated that between 44,000 and 98,000 Americans die each year as a result of medical errors.

Anecdote

"When a man says 'no,' it is the end of a conversation. When a woman says 'no,' it is the beginning of a negotiation." (Gavin de Becker)

Story

I have a love affair with suicide. I used to be obsessed with how I would kill myself. I'd think about it all the time. I'd plan it, get lost in the reverie of it. I would hang myself because my mother was hanged and I watched that happen when I was a child from the inside of a basket in our hut. I wanted so badly to join her. I would clean my house, give away my possessions, pay bills, not leave any work for anyone, go to the forest, dressed like mother in a white dress, a blue ribbon in my hair. I would leave a warning sign for hikers so I wouldn't surprise or frighten anyone. Then I would hang myself with a rope from a tree. I would be free from pain and reunited at last with my beloved mother. (Paraphrased from when I media-coached Elizabeth Kim, author of *10,000 Sorrows*)

One-liner

"The best mind-altering drug is truth." (Lily Tomlin, actor)

"Elegance means elimination." (Madame Errazuriz, a Chilean-born minimalist interior designer in the 1920s)

Find your own voice

Your voice is as personal as your thumbprint. You may not recognize it as such, but your pets, neighbors, loved ones, and colleagues do. You use phrases and have mannerisms that are like the billboards that holler over city highways. Ask your friends and family what your billboards are. They'll be able to tell you right away. Ask yourself which of these patterns should be amplified, and which should be toned down. Do you have a signature story that you tell over and over again? These stories are one way we frame our lives. Begin to notice how you talk about your experiences.

Know your music

During media-coaching Dean Sharenow, a sound engineer and pop and Broadway musician, explained the two ways to approach music with complete freedom:

1. Come to a piece of music for the first time with no expectations.

2. Know the music so completely that you are open to all possibilities.

While some people thrive on the pressure to perform by going to an interview unprepared and with no expectations, most don't. The time constraints for media interviews are typically so tight, your ability to know and condense your material is of utmost importance. Once you know your "music" intimately, you can experience the freedom of spontaneity and improvisation.

Another reason to practice thoroughly relates to brain chemistry. A recent study at the University of California at Irvine revealed that cortisol, a hormone that gets released during stressful situations, blocks the brain's ability to retrieve information. "Our studies show that information stored really well in the brain is not affected by cortisol," explains Benno Roozendaal, Ph.D., a researcher at UCI's Center for the Neurobiology of Learning and Memory. By preparing and practicing your sound bites you will establish a strong foundation. You will then be free to be spontaneous. When you are relaxed, you can allow insights a place in your patter.

Practice out loud

A woman who was one day away from appearing on a major TV show came to my office for an emergency media-coaching session. We had done a number of practice interviews by phone and had honed her sound bites down to three key points for every question she was going to be asked. I then wrote the points out and sent them to her so she could practice at home before our in-person meeting. We even timed each sound bite to ten seconds so she could be sure to get in all of her points. But she still had difficulty saying each one succinctly. When I asked her if she had practiced speaking her points out loud, she confessed she had only read them on the page.

Rehearsing in your head is good. But in order to sound natural and spontaneous, practice talking your points out loud. To ensure that your words will become embedded in your muscle memory, practice them in the same position that you will tell them. Each time you rehearse them, act as if you were saying them for the first time. Each moment is different from every other moment. Allow all the subtle new details to arise as you practice.

Someone said of Frank O'Hara, "He wrote poetry that was so conversational, casual, easy to like, colloquial, that it was very easy to fall in love with his poetry. He made poetry seem as natural as breathing." This is the goal of your sound bite delivery. To make it as natural as breathing and to invite people to fall in love with you, and whatever you are selling or offering. Your sound bites evolve as you do. Bring freshness to them with expression, enthusiasm, and delight.

Create fresh word flowers

Buddhist Zen master, poet, and peace activist Thich Nhat Hanh says, "There is a gatha (teaching) that says, 'Words can travel thousands of miles.' They are to build up more mutual acceptance and understanding. I vow that my words will be like gems. I vow that my words will be fresh like flowers."

If you can, use your gems and flowers to encourage justice and good in the world. We, as women, are often consumed with how to make things beautiful. This extends just as much to the way we speak and move as it does to making our homes a sanctuary for solace.

Edmund Morel, considered the greatest British investigative reporter of his time, was largely responsible for putting an end to the slave trade in the Congo through his one-man publicity campaign in the early 1900s. He almost single-handedly created a worldwide human rights movement with his efforts. He convinced Mark Twain and Booker T. Washington to go on a speaking tour to stop this African holocaust. In England he enlisted Sir Arthur Conan Doyle, the popular author of the

Sherlock Holmes books. Their aid in protesting against the United States for being the first country to recognize the Congo as King Leopold's possession helped incite international fervor and forced Leopold to turn the colony over to Belgium. Working with Morel, Mark Twain took his own intentions to heart when he acted on his words, "Always do right. This will gratify some people and astonish the rest."

CHAPTER 8

Handle the Five Main Types of Interviewers

Conversation is really just the art of connecting with another person. Can you connect with this person for 5, 10, 20, 30, 60 minutes?

In this chapter you will learn how to get your information or message out under any circumstances with the five main types of interviewers. They are

The Nice.
The Unprepared.
The Interrupter.
The Rambler.
The Hostile.

I am using the term "interviewer" for hosts or any media person who is involved in receiving a "presentation" from you. The things to remember in every interview are your purpose, your intention, and your reason for being there. One way to do that is to become a clear channel for listening. Rather than planning what you are going to say when the other person is talking, focus your total attention on him. Try to take the information in a neutral way, watching for your judgments and letting them go as they arise, so you can hear what is really being said. Let's begin with the easiest interpersonal interview style, the Nice.

Relish the nice interviewer

Getting the Nice Interviewer first is a pleasant way to get acclimated to the give-and-take of a genteel conversation. You will be able to relax and focus in on your points knowing that you probably won't be thrown for a loop. The Nice Interviewer doesn't make waves, he surfs. He wants to make it easy for you; he wants to get along. He may have prepared for your interview, a little or a lot. He wants to know enough to make a conversation continue. You really already know how to handle the Nice Interviewer: Have your sound bites ready, state them succinctly, and be yourself.

The Nice Interviewer may need the slightest bit of nudging to give your conversation some pep. Look for opportunities to interject your points and do it in a conversational way. This is the time to bring up something that is just a touch sassy. Here are some methods for responding to the Nice Interviewer:

The Offer

When you sense that an interview is lagging, ask to read a passage from your book, provide cutting-edge research, or describe your service or idea with a tightly condensed and powerful phrase. You will, of course, have chosen in advance to read a paragraph or two that is particularly exemplary. Don't feel shy about offering. When she was being interviewed on the radio for her book, *Some of Me,* Isabella Rossellini asked, with her exotic accent reminiscent of what is most intriguing about Italy, "Should I read something?"

The Joe Friday

Many times, though an interview is going smoothly, it may still be moving forward on a different track than you prefer. When asked a question you don't want to delve into deeply, state facts or statistics or quote someone else who has information relevant to your point. Surrounding yourself with other experts who agree with you creates a fortress of facts that support your views.

THE KEY: SET YOUR OWN PACING AND AGENDA.

It's up to you to be informative and entertaining and not to depend on the interviewer to ask you interesting or provocative questions.

Correct the unprepared interviewer

Unlike the Nice Interviewer, you are going to have to work hard here. The Unprepared Interviewer can be like meeting all your lover's relatives at one time. Most of them don't know a lot about you and what they do know is probably wrong. The Unprepared Interviewer is the person who wings it. He may know little or nothing of what is being discussed or promoted. He may even ask questions that make minimal sense or are totally offtrack. Don't count on the producers to have your biography, questions, or product available. You never know what kind of a day they've had. They will be grateful that you are prepared if they can't be.

When there is a commercial break in the interview, you can gently give the interviewer some clues about your subject matter by synopsizing a few main points and let him know in which direction you might proceed. Be perceptive in observing which interviewers would be grateful for such information and which might like to give you a tonk on the head for being out of line.

You can begin by saying, "Would it be helpful if I gave you a quick rundown of some main points of my (work, product, service, business, book) given that I know I wasn't scheduled for this time slot?" Or if you are pressed for time, say, "I thought it might help if I gave you a quick rundown of some main points of my (work, product, service, business, book) to make your job easier."

The Unprepared Interviewer frequently asks questions that may not be applicable to your subject or your main points. The following phrases and techniques will give you ideas about how to deal with this issue:

The Ignore and Divert

Most men know how to give a nonverbal message and have it be heard like a cannonball boom. The technique is this: You act like you didn't hear the question and then do or say something that completely changes the subject. For example, let's imagine someone asked, "Why is it that women aren't as successful in business as men?" You'd say, "Understanding that you have one job and one job only—to make your boss successful—is the one factor that will help anyone move up the corporate hierarchy."

The Transition

It is up to you to carry your end of the show and politely correct the interviewer whenever an error is made without appearing to do so. Use the inaccuracy as a transition into a point you want to cover like this: The interviewer says, "Isn't it true that entrepreneurs care more about getting a product into the marketplace first even if it's defective?" You answer, "It's commonly believed that entrepreneurs value speed, but the majority have become well known because their products fill a desperate need. People don't continue to buy products that don't work."

The Wonderer

Sometimes all you need is a smooth transition to get you into the subject of your choice. At times when things are bump-bump-bumping along, ask yourself a specific question and then answer it. Professional speakers and seminar leaders use this tip all the time. The nice thing about "the wonderer" is it sounds natural to encourage a conversation with yourself. You might say, "I sometimes wonder how I could have written/said . . ." Then launch into a story, an anecdote, or an epiphany. A rule of thumb is to create small stories with the format: situation (set the scene), action (what you did), result (dramatic conclusion), as you learned when you created your six sound bites.

The Entrainer

As much as you embrace or resist the idea, you are on the air because you can provide entertainment for an audience. Rather than just entertain, *entrain. Entrain* in the French sense of the word, means "to transport" or "carry away." Entrainment has an element of trance, the quality to mesmerize on a deep level. Entertainment doesn't have that same kind of holding power. When you are asked a question that doesn't pertain to your topic, it helps to be entraining. Sharing information with the audience that you know is fascinating makes the interview move at a swift pace while making the interviewer appear as if he's doing an excellent job. For example, say, "What most people want to know is . . ." Or, "What many people ask me about is . . ." Or, "What people find most surprising/useful/entertaining is . . ."

The "I know"

At some point you will get asked a question that seems to have been launched from the moon. When asked such a question for which you don't have a clear answer, or any answer for that matter, stay within your area of expertise and reinforce the impression that you are knowledgeable in your field. You might say, "I don't know about that, but what I do know is . . . which I discuss in . . . (name of book, article, brochure, report)."

The Share

There are times during interviews when you have not been asked about something you want to cover. Shyness be gone! Worse than in a relationship where you expect your significant other to read your mind, interviewers don't know the terrain of your gray matter. Offer to share something the interviewer hasn't thought of. Most often he will greatly appreciate your thoughtfulness. Use a teaser tidbit. "I could tell you about . . . if you'd like."

THE KEY: COURTEOUSLY INSIST ON ACCURACY.

Don't let any untrue bit of information perpetuate itself in the media. It may come back to haunt you.

Interrupt the interrupter interviewer

Many radio and TV stations are under tremendous time constraints. The hosts of those shows have developed a real conversational rhythm to keep the program moving according to schedule, commercial breaks, and the cues of the producer, all while managing their guests. This is much like sticking your finger in a dike while balancing a ball on your nose.

Of course, there are the interviewers whose personalities dictate that they cut off their guests before they have finished speaking, but that is the exception rather than the rule. This interviewer style is a tough one for women because we have been habituated into believing that interrupting to gain the floor is rude.

Time to change that dynamic. In her book *You Just Don't Understand*, Deborah Tannen points out that men often interrupt to speak at length, or give a "lecture." She labels this "report talk," which is to speak until interrupted by someone else competing for the floor. When women interrupt, it is often (though not always) to establish rapport rather than to one-up the speaker. She warns that while men accept and even welcome this form of contest in one another, a woman is often viewed as aggressive if she employs the same strategy. Knowing that risk, I still advise you to take it with the knowledge that you *might* stub the toe of a well-meaning man or woman. In any case here is what to do when you find that you are prevented from finishing a sentence or a thought.

The Pretty Please

The most polite way to deal with the Interrupter is to pick up where you left off when you were interrupted. You may find you are doing this continually if the interviewer is in the habit of cutting off guests when he deems they are done. You can also say, "I wanted to add one more thing to *your* thought," which is a charming way to compliment your interrupter while still making your point. Even if he's already gone on to the next point, you can say, "I want to say one more thing about . . ."

The Yes

Interrupt with agreement. Say, "Yes!" and then state your point.

The Polite Please

Raise your voice and say, "Pardon me!" If that doesn't work, try a slightly sharper-toned one-word "Please!" Or, "Please! I'd like to finish." Or, "May I finish?" Don't hesitate or wait for agreement, just finish. This technique works well for panel discussions, when other guests momentarily forget their manners, rather than for a one-on-one conversation.

The Lean In

If you find the polite please doesn't work, intensify your position by leaning toward the offender, intruding into his "safe" space zone, and say more forcefully, but still neutrally, "May I please finish? I will give you the same courtesy."

The Finger

(No, not that one!) If you are being interviewed in person, hold up a finger. If a person is more belligerent, hold up your hand like a stop sign. In the case of a panel discussion or meeting you can actually say, "Stop!" to another guest if that person is really blockheaded.

The Pound
If he continues to be loutish and unruly, then escalate it to the next level of intensity. Do something that creates a disruptive or startling noise. Pounding a fist on the table makes a lull so you can then jump in.

The Low Rumble
Speaking in a lower voice immediately commands authority. When others are excitedly talking in higher voices, lowering yours will attract attention.

The Startle
You can verbally startle your interviewer into stopping by interrupting him right back. The result will be a quick peppering kind of conversation, which can be quite nice.

The Shin Crunch
In all those political roundtable discussions I'd like to give you permission to kick your opponents under the table. Not too hard, just enough to startle them into shutting up. Wouldn't this be great if someone had the guts to do it?

The Joiner
Short of kicking someone to make an opening, there are times when it is appropriate to join into the festive fight. Many producers relish on-air fights because the energy is high and it is exciting for the audience. A friend told me about a time when she watched helplessly as her airtime dwindled when two guests on a show got involved in a heated argument. When the show cut to a commercial break, the host turned to the two shouters and said, "Keep it up!"

THE KEY: DON'T GIVE UP ON THE INTERRUPTER.
Sure, it can be really trying, but consider it one of the many styles of interviewing you will encounter. As a last resort you can try talking over the Interrupter Interviewer in hopes that he'll stop

first. If that doesn't work after a few seconds, I'd advise you to stop. In most cases the audience is loyal to the interviewer and you will be perceived as the rude one. Zip in those points whenever you have the chance and let the Interrupter indulge his rudeness in the glare of his own spotlight. Trying to change his style isn't going to get you anywhere. Adapting to the pacing and rhythm of being interrupted can be like bouncing along on a pony without a saddle. You may be a little sore, but make up your mind ahead of time to consider the ride a pip.

Reel in the rambler interviewer

The Rambler, or constant talker, is a person who rarely asks a question and babbles on about inconsequential or irrelevant subjects. This person can be pleasant as they ramble, but often sees the meeting or interview forum as a chance to chatter about whatever comes to mind. He sometimes talks just to show that he has a close relationship with the presenter or guest.

The Rambler tends to give women the most trouble. We are trained not to interrupt. A rambling interviewer can seem nice, which is a double problem. Who wants to interrupt a pleasant, well-meaning person? You do. Get comfortable with interrupting because some ramblers don't even ask a question. It will serve you well in business meetings as well as in media appearances. To make your points when you have a chatty host, use these helpful word wranglers.

The Lock

Lock onto one word that he's just said and begin your sentence there. Example: The Rambler says, "You know we're all just ticktocking away at our future no matter what age we are because timing waits for no one. . . ."

You say, "Timing is the one thing you must master if you want to get really good at being on the radio."

The Perfect Point

Tell him how happy you are that he has touched on a point you want to cover. You will establish rapport and get in a few words. "I am glad you brought that up." Then launch into your point, relating it in some way to his meanderings.

The Speed Demon

Match his speed. Many ramblers don't like dead air. They can't stand silence and may even see it as wasted time during an interview. By stepping up your pace and matching his, you will satisfy his need to keep things lively and constant and may even be able to get in a few extra ideas.

The No Breather

Don't breathe at the end of your sentence, breathe after the word "and." Lengthening the word "and" and then continuing until you are done disrupts the natural rhythms in which most of us speak. The majority of people will unconsciously feel uncomfortable interrupting you in that rhythm pattern, which is slightly unnatural.

THE KEY: PERSIST IN *YOUR* INTERRUPTIONS.

One impatient client of mine coped with the Rambler by not coping. She got mesmerized by the continuous chatting and zoned out. No zoning! Take back control. The Rambler may never be done. His run-on sentences are the kind that the teacher dinged you for in school. You must plug him up over and over again as if all your precious resources were being poured down the drain (which they are). Time is of the essence. And so is politeness. Don't ever get exasperated or impatient. It will reflect badly on you. Swoosh in when he takes the slightest breath. This takes some practice and tuning in. You will be able to do it easily once you get used to the breakneck pacing of continuous-stream chattering. He breathes; you talk. He pauses midsentence; you jazz in.

Herd the hostile interviewer

The hostile or skeptical interviewer is the one most people fear. But you really don't need to, once you understand the game. Most curmudgeons just want to have a good show or presentation filled with animated discussion.

For women the Hostile Interviewer is more likely to be condescending, or to ignore or embarrass them, than to be aggressive. Men tend to enjoy this type of verbal interplay, which they view as lively competition. They are comfortable with their testosterone levels rising with the volume of their voices. In the best case, when a man challenges your authority, he's inviting you in a friendly way to defend yourself. In the worst case, he may be a person who questions your authority and tries to find any weaknesses in your presentation in a game of one-upmanship. He may deliberately try to make you look foolish, irrational, or unprepared so he'll look better.

Whatever the case, it is not really important.

What is important is to remember the reason you are there. Is it your mission to enlighten your audience about a cause you feel passionate about? Are you looking to make your product the best of its kind? Do you want your team to continue to be asked to work on the core issues of your company?

Bring yourself back to your mission over and over again. If you believe that this is the best way to get the word out on what you want to promote, remind yourself of that.

Some of my clients were surprised to find the hostile interview the most fun and energizing once they got into it. Because it tapped into subjects about which they were passionate and had strong opinions, they found that they were increasingly focused and alive. And they were much more compelling to hear and watch.

Something to remember: No matter how much you are enjoying the intensity, never fall into the trap of insulting someone back. Maintain your own equanimity and be able to back up your point of view. One more thing: Research shows that it is harder to say no to someone who makes a request accompanied by a touch. Make your point with a light or lingering touch to turn the attention in the direction you want. Here are numerous ways you can "touch" the Hostile Interviewer. By the way, this works with his hostile guests or your peers as well.

The We

Try aligning yourself with others before a disagreement sets in. Decide to agree before you disagree. Find an area of commonality before you broach something that might bring up strong feelings of contrariness. Use language like, "What if we . . . ?"

The Agree

Before you counter with your reply, disabuse the hostile person of his notion by first acknowledging that many others agree with him. He'll feel like he has support for his ideas and you are just one small voice in a crowd of cheering fans. "Many people think as you do and that is why I did so much research and have found otherwise." Explain what you have found in anecdotal evidence, facts, or statistics.

The Defuser

Another way to agree with the hostile person is to defuse the tension quickly by stating your understanding. "I see how you can come to that conclusion and . . ." Then state your point. Notice I used the word "and" and not "but." The word "but" is an unconscious cue to butt heads. "And" is a word that smooths things over.

Another tack you can use to defuse is to show that an idea must have validity because a number of people subscribe to it. "People who disagree with me might say . . ." Or, "Other people who have opposing ideas may say . . . and I believe . . . for these reasons . . ." Or, "What I am about to say may make a number of people angry . . ."

The Compliment

Compliment the hostile person. Sometimes he just wants to be recognized. "Really! That is fascinating."

Then tell why you disagree.

The Impersonal

Take the discussion out of the personal to the objective by stating facts. "Statistics prove otherwise." He won't feel like you are attacking him for a second or two.

The Accuser

Avoid accusing. Relationship counselors are always advising us to use "I" versus "you" messages when describing an aggravating issue. Better to focus on your own behavior, thoughts, and feelings than to judge someone else's. Don't point a finger at someone and say, "*You* don't know what you are talking about." State how you feel or your point of view, backed up by statistics or other authorities. An opinion is just that. An opinion backed by your own personal experience or facts becomes a reason to listen to you.

WARNING! **USE "YOU" LANGUAGE WITH A BULLY.**

If you are truly dealing with a raging bully, Sam Horn, author of *Tongue Fu!* recommends using strong "you" statements because bullies think that you're the one who has the problem. "I" language just gives them an opportunity to show you you're wrong. Say something like, "You need to understand that ..." Important: Then move quickly to your point to keep the conversation running. Don't give the bully the chance to derail you.

The Controversial

Jean-Paul Sartre said, "Words are loaded pistols." When you want to deliver your own controversial ideas, you can use words' explosive power in your favor by learning how to soften your introduction before you speak. Acknowledge a difficult issue or position while respecting your critics' or opponents' ideas by mentioning an opposing view in your response. By bringing up his viewpoint, you automatically defuse it. Examples: "People who agree with you have every right to do so." Or, "Your ideas make a lot of sense. I agree with . . . and not with . . ."

If, on the other hand, you really relish a good tiff, you can follow the Gaelic proverb "If you want an audience, start a fight." I remember accompanying a client to a live radio show whose premise was to cover controversial issues. He and the other panelists went at it with gusto. Afterward they all sat around a table chatting amiably. I didn't know it, but they knew each other well and had a healthy respect for their individual opinions. Later on in the car with my client I found out that they all agreed on most topics in their common field, but chose the areas where they disagreed to throw some hot pepper in the eyes of their audience.

WARNING! EXPECT TO BE CHALLENGED IF YOU CALL YOURSELF AN EXPERT.

Naming yourself an expert is often considered an invitation for a challenge. If you don't want to be challenged, then position yourself as an "observer" or a "witness"—someone who can share personal experiences and observations rather than prove something with evidence or logic. Men especially relish the chance to test an expert's abilities, while women sometimes view these challenges as a way to demean or disrespect their authority. See this as an opportunity to bolster your authority rather than as an attack upon your credibility by preparing additional points to support your side.

The Abrupt Interrupt

Stop the hostile person in his tracks with an abrupt interruption. Using the same type of energy for a moment aligns you with his and also startles him and makes an opening where there might not have been one. *"No!"* Then lower your voice and give your explanation.

The Switch

An interviewer might not know where your sensitive points are or he may seek them out. Either way, to switch the subject you can employ a few different techniques. When Terry Gross pressed a leader of a rap group about one of the members of his group making anti-Semitic remarks, he answered vaguely a number of times and then said bluntly, "Let's move on," which made him appear rude. Instead, he might have said, "I have really said all I can say about this. Can we go on to the next question?" Or, "I have really answered this to the best of my knowledge at this time with the information I have available."

Another way to handle persistent questions on a topic you wish to avoid is to give a series of very short responses, or to answer them with information that is so charming or captivating, the interviewer won't notice you have deviated from his request. He will then feel as if his questions have been answered satisfactorily without being embarrassed by not being able to elicit a direct response from you.

The White Elephant

Don't let the unspeakable or unsaid lurk in the background, huge and invisible. If you are hiding something, the audience will know it. Be the first one to speak about it so you can frame it in the way you want it received. Don't wait for the Hostile Interviewer to skewer you with some large wild beast of a thing while we watch you get charred in the cooking. In advance of the interview make a list of all the potentially difficult negative questions that oppose your views or accentuate your weakest character points. Really almost anything can be turned into a point in your favor with some advance role playing.

The Reframe

When asked an embarrassing or inappropriate question, reframe the question by beginning with "What I feel is . . ." Then focus attention on a broader social issue or expand your answer to encompass what many people might feel.

In her very first TV show ever, one of my clients told the story of her rape by a prominent sports entertainment lawyer. The insensitive host of the program asked her bluntly: "Did you feel dirty, unlovable, ashamed?" Instead of answering "Yes," she might have responded, "Many women, whether they've been raped or not, have been made to feel that way about their bodies or sexuality at some point in their lives. That is why I have chosen to speak out on this sensitive issue now. To give a voice to all of us, even those who have no voice." Which was her whole reason for doing publicity in the first place.

WARNING!   **INTIMATE QUESTIONS CAN BE HOSTILE QUESTIONS IN DISGUISE.**

A woman typically will be the one to ask an overly intimate question, while a man will ask a challenging one. Keep your wits about you and respond by reframing the question with the above format.

The Humorous

Use humor. A light touch can be transcendent. Change the level of energy dramatically by refusing to engage in hostility in the first place. Humor is one of the best ways to create an opening and change the tenor or direction of the discussion. Just the other day speaker and author Debbie Gisonni and I were doing a media-coaching session on the phone. She had asked me to come up with some "zinger" questions, so I threw in the one that Howard Stern had asked one of my clients. "What is your bra size?" She laughed and said, "My bra size is hardly newsworthy." And then she quickly transitioned into saying, "But, speaking of breasts, one of the people I talk about in my book is my aunt who died of breast cancer. When they removed one of her breasts she had a lot of trouble finding the right kind of mammary glands to replace the ones that had been removed. She had only one breast removed and because there was a moratorium on silicon at the time, it was filled with saline. That's why it never looked quite like her other 'real one.' One tipped up; the other hung down. But after surviving her surgery, breasts became so inconsequential to what was truly important in her life."

Humor is particularly good when asked a question that is too personal. You can change the nature of the question gracefully by saying, "What I'd really like to say is . . ." Or, "The question I'd really like to answer is . . ." Or, "In my book I say . . ." Or, "I'd like to keep that part of my life private, and I would like to share this. . . ." Then offer something else delicious and intimate.

THE KEY: RETURN TO THE QUESTION "WHAT DOES MY AUDIENCE NEED TO KNOW?"

To keep on track in any situation, including a tussle, an inappropriate question, or a surprise question, ask yourself, "What is the real question here? What does my audience *need to know* to understand my offering?" Take out the tone, the churlish personality, or whatever isn't sitting right, from the person asking the question and address the underlying issue. Lifting yourself away from any kind of personal entanglement will give you the clarity of mind to answer any question with detachment. Even when caught off guard, take a deep breath, reflect, and then say something that people will remember.

CHAPTER **9**

~ ~ ~ ~

Become Mediagenic

The power of presence is underrated in our society. It may shock you to find out that it takes a person less than seven seconds to sum you up. Seven seconds. People "get" you instantly on a primal level. They take in the total picture of who you are.

Whenever you are in the company of someone who has a strong positive energy, you know it in a blink. They don't need to *say* anything. I remember an incident that startled me over twenty years ago when I was living in Paris and learning to meditate. The leader of the spiritual order I was studying with came from India to pay a special visit to the group. Hundreds of people crowded into a small room filled with incense and expectation.

When the guru entered, gracefully floating toward his throne at the head of the room, I couldn't believe my eyes. He was golden. Not only could I *see* this radiance, but I could *feel* it everywhere in my body. I turned to my friend Sheila and said, "Do you feel it?" This man was more than electric. He had the power to bring you to another level without saying a word. Presence is undeniable.

Before you subject yourself to a camera with millions of people inspecting you head to toe while they listen to your two-minute message, here are a few things to help you embody your message.

Start with one true thing

To continue to develop your presence I advise you to listen to the great American writer Ernest Hemingway, who stated, "Start with one true

thing." One of my clients has the same great talent as Dorothy Parker—
she's bulldoggishly witty. This is her one true thing. Ironically this quality was her worst enemy as well. She used her swift tongue to intimidate
her employees when she wanted something done fast, which was all
the time. As we practiced handling different interviewers, great lines
came flying off her tongue, which she immediately censored. Her main
fear was not being perceived as a nice girl.

In her efforts to be nice she became a bland and banal Barbie-dollish
caricature, all perfect curves and tiny waist. This kind of censorship
didn't serve her. After months of encouragement she began to realize
that the harsh-edged meanness directed at a target could be shaped into
its mellower cousin wit, without the slap of intimidation. Through this
process her worst quality became her best.

Try trusting yourself. Faking trust is like carrying a picture of someone else's family in your wallet. Take a look at where you are holding
back and I bet you will find a rare and juicy center. At first this blood
man seem barbaric. But if you begin to play with this barbaric part of
yourself and let it out of its confines, you will have the chance to refine
this wildness rather than keep it pent up.

Become the message you want to give

Your essence plus your presence conveyed through your face, body,
language, and voice is the quality of your being. You are a walking, talking message. Are you the message you want to give people? A man
about to give a talk at an architectural convention expressed his nervousness to the American architect Philip Johnson sitting next to him.
Johnson reassured him, saying, "There is no need to be nervous before
a talk because the audience won't be listening to what you are saying.
They will be deciding whether you are an honest man or not."

The most important thing is to be honest with yourself. I am talking
about in even the smallest ways, which you might want to dismiss: taking a neighbor's paper when yours wasn't delivered, for example; the
tacit smile of agreement the moment someone at a dinner party makes
a racial slur. Everything that you do, say, or think that isn't in alignment
with who you are chips away at your core presence. Staying true to
yourself at all times does not mean that you are to beat yourself up
when you slip. Like most things, this is a process of awareness. Begin

to notice all the areas where you might be "leaking." Try to recognize these leaks in the moment and then forgive yourself. Let them go, and move on.

WARNING! **DON'T APOLOGIZE BEFORE YOU INTRODUCE AN IDEA.**

Even experienced politician Senator Dianne Feinstein apologized on an all-male (except for her) panel on *Larry King Live* during the 2000-presidential-vote-count issue. While the men were introducing their ideas with a sentence or two about their weighty experience, Feinstein was asking permission to add an idea before launching into her opinion. While this might be an acceptable mode of conversation in a social context to establish and keep rapport, in a media situation it diminished her respect in the eyes of her male peers and viewers of both sexes. Accommodate your natural speaking style to the context in which you will be judged.

Elevate your energy

A client asked me how she could get her energy up at the beginning of an interview instead of in the middle or at the end. Besides beginning with a juicy story or phrase, remember a time in your life when you felt the rush of exhilaration. For example, a man told me that when he got his first patent, he felt elated for days. You can remember something from the recent past or from your childhood, adolescence, or young adulthood. What is important is to recall an experience in which your energy was at a peak.

Allow this feeling to circulate through your whole body. If you like, you can imagine a golden flow of warmth starting from the top of your head to your toes infusing your insides with a gentle honey-like smoothness. To enrich the experience call upon all the sensory details of the moment—the environment, the people with you, the clothes you were wearing, the look on your face, the sights, sounds, smells, feelings. Bring all of these memories into the present moment to re-create this strong and powerful feeling. Breathe into it to expand the feeling so it encircles you as well as fills you. Once you feel you are fully in it, push your feet more firmly against the ground/floor to anchor the memory. Since you will be standing or sitting whenever you want to recall this peak state, pressing into your feet will allow you to do so without bringing attention to yourself.

Opt for being expressive rather than perfect

Many of us forget that people don't want you to be perfect. They want the opportunity to relate to you. And they want to like you, too.

One of my most delightful clients, Susan Bremer, is in the business of making women feel good about their bodies. The essence of her class on how to strip for your lover is to make friends with your mirror.

Susan tell the story of how she was a buttoned-up techie type who shrouded her femininity in clothes that covered her sensuality and most of her body. She understands what it means to be uncomfortable with her body, and so can help women who feel similarly loosen the grip that self-criticism has on them. She deliberately points out her physical faults and talks openly about her emotional ones.

Her honesty lets her address women frankly about how to accentuate their best features in the process of accepting themselves no matter how they look. Your honesty about where you have been and how it has helped you arrive in the place you are now will assist others in doing the same. Her credibility comes from her own experience and her willingness to discuss her mistakes and insecurity freely. So can yours.

Attune to your tone

An executive at an investor relations firm asked me to media-coach one of her clients, the CEO of a well-known dot-com, because members of the investment community called him a dead fish, a dud, a bore. "He's smart and personable, but doesn't come across well," she told me. She went on to explain to me that when the CEO spoke to investors on a conference call, they interpreted his *tone* as a measurement of how his business was doing. If his tone wasn't upbeat, they didn't think the business was doing well.

How you say something is as important as, if not more important than, *what* you say. Start tuning into your tone. When you tape your practice interviews, try listening to yourself as if you were a stranger.

Ask yourself what your tone conveys: confidence, happiness, indifference, insecurity, defensiveness, openness. Your tone gives away subtle underlying feelings you have about yourself. Begin to pay attention to the tone others use. People are listening for cues to who you are in your tone. Get attuned to tone and you will hear what people are really saying in spite of, or in support of, their words.

WARNING! ## WATCH THAT YOU DON'T RAISE YOUR VOICE TOO MUCH.

A higher, softer-toned voice can be interpreted as submissive behavior. When you sound like a small girl, you encourage people to treat you as such. When women want something from a man, they automatically make their voices softer, higher, and lighter. I am not saying never to use this kind of voice. It is a natural part of the way we behave as a gender. Save your flirting for *before* you are on the air. Otherwise you might be perceived as less credible—especially by other women.

Master flexibility

The one secret that puts you in a league of your own is . . . flexibility. In the movie *The Matrix,* Neo, the man chosen to save the world, played by Keanu Reeves, goes to see a fortune-teller who is the only person who can tell him if he is "the one." Waiting in the outer room with children showing off all their unusual powers, he encounters a bald-headed little boy who holds a silver spoon up to his face. Neo watches with total attention as the spoon bends like melted butter on its own. By way of instruction the boy tells him, "Don't bend the spoon. The spoon does not exist. Bend yourself."

Fire captain Bob Smith (who goes by "Captain Bob") knows how to bend himself. When he was invited to talk about passion and relationships on Barbara Walters's ABC show *The View,* he had a bit of a surprise. The show originally was just going to include Captain Bob and host Meredith Vieira. However, the last week before the show aired, the producers changed the content four times.

The morning of the show, they changed some of the content again and added an additional host. Five minutes before he was to go live he and the producer were in the green room (the waiting room, which is rarely green) watching the show in progress. One of the other hosts mentioned something about shopping with her boyfriend and the producer turned to Captain Bob and asked, "Can you go with that?" The answer, which he spoke without hesitation, was one three-letter word: "Yes."

You will be an honored and requested guest if you can go with the flow and be flexible. As often as things change in our nontelevised world, they change even more so on network TV. Crises happen in your world once in a while, but world crises occur every day in the news. Hosts need to adjust their agenda to accommodate these large and small crises that happen on and off the set. If you are able to respond on the spot to anything that arises, you will be prized for your ability to shift your expectations to fit the agenda of the moment.

Display vulnerability

That one essential quality that will make you forever beloved is vulnerability. Show your vulnerability, then balance it with your expertise. Too much vulnerability and we won't see you as a strong leader. Too little and we'll consider you arrogant. Vulnerable means approachable, down-to-earth, on our level.

When Nelson Mandela came out of jail in South Africa after twenty-seven years, he asked his people to forgive those who had wronged them. At first some were outraged. But many realized that Mandela's moral stature and suffering gave him the power to ask others who had suffered, to forgive, because he had truly done it himself. He not only balanced his vulnerability with his expertise, but he aligned his presence with his message.

Take "fearless moral inventory"

Alcoholics Anonymous calls looking honestly into what is healthy and unhealthy inside ourselves taking "fearless moral inventory." If we are to see clearly where we are holding back from acknowledging a tough truth about ourselves, then we must begin to look at ourselves stripped of the veil of illusion. Body language is mostly unconscious, so that is naturally where all your insecurities show up. Therefore your body-speak is the most difficult language to disguise. The expressions "giving yourself away" and "wearing your heart on your sleeve" become literal when you are on camera. That is one of the reasons so few people like watching themselves. But it will help to know these things about yourself first at home, or in a media coach's studio, before seeing them reflected on a TV in front of millions.

When I do a client's first media-coaching session on camera, I turn off the sound so he can see what his body and face is saying. Everyone is so self-critical, myself included! I recall one client saying, "Oh, look at her! That is a lie; she's lying! Look at that fake smile. Who does she think she is?" all the while talking about herself in the third person.

Seeing the difficult truth about yourself will determine how willing you will be to investigate your own difficulties and to allow your marketing and publicity campaign to offer you freedom from your fears and desires. Often, as you examine yourself from the outside, you can begin to make shifts from within. Each time it gets easier and more pleasant to watch yourself. By the end of an hour or so, most of my clients like themselves a little more and have a certain sympathy for their own inner plights and for the plights of others who are brave enough to show themselves on TV.

See the face of God in everyone

Look for ways to connect with people instantly by finding something you have in common or something you like about them no matter how small. I love the concept of bowing to another human being. Daily, in places like India people say, *"Namaste,"* or "I bow to the Divine in you." You can symbolically bow to every person you meet by choosing to see their true nature.

At one point in her career Mother Teresa was asked, "How can you take care of so many children?" "I don't," she said. "I take care of one." She explained that she saw God in the face of every child. We are all children of God, however you define God. If you see God in the face of everyone you come in contact with, you will be able to make a connection with every single person, and it won't make a difference where you are or who they are. In those moments of connection, there is no separation.

Trust in your own authority

When I was a senior in high school, I volunteered to participate in a psychology experiment at Stanford University. After I signed a contract that stated my anonymity was guaranteed and that I agreed to complete the entire experiment, I was ushered into a windowless room furnished only with a chair and a device with a sort of meter reading. A man explained to me that the experiment was to test the pain-tolerance levels of people. I was responsible for shocking a man in the next room when he answered a question incorrectly. Each time the man answered a question incorrectly, the intensity would increase. The administrator then gave me a shock so I would know what it felt like, pointing to the meter that registered the shock level. My job was just to press the button each time I was told that the answer was wrong.

By the third or fourth wrong answer the man's cries became loud and distressed. He begged me to stop. When I refused to press the button to give the man the next shock level, the administrator calmly told me that I had agreed to the experiment and that I was to press the button. I said, "No." He loomed over me and more firmly said, "Press that button! You are obligated to do as I say!" Still I refused. He got even angrier and started yelling at me that I had to press the button!

I stood up and said, "Look, you can have your money back. I am not playing this game anymore. Let me out; I am going home." At that point he relaxed and told me to sit down. He explained that this was all part of the experiment and that it wasn't to test the pain-tolerance levels of people at all, but a test of how people responded to authority figures. In that moment I vowed to always listen to my own inner voice.

Most people who were told to do so administered the shock all the way up to the maximum or close to it. When they were asked why they did it, they said that they were obeying the person in authority who insisted they had to comply.

You see, most people are kindhearted and don't want to hurt another person, but when they are under pressure of authority, they often succumb. What mysterious part of human nature allows us to discount our own feelings in favor of someone we perceive as an "authority"?

Whether in the rooms with no windows at Stanford, in business meetings where you are the sole vote in disfavor of a project, on radio and TV shows where someone wants you to act in a way that goes

DON'T FORGET YOUR VOICE

Here are some insider secrets to packing your travel bag with products to take care of your voice for those all-important interviews or presentations:

DON'TS

- Don't drink coffee or black teas, as they dehydrate you and can dry out your mouth.

- Don't drink milk, as it can cause excess mucus, which coats your throat.

- Don't drink cold drinks or drinks with ice, as they can cause your throat to constrict.

DOS

- Do drink lots of water and keep it handy.

- Do moisten your throat with chamomile tea (good for colds).

- Do drink honey-ginger water. The honey will ease any throat pain and the ginger will warm up your stomach and aid digestion.

- Do use salt water to cleanse and clear your nasal passages. Keeping your mucous membranes moist will aid breathing and speaking.

TWELVE COMMON SPEAKING SNAFUS

1. Monotone.
2. Nasal.
3. Too fast.
4. Too slow.
5. Mumbling your words.

6. Using a shrill tone.
7. Using a singsong or an overly sweet tone.
8. Raised or up inflection at the end of a sentence.
9. Too soft, the itty-bitty syndrome.
10. Too loud, the loud lout syndrome.
11. Shallow breathing or gasping.
12. Sound interruptions—clicking, smacking, sniffing.

against your intuition, ethics, or common sense, stay true to yourself. If you believe that anyone has authority over you, you are indeed in a prison of your own making. Famed bird-watcher John James Audubon said, "When the bird and the book disagree, always believe the bird." Trust in your own authority. Never give it up.

PART VI

Create a Clear Message—in Print, on Radio and TV, and on the Internet

CHAPTER 10

Prepare for a Print Interview

In her fabulous book *Bird by Bird,* Anne Lamott describes the thrill of seeing her work in print for the first time: "It provides some sort of primal verification: you are in print; therefore you exist. . . . Seeing yourself in print is such an amazing concept; you can get so much attention without having to actually show up somewhere."

Not only does being profiled or quoted in print allow you to sit at your home or office and expound upon your knowledge, but it also gives you a wonderful opportunity to leave a legacy about yourself, your business, book, product, or cause. An article is a way for you to share your knowledge, expertise, and joy. When a reporter interviews you for print, view it as a chance to spread a good laugh, a singular insight, or a simple story that is a complete pleasure in itself. And remember, it's supposed to be fun. You are talking about what gives you zing, zest, and exuberance. You are passing on those feelings in some fashion, no matter what you are talking about.

Many of you may be hesitant to be written about in the news because you have little control about how you are portrayed. This is both true and not true. One of my first clients, the president of an all-natural-clothing company catalog (even the packing peanuts were organic), was dismayed when an article in the *San Francisco Chronicle,* written by a reporter with a sense of humor, had a little fun at his expense. The piece was about

Earth Day and the tone was light and slightly dismissive about people who were "green" obsessive. Still, he got a great mention, which spurred sales. I explained to him that a reporter always needs an angle or a slant.

The journalist's job is to keep the interest of his readers while "accurately" reporting on events. "Accurately" means including facts and examples that support the angle he thinks is newsworthy. Watergate reporter Carl Bernstein's definition of good journalism is "to arrive at the best obtainable version of the truth." Self-publishing expert Dan Poynter explains, "The mission of the reporter is to listen carefully, record it all, look for a hook and to boil it down by separating the 'wheat' from the 'chaff' . . . So she can print the chaff." The truth is probably somewhere in between.

As a publicist who has spent thousands of hours on the phone with reporters, I will tell you how false facts or inaccuracies can be avoided much of the time. I said much, not all. Below are ways that will help you keep as much control over *your* story as possible while keeping a good sense of humor about the rest.

The five things to do before you call a reporter that will save your sanity

1. Put yourself in the mind-set of the reporter.

There are two words that sum up what you need to know about dealing with reporters: "Be helpful." Take the attitude of willing servant to their needs and you will be glad you did. Women tend naturally in this direction, so you will probably find this pretty simple to do.

If you realize that the job of a reporter is not to make you look good, but to report the news as fast and accurately as possible, it is easier to keep your perspective. Figure out how you can help him get what he needs—even if you are not included in the story. Always bend over backward to make time in your schedule—no matter how harried you are—to help. Reporters remember people like you. Even if some don't, you have done a good turn. This can be a kind of community service.

2. Set your personal limits before you meet.

One journalist told me she always wore her glasses when she interviewed anyone to appear plain and unintimidating. As a woman she didn't want her good looks to be a hindrance. Her subjects viewed her unthreatening appearance as a comfort and spoke more freely. Glasses or not, whatever you tell this one reporter, you tell hundreds, thousands, possibly millions, of people.

A reputation can follow you like a golden sun or a piece of rotten meat. Setting your own limits in advance is important for your future because whatever you say may be stamped into the national consciousness like a tattoo on a body.

3. Protect your privacy while being personable.

Never answer a question that would compromise you or your business in any way. One of the most important things I can impart to you is, silence is your friend. Your next best friend is a well-prepared phrase that gets you back on a subject of your choice.

I know that this aspect of an interview can be worrisome, since many of my women clients mention they want to talk about it first thing. One of my clients was widowed in her thirties when her husband committed suicide. It was an issue she didn't want to be raised, but we knew it would come up. We practiced answering questions about this subject in different ways such as, "For many women who are widowed, the bigger question becomes how to survive both physically and emotionally." Answering a question this way does two things. It divorces the question from you personally and deflects it onto another subject. You can satisfy the reporter while keeping your personal matters private.

4. Prepare your points.

Putting your points on note cards and keeping them with you during the interview will help give you the confidence to stick to the information you want disseminated and not to allow your private matters to show up in the gossip column. Feel free to refer to them at any time and don't let the reporter intimidate you into veering away from what you want to communicate.

If you are not used to being interviewed, it can be a heady experience to have someone lost in the landscape of your eyes, bewitched by your every word. Beware the seductive power of a good listener! One of my friends likened it to being in a therapy session where the most fascinating subject in the world, you, is being discussed. Even if you are speaking about yourself, your business, book, product, or cause, the same hypnotic effect can overcome you. The less you say, the less there is to edit out.

5. Manage your image during photo opportunities.

Photographs give your audience an immediate sense of you that often creates a greater impact than words. This "snapshot" or impression can be what someone remembers most from the article. That is why a great photograph sometimes just needs a caption to make it a complete story.

Part of controlling your image is to control your images. It is important for your media well-being to find out if the reporter is bringing a photographer to your interview. Often photographers will be at your place of business anywhere from two hours to an entire day. They want to get just the right shot, so prepare accordingly.

Mapping out some possible shots that include the way you want to be represented will help you be seen in the way you choose. Present these suggestions to the photographer casually, in the course of conversation, as he will have his own ideas in mind.

Twenty-four-year-old Jenai Lane, who in 1993 founded Respect, a company with $2 million in sales, had a real learning experience when doing a big spread for a magazine. Lane, who is committed to designing jewelry that is both fashionable and meaningful, had no idea that she could be compromised with a few clicks of the camera.

> The photographer dressed me up in this little baby-doll sexy thing, painted my nails, and put little barrettes in my hair. After all, I was the CEO of a company! And when I walked out the door, I just started crying. I felt I had a serious mission showing women and girls how to get respect and I am coming across as a sex object. Even though I had done dozens of interviews for over a year (*Inc., Entrepreneur,* CNN, Rosie O'Donnell, Fox News, *Glamour, People,* and more) and had had major press in top business publications, I didn't know that I could control my own image.

Janai says that her experience was a really good lesson. "I consider myself a feminist, very socially conscious. And I still gave up my power. In that moment I let them make me into what they thought I should be. So it is really important to maintain who you are at all times."

HOT TIP!

BRING A PROP.

First ask if there is anything the reporter would like you to bring. Even if he is not planning to photograph you or your surroundings, bring any visual representation that would clarify the points you plan to make. The photograph can become the center story or the hook that draws readers into the story. Your prop may not make it into the publication as a photograph, but the journalist may be intrigued enough to describe it.

Eight factors to make your call to a reporter go smoothly

1. Ask one crucial question.

Before you launch into your well-prepared pitch, always remember to ask the reporter if he is on deadline. Even the best idea offered at the wrong time could get nixed if a reporter is rushing to get in a story on time.

2. Don't beg.

Your lips are made for talking. While it is imperative to be attentive, don't bow, scrape, or otherwise raise your lips to the posterior of the reporter. You are there because you have valuable information to impart. Much as some reporters pretend they don't need you, you are a critical part of their job. Focus on their questions and your message, and you will make a good interview.

3. Give a reporter an exclusive.

One thing you can consider is to offer your story exclusively to a particular reporter or publication suited to the kind of coverage you want. Everyone likes to be first. Play a little on the reporter's vanity. Tell him about the stories he's just written that you liked. Yes, flatter, but don't slather it on too thick. Be truthful. As a good promoter you will be familiar with his work, style, and penchants. Tell him why you liked his stories and why the one you are offering is right for him.

When you can emphasize why your story is important to his readers rather than to you, your company, or your client, he'll understand that you are on his side. After all why would you be sending your precious material to this person if you didn't want him to bless you with his words?

4. Return the reporter's call ASAP.

Timing is crucial to get included in a story. A reporter is on crushing daily deadlines in between breaking news stories. It may be a five-minute or five-day deadline. But what is hot right now may be passé in an hour. When a reporter calls you, he has (hopefully) left the time frame and the nature of his story on your voice mail message. If not, don't panic. You will find out.

Taking a minute to compose your thoughts will be well worth your effort. Breathe a few times and sip some warm water to soothe yourself. There is no rushing inspiration. If you know you have some time, you may want to make a quick list of the points you want to cover. Keep your press package handy so you can quote directly from it (no reading, please!). Be conversational and keep to your points. Reporters greatly appreciate brevity.

If a reporter reaches you on the phone, don't feel like you have to talk at that moment. He may try to press you. It is perfectly proper to tell him that you will call him right back. Using these few extra minutes to collect yourself can mean the difference between a hot story and a tepid one.

5. Find out the reporter's agenda.

Before you speak, assume the role of the reporter by finding out all you can about *his* agenda by asking what he hopes to receive from you. You will also want to know how he found out about you. Make sure you know his beat (the topic he covers—e.g., health, crime, food, fashion, technology), which will give you a clue about the context of the story.

A reporter calls you for all kinds of reasons. He may want to verify or expand on an item in your press materials. He may need a quote from an expert. You *must* fact-find: Is the story linked to an event that just happened (breaking news) or is about to happen? Who else has been interviewed? Who does he plan to interview? Once you know these answers, you will be better able to offer assistance and information to help shape his story to include more of you and whatever you are promoting.

What do you do if the reporter's agenda is biased against you from the start? What if he's preparing a story that negatively positions you, your company, or your industry? Use your good judgment and realize that this is still an opportunity to influence. Even if the article looks like it would put you, your business, or your perspective in a poor light, ask yourself if you can set the record straight or provide evidence contrary to the intended angle. You can always ask for the things you want. The worst thing that can happen is you will become friends with the word "no."

HOT TIP!

GIVE THE REPORTER CONTACT INFORMATION FOR OTHER SOURCES.

Suggest that the reporter talk to other people whose views support yours and the story or the slant that you want. Make up a list ahead of time of your recommended contacts. By taking the time to educate him you will lighten his load a little. When you help him, be as thorough as possible—he'll be appreciative. It is time-consuming to track down leads and research facts. Provide the information, phone numbers, or Web sites of any pertinent contacts to eliminate extra work for him. Make his job easy by being resourceful.

---

6. Arrange a mutually convenient time and place to conduct the interview.

Often a reporter will want to meet you at your home or place of business. If you feel this is an invasion of your privacy, politely suggest an alternative. A reporter may need a quiet place to record the interview. Feel free to ask if a secluded booth in a discreet spot would be preferable to your lively local café. A reporter may welcome being treated to lunch if it is not against his publication's policy. Ask if he has a favorite place he frequents so you can enjoy your interview while pleasing his palate. Most reporters' salaries are about the size of a pea, so be sure to pick up the bill as a thank-you.

7. Set your time limits before you meet.

While you want to be accessible and cooperative, observe your own time constraints. As women we sometimes tend to be overaccommodating. If you don't have enough time in one phone call, offer to continue your conversation at another time. A half hour is usually enough for a phone interview. An hour to one and a half hours will be ample time in person.

8. Understand that you don't ask for or accept payment of any kind.

Deemed highly unprofessional, you may appear to be the money-grubbing equivalent of an ambulance chaser. The *National Enquirer* may pay to see you flaunt your wares to the wind, but most reputable publications will not.

Three essential components to conduct a professional interview

1. Record the interview.

A taped interview gives you several things. First, it keeps the reporter honest. Second, you can verify your own quotes, so the reporter won't have the urge to polish them for you. Third, you will be able to review the conversation and see how the reporter shaped the story from what you said. Fourth, you will be able to review your dialogue and sharpen it for the next interview. Tell the reporter *before* you turn on the tape that you will be recording the conversation. In fact, it is a good idea to get your statement with his agreement on the tape. Recording the interview makes the reporter a tad more responsible for the ensuing verbiage. I recommend it.

One of my clients, who knows better, gave an interview to a columnist at a prominent national paper. She thought they had a jolly rapport and became a bit loose-lipped about the fortune the business had amassed in a hard-won deal. The interviewer positioned her as a spoiled and arrogant twit who had, to a certain degree, lucked out. She called me fuming and at the same time knowing it was her fault. The reporter is not your therapist, so this is not the time to discuss your innermost workings. The reporter is there to do one thing—get a good story. If you don't want to see it in print, don't let those precious words leave your lips. Period.

> **WARNING!** **YOU ARE ALWAYS ON THE RECORD.**
> Anything you say can and will be used for or against you. Remember, if your mouth is moving and sound is coming out, you are on the record. Even when the tape recorder is off, even when the reporter has put away his pad, even when you think that the reporter thinks you walk on water, you are on the record.

---

2. Respect the reporter's time frame.

Maybe you have all the time in the world, but the reporter doesn't. If he says he wants to interview you for fifteen minutes, don't try to extend it into an hour. If you have more to say and your time is up, ask permission to continue. "I know we agreed upon fifteen minutes. Our time is up. I still have a lot more information if you are interested." This allows the reporter to maintain the illusion of control over the interview and also confirms his interest. If you are on the right track, don't worry, he'll let you know. He isn't going to lose a good story.

3. Be forthcoming and helpful.

A reporter has contacted you because he believes you have information that will add something pertinent to his piece. He will be forever grateful to you if you can deliver this information in a brief and captivating way. He wants experts to quote. He needs experts to quote. He's hoping you are that expert.

Now, if you are not the expert he's looking for and aren't 100 percent sure about something, don't say it. It will haunt you forever. The Lexis-Nexis search system contains a comprehensive library of news and business information in various media that journalists use to research stories. Once your words are in print, consider them written in permanent ink.

Every journalist who has access to Lexis-Nexis can read your statements, can take them at face value, and has license to reprint them attributed to you in his article. He isn't going to call you up and ask you if that is what you really meant. So your mishap could get repeated in dozens of articles for years upon years, like the ripples from a stone tossed into the pond of bad dreams. Vincent van Gogh said, "I have walked this earth for thirty years, and, out of gratitude, want to leave some souvenir." Ask yourself, out of gratitude for being on this earth, is this the legacy you want to leave?

Six secrets to keeping as much control over your content as possible

1. Put your key points in writing.

My brother, Joshua Horowitz, an acclaimed klezmer musician in Europe, knows how to keep his sense of humor when dealing with out-of-control reporters. He has been interviewed hundreds of times for his group, Budowitz. Time after time his interviews would be truncated, edited in such a way as not to make much sense. At first he was furious. But there was nothing he could do. He had no control over the editing process once he spoke. So he learned to speak in such a way that his sentences couldn't be edited.

By applying that same skill to his written materials he was able to stop basic facts about his instruments and their history, as well as his own history, from being mangled beyond recognition in print. First he decided he would embellish his own (our) family history so enticingly that it would roar to be printed word for word. Then he interviewed himself so all historical and technical information was ready to be handed to a reporter after the interview.

This allowed the reporter to do two things: focus on questions that Joshua didn't cover, and receive the factual information in a clear, easy-to-read format so he didn't need to rehash it during an interview. Did the reporters always use his information? No. Did they still make errors? Yes. But it lessened the frequency and Joshua's frustration.

HOT TIP!

DEVELOP YOUR OWN FAQS—FREQUENTLY ASKED QUESTIONS—FOR ANY SPECIALIZED TERMINOLOGY OR DIFFICULT, COMPLICATED, HISTORICAL, OR TECHNICAL INFORMATION.

Hand this compendium to a reporter before the interview and explain its purpose, or offer to fax or e-mail it if you are being interviewed by phone. A reporter will be pleased to have this information if you explain that it saves him time and work. Keep it short and to the point so the information is immediately accessible.

You can then speak fluidly knowing that he can refer back to that document. Let him know in advance that all the unusual spellings are covered on your one page. In the event it is just a word or two, take the time to explain your meaning and the exact spelling. New or junior reporters are sometimes reluctant to ask because they don't want to appear inexperienced. Save them the effort (and yourself a mistake) by offering.

2. Repeat your points

Get in the habit of telling your stories in a variety of ways so you don't sound like a merry-go-round. Odd as it may sound, people listen selectively without knowing it. People hear and remember things that capture their interest. A reporter may be unconsciously listening for things that support his angle so he can write his story more efficiently.

HOT TIP!

REVIEW ALL THE INFORMATION YOU WANT COVERED.

Wrap it up, summarize. Watch to see what a reporter is writing down. If he isn't writing when you think you are making a remark that you think should go down in history, one of three things is going on: He isn't paying close enough attention, your remark is irrelevant to his angle, or your remark is dull-witted. Say it three different ways and see what happens.

——————————

3. Ask to verify your quotes.

Author Bill Barich describes his first media encounter for his first book, *Laughing in the Hills*.

So I flew off to New York in February with a borrowed suitcase, feeling for all the world like John Boy Walton, the would-be writer of television fame. The magazine *(The New Yorker)* put me up at the Algonquin Hotel, directly across from its headquarters, and soon I was seated in the regal lobby bar and conducting an interview with a journalist from (of all places) *Women's Wear Daily*, who'd been dispatched by the Viking Press for some advance publicity. Hardly a pro and suffering from years of isolation, I delivered an impromptu lecture on the importance of literacy in a democratic society (a surefire topic for the poor guy's audience) and forgot to mention my book. When the story ran, I had my first experience of being misquoted. My entire lecture was boiled down to a single remark, "If you can't read, you shouldn't be allowed to vote."

To avoid a similar fate, prepare your sound bites well. Offer to have the reporter call you back to verify quotes before the article goes to press. While reporters often condense what you say while trying to maintain meaning, something may get lost or changed in the translation. The exception to this phenomenon is the *New York Times*, whose editorial and style and usage manual dictates that its reporters not "doctor" a quote.

Magazine writers have a longer lead time and some have a policy to fact-check (though increasingly rare with cutbacks and time deadlines). Newspaper writers are on stricter deadlines and may not have the luxury of time to do so. Don't be surprised if the reporter turns down your request. More frequent than being misquoted is having your words taken out of context. The surest way to keep from being misquoted is to repeat your points, then sum them up at the end of your conversation.

4. Request your contact information be included.

Be very clear on how you would like to be identified and contacted. Request that the reporter include the correct spelling of your name, your title, business, phone number, URL (universal resource locator for your Web page or Web site address), and any other relevant information. Ask for what you want. Think about what will bring you the maximum clients, exposure, whatever it is you desire, and ask that those things be listed first. Many publications have a policy in place regarding how they deal with bylines and mentions.

HOT TIP!

MAKE YOUR REQUEST BEFORE YOU ASK ABOUT THE POLICY.

On the other hand, just as many publications don't have a policy and you don't want to give the reporter the idea and cheat yourself out of a better plug. At the very least your name or the name of your business and the city should be included so people can find you. Most publications are gracious enough to provide this information to their readers.

---

5. Find out when the article goes to print.

Publicity can generate a huge rush of orders and requests for information. One of my clients who runs a seminar business and consulting practice got over 100 calls over the course of a few days. The results of a one-column piece packed her schedule for the next year. Be prepared for the best by alerting your employees, or by hiring temporary workers to answer phones if necessary. To save yourself any grief, have brochures and products ready to ship.

6. Invite the reporter to call you back with any additional questions.

Once a reporter gets back to his desk, he may find that he forgot something he wished he had asked—but may not want to seem unprofessional or negligent. He might prefer to leave something out rather than keep it in, in error. Another reporter may be one sandwich short of a picnic. To cover all types of reporters, ask if *you* may call the reporter back in the event that you think of something you'd like to add. This is a great way to ensure accuracy and save face.

Five more secrets to managing the critical content of your story

1. Do correct a reporter.

When a reporter paraphrases your sentences inaccurately, always correct him on the spot. Say a firm "No, that is not what I said." Then repeat what you want printed. Continue to assert the sentences you want quoted even if the reporter persists in paraphrasing you incorrectly.

2. Do reiterate your answer to a question that is asked repeatedly.

You can vary your answer slightly if you like, but often a reporter will try to get you to slip up if you are discussing a sensitive issue. Best to stay with one answer like a mantra when you are handling a sticky subject.

3. Do allow the reporter to finish asking his questions.

Interrupting shows defensiveness. Have the good grace and courtesy to let the reporter continue with his indignities as long as he likes.

WARNING! **DON'T CENSOR YOURSELF FOR THE SAKE OF PROPER PROTOCOL.**

We women are brought up with keen inner censors that measure everything from hurt feelings to disapproving looks. Anytime you find that you are censoring yourself for anything because you believe it is not proper protocol, assume you can say it until you find out otherwise. I am determined to let everyone who reads this know that you are driving your own bus. The reporter is along for the ride. Give him the tour you want him to see.

---

4. Do shape the story.

I am so surprised that many of the smartest and most talented women I know don't have a clue about the rights they have during an interview. I want to give everyone permission to use their good common sense. One woman whose company does corporate seminars for major firms was thrilled to know that she could keep her notes with her during an interview with a business journal reporter. How else to remember all your great points unless you have been interviewed hundreds of times or have a photographic memory? Get in the habit of controlling your destiny by measuring your words while conducting a natural conversation.

5. Do draw your own conclusions.

Interpret the facts, stories, statistics, for the reporter. He is interviewing you for your point of view. Make the most of it. It can work to your advantage with a lackadaisical reporter who may welcome your observations. It can shift the entire perspective of the piece. Don't hesitate to (politely) disagree with the reporter's angle if you think it is off. The reporter always has the last word and can choose to use what you have to offer or not.

Five mistakes you must not make when dealing with hostile, pressuring, and lackadaisical reporters

Some reporters are abrupt by nature. Others' etiquette gets abridged by shorter and shorter deadlines. Still others may not think it is necessary to get things exactly right for whatever reason—time, personality, or a poor work ethic. The reasons don't really matter. First, learn not to take anything personally. Most of the time the reporter has nothing against you. He may be trying to get a rise out of you to add some zip to the story.

The song of controversy has a sweeter ring than one made of a single agreeable note. Radio hosts Howard Stern and Dr. Laura Schlessinger have made a regal living out of abrasiveness. To them rudeness is a style not a character flaw. If you are a person who doesn't want your trademark to be rudeness, follow these don'ts to turn an unmanageable person into a manageable one.

1. Don't lose your cool.

A sarcastic or snappish response is not acceptable. The two things you want to convey are authority and credibility. Your job is to maintain your aplomb and deliver your message in a neutral tone that matches your material.

2. Don't say, "No comment."

Never, ever speak this death knell aloud. You can still be open while not revealing any compromising information. When Ileana Sonnabend, owner of the Sonnabend Gallery in New York, was asked by a journalist her thoughts on her ex-husband Leo Castelli's marriage to his third wife, she replied, "I have many thoughts, but no statement." Sonnabend gave the journalist a snappy sound bite he could use.

HOT TIP!

DEFER TO THE INDUSTRY STANDARD.

Take the personal onus off you by stating that in keeping with the industry standard, the information you have been asked to reveal must be kept quiet. Many a reporter has persistence running in his blood. To him you can say, "Thank you. I can think of nothing else to add."

---

3. Don't answer a question that has a built-in assumption with which you disagree.

Some reporters will play the game "go fish" and bait you with a statement like, "I have heard that . . ." intimating they know more than they do. For the most part reporters are not a sneaky bunch, but it only takes one. Set the record straight before attempting to formulate an answer. Another might use a more direct approach, saying, "How did you embezzle your employer's fortune?" which implies that you did it. Correct the inaccuracy with a statement that refutes the question.

4. Don't feel obligated to talk when a reporter is silent.

Silence can create a deafening vacuum. Many of you will be tempted to fill the void. Reporters count on you being uncomfortable with long pauses. They may look down at their notes or just look at you and wait. You can calmly return their expectant gaze.

5. Don't ask for a list of questions.

A reporter wants you to be candid, not canned. He wants to talk to someone who is thoughtful and can communicate an original perspective. That is why he's come to you.

Three things to do after the interview that will help you get the best story possible

1. Follow up with a fax or an e-mail.

Make a list of your main points with your correct contact information on one page and fax or e-mail it directly to the reporter after the interview. (Ask for his direct fax number, as many large publications have fax numbers for different departments. Ask for his e-mail address as well.) He may not use your information, but he has it if he needs it. This is a good opportunity to remind him casually that you would like to verify any quotes. (Persistence pays!)

2. Call if you are unhappy with the article.

While you can't change what has gone to print, you can still continue to influence the reporter. You may want to suggest additional facts that didn't get included or an idea for a follow-up piece that shows you in a more positive light.

3. Express your gratitude.

Even if your interview doesn't make it into the article, send an e-mail or a hard-copy (yes, paper) thank-you note expressing your appreciation. This ancient form of prayer still has a profound effect on people. Include your business card to make it convenient for a reporter to add you to his Rolodex. It's both a practical and a nice gesture.

Your presentation on paper is the ambassador of your product, presence, or cause. Long after they've met you, people may forget your face, but the business card, thank-you note, or article will remind them of the pleasant encounter.

CHAPTER 11

Prepare for a Radio Interview

People you want to reach are tuning into the airwaves at all hours of the day and night to hear what's happening out in the world. The average American listens to three hours of radio every day. Over 11,400 radio and TV stations are licensed with the FCC (Federal Communications Commission) in the United States.

This makes radio an easy place for you to begin your publicity campaign for two reasons: You have a large and eager audience, and most of the time you don't even need to leave your home to do an interview. What your audience "sees" is only the picture your voice paints. They don't know you are wearing your favorite flannel shirt with your notes propped up in front of you. Considered "promotion friendly," in the words of Steven Harrison, president of *Radio-TV Interview Report* (a book that profiles people like you who want to get interviewed on radio and/or TV), radio hosts are used to doing paid commercial ads themselves. If they like what you are promoting, they feel completely comfortable plugging it to their loyal listeners as if it were another "ad."

Most of you will have the chance to do print or radio interviews before you consider being on TV. That is how it should work. Being on the radio is a lot less complicated than TV. And you don't need to get gussied up to do it.

What you do need to do is allay the three biggest fears radio producers have about you. Steven explains it this way: "They're afraid you will be boring on the air. They're afraid you will turn their show into a nonstop commercial for your product. They're afraid you won't show up."

By the end of this chapter you will be able to address all three fears eloquently. All you will need to get started is a phone, a strong voice, and an open attitude.

How to get booked on a radio show: what to say to producers so they will rush to interview you

Give good phone

A producer's mailbox is jammed with jabbering publicists and people like you seeking publicity. A colleague told me that one local radio station producer gets over 200 faxes a day! Worse, he doesn't bother to read them, he's so swamped. Your pitch must be something special to catch the attention of the producer who is mired in paper and pitches. Learning to give good phone is essential.

It is crucial that you have your pitch down to fifteen seconds. What goes into a pitch? State the one or two lines you created when you developed your "hot hook." For the author of *The Computer Privacy Handbook*, I said, "Find out how computers are using you even if you don't use a computer. Computer privacy expert André Bacard says that Cyber snoops may already have information on you that could destroy your credit or your livelihood." Notice I didn't focus on Bacard's book. Producers don't care that you are trying to sell something. They want to know what you are going to do for them and their audience.

Leave your name and phone number first, give your pitch, and then repeat your number again slowly. Producers get infuriated by long-winded messages from nonprofessionals who then wait until the end of the message to leave their phone numbers. It is becoming increasingly rare to actually speak to something that breathes on the other end of the phone. Most of the time you will be called back (or not) based on the quality of the pitch, which means your pitch needs to fit the needs of the producer like new skin.

~ *Invitation* ~

Write out your fifteen-second pitch now. _____
Name and phone number: _____

Once you've completed it, say it out loud a number of times until it sounds conversational. Time it to make sure it doesn't exceed the fifteen-second time limit.

HOT TIP!

CALL IN A QUESTION.

According to some statistics, 90 percent of radio call-ins come from men. What is especially curious is that the same high percentage of men call in even when an audience is split fifty-fifty between men and women! Though it's commonly thought that women talk more than men, it's not true. At public venues men often claim more time making statements and comments than women. Sometimes they keep the floor by communicating their opinions before even *asking* any question.

~ *Invitation* ~

Practice calling in to a radio show and talking solely to claim attention and disseminate information. Call in to a talk show every day for two weeks. Get used to stating your view before asking a question. It may feel very uncomfortable at first, but you'll soon find it exhilarating. This will help prepare you for both pitching your ideas and being an on-air guest.

Deliver irresistible phone pitches

- *Give your pitch an expiration date.*

    If your pitch is related to the hot news of the day that could expire by tomorrow, you can get a priority booking on a show. Creating urgency by linking your pitch to a news event gives it inherent relevance. A built-in time limit makes your call a priority.

- *State what people have to lose by not taking your advice.*

    Tell the producer that not only are you offering a solution to a pressing problem, but his listeners will lose by not putting your words into action. Sad as it may seem, most people are more motivated by what they will lose than by what they will gain.

- *Include health, wealth, sex, and happiness.*

    Researchers have found that what motivates people is pretty simple. They want health, wealth, sex, and happiness. Which means most of us are searching for a sound body (health), an easier life through creature comforts (wealth/money), loving or thrilling relationships (sex/love), and some sort of connection with the divine (happiness). You may not think your topic relates to any of these four hot buttons, but it may surprise you that it might. I am encouraging you not to sensationalize, but to find the sex appeal in what you are selling and turn it into sage advice.

HOT TIP!

HIGHLIGHT THE HOT BUTTONS.

Your pitch will include who you are, your solution to a problem, and whom it benefits. Keep it short and snappy. If you have been on other shows, mention them so producers will feel confident that you are already an experienced guest. Remember to include any dramatic or unusual results that you have achieved for your clients.

Offer to do a membership fund drive

Suggest your product as a premium for a membership fund drive. Public radio stations are always looking for premiums (products to entice customers to buy) to give away in order to entice their listeners, who listen for free, to become paying members. This is a really nice way to support a public radio station and at the same time spread the word about you.

The producer is the one to talk to first. He will then connect you with the department that deals with the logistics of the drive. One of my clients regularly did interviews with a public radio station in New

York. Every few days they would rebroadcast the entire half-hour interview in conjunction with their fund drive. He never would have been able to get that kind of airplay on any other station. His publisher gave away about 100 books. In return, book sales soared, which helped him sell over 100,000 copies, to become a best-seller.

HOT TIP!

CLOSE THE SALE ON THE SPOT.

Once you have gotten a producer's interest, set up a time right then for an interview. If he isn't ready to commit before seeing more materials, ask to set a tentative time for an interview that you will confirm once the materials have been reviewed and formally accepted. On those materials you can list quotes from other producers who have had you on their shows and adored you. This is one way to handle a producer's fear that you will be boring. They trust the opinions of their colleagues.

Once a producer has made a commitment to place you in his calendar, he is unlikely to cancel—unless he reviews your materials and deems them unacceptable.

Ask for referrals

If your topic or angle truly doesn't suit the nature of the show, you may just have the wrong producer. Ask who else at the station has a show that would be relevant to your topic. Often a producer will make a suggestion that puts you in a good position to call the appropriate person. Always ask for that producer's direct number, then start your conversation with, "[Name of producer who referred you] thought my idea might be right for your show."

Producers are so busy, they aren't thinking about how you could help another producer. If that producer doesn't have time for you, call back the main switchboard and enlist the help of the receptionist. Tell her your fifteen-second pitch and ask her the names of the shows and the producers it fits. Then get those producers' direct numbers and start again.

HOT TIP!

MULTIPLY YOUR CONNECTIONS.

After you have been on a show where they have adored you, ask the producer who else at other local or national stations might like to have you as a guest. What friends of their audiences might appreciate the kind of information you can offer? Does he have that person's direct number? You get the idea.

~ *Invitation* ~

You Are Booked: What You Need to Ask the Producer to Create a Smooth Show.

Essential Information about the Station and Program

What is the exact name of the station, the call letters?_____

_____

Name of host? _____

Name of producer? _____

Station hours? _____

Directions, including parking? _____

What time should you arrive?_____A.M. ❏ or P.M. ❏

   Time zone: EST ❏ PST ❏ CST ❏

Program: Live? ❏ Taped? ❏

Will listeners call in for questions? Yes ❏ No ❏

Will you interact with a studio audience? Yes ❏ No ❏

   Phoner? ❏ In-studio? ❏

You call the producer? ❏ The producer calls you? ❏

   Give the producer your phone number either way, so if an emergency comes up on his end, he can contact you.

   Direct studio phone number for the producer? _____

Show Length

Less than 10 minutes? ❏ 10–20 ❏ 20–45 ❏ 45–60 ❏ 60 ❏ 120 ❏

How much time should you allot for the show?_____

How much actual airtime can you expect (with commercial or music breaks)?_____

Show Format

Interview? ❏ Forum? ❏ Panel? ❏ Zoo? ❏

Local? ❏ Syndicated? ❏

Number of stations?_____

    Can they fax or e-mail you a list of the stations it will be on?
Yes ❏ No ❏

Is the station news-driven? Yes ❏ No ❏

What are the listenership demographics? Number of estimated listeners? _____

What is the typical listenership for that hour? Males age 22–35 ❏ Women age 22–35 ❏ Seniors ❏ Businesspeople ❏ College educated ❏ Other_____

To Do

Fax the producer your bio and questions? Yes ❏ No ❏

Bring or send a tape for duplication for your records?
    Possible ❏ Not possible ❏

Who announces your 800 number, Web site, or other contact information? You ❏ The host ❏

Keep this checklist handy in electronic or hard copy whenever you book an interview for yourself.

Review the different station and show formats

Understand these terms so you can set your expectations properly for the kind of show on which you'll be interviewed.

Type of interview

- Phoner:

     You are at your home or office on the phone. The producer is in his studio in a different city, state, or country.

- In-studio:

     You are physically at the station location.

Demographics

Who listens to the show? Demographics profile the age, gender, and attitude. You will want to know who your audience is so you can tailor your information accordingly. Realize that attitudes and politics vary widely in different parts of the country.

Show format

- Interview show:
  One-on-one interview where the host asks you questions.

- Forum discussion:
  Two or more guests of opposing viewpoints.

- Panel discussion:
  Three or four guests is the norm for a panel. Many times you will be in different studios in different parts of the country. A panel is often purposely designed to include people who disagree with each other, so you can plan for fast-paced, perhaps hostile debate.

- Zoo show:
  Morning-drive shows often have wacky repartee between a number of hosts. You will be expected to jump into the conversation, as there aren't many questions.

- Taped show segments:
  Short thirty-second to two-minute segments on a single topic and aired at a predetermined time. You go into a studio and speak about a subject without being interviewed.

Station formats

- Syndicated station:
  Syndicated stations license their shows to other programs throughout the country. The program on which you're a guest can be broadcast from a handful to dozens of stations.

- News-driven stations:
  News-driven stations' main focus is to bring up-to-date coverage of the day's events. Be aware that your spot could easily be bumped off the air by a breaking story.

What to bring to the studio or prepare ahead of time

- *Fax the producer your bio and questions.*

  Fax your biography and ten questions at the time your interview date is confirmed. I often put the bio right at the top of the questions. It is polite to first ask the producer if he would like to have these exquisitely formulated questions before you assume he would. Most of the time he will give you an eager "Yes!" Expect an ogre "No!" if the host prides himself on being an improvisational genius. On your fax write down the date and time that you have agreed to. If the station is in a different time zone, then use their time zone to avoid confusion.

- *Bring or send a tape for duplication for your records.*

  If you are in-studio, many producers can pop the tape onto a high-speed dubbing/duplicating machine right after the show if they have time. Most studios are so busy that you can't count on getting a tape back even if you send in an SASE (self-addressed stamped envelope) with it. Be advised. They're all overburdened as it is with their regular job duties, so they may not comply.

HOT TIP!

TAPE YOURSELF.

For phoners I recommend getting your own tape recorder that you can hook up to the phone so you can record your interview yourself. You will save a lot of time and aggravation that way. And you will have the tape instantly so you can review it and make any changes to your presentation before your next show.

Show interview details

- *Address the producer's concerns.*

  Talk to the producer briefly about his needs. Steven Harrison recommends you ask, "What can I do to make your show great? Is there an area you'd particularly like me to focus on? How can I make this your hottest show ever?"

  Remember, a producer's second concern is that you will turn

his show into one long dreary commercial announcement. Allay his fears and focus on what would entice his audience. He knows his audience preferences, since he chats with them every single day. He can help you become a better guest and you can help him have a terrific show.

- *Know who will announce your 800 number, Web site, or other contact information.*

Stations often have a policy about giving out ordering numbers, so find out ahead of time what you are allowed to do. Sometimes the host promises to do it and is a bit lax. He has a lot of things on his mind to make sure his show is great. You can gently remind him at the commercial breaks as a kindness. I always put this information on the question sheet so he has it available at his fingertips. Whether he uses it or not is often not up to you. Repeat all the information you have confirmed so that there is no misunderstanding.

HOT TIP!

TRACK YOUR SUCCESS.

By giving out your 800 number you can track your response record for shows, which will indicate what venues are more successful for you. Then you can do a vertical marketing campaign to those types of stations or shows from which you received the most calls.

HOT TIP!

ASK TO BE PUT ON HOLD.

To get a sense of the host's style call the station at the time the show airs and ask to be put on hold. Most stations play the current program as the "music on hold" and you will be able to hear the show live. This is especially useful when the show is out of your local frequency or in another state. To prepare well in advance, call up during your scheduled time slot a few days before your interview to give yourself time to get acclimated. As you can access many popular radio stations on the Internet, you may be able to listen to past programs in the station's archived files through your computer sound system.

~ *Invitation* ~

Have your friends and colleagues listen to your voice as you tell them in three minutes your main points. Ask them to tell you what they "see." Find out which are their favorite parts. It may surprise you to discover what other people are hearing and seeing when you speak. Refine your points based on their feedback.

The day of the show: nine ways to handle the details like an executive assistance

1. Reconfirm your interview the day before and the day of the interview.

For shows that cover breaking news you will be glad you did. I know lots of guests who have been bumped for a breaking story. Also reconfirm for the peace of mind of the producer who fears you won't show up—you will help him sleep better.

2. Keep your notes handy.

If your interview is not in-studio, keep your sound bites and questions in front of you. Even if you are in-studio, bring them along for quick reference. Keep them all on note cards or on one page so listeners won't hear any paper rustling. All sounds are amplified, so you will need to sit still. Take off any clothing that could cause a distracting sound. Remove jewelry, keys, change, and anything else from your pockets that may make noise.

HOT TIP!

BE YOUR OWN POSTER CHILD.

Always bring your book, product, or information about whatever you are promoting with you. Also bring your bio and questions for the interviewer. If you are doing a phoner (phone interview), keep these ready by your fax machine to send to the interviewer just prior to going on the air.

———————

3. Memorize your bio.

Be ready to spout off your brief introduction orally to a host who hasn't had the time to glance at your materials. I have dealt with many frantic producers seconds before the show was about to air who weren't near a fax machine and didn't have the materials that were sent to them, sometimes several times, aeons ago. I'd blurt the essentials while they jotted frantic notes. When you hear it on the air, you'd never know that everything wasn't beautifully orchestrated. They are used to thinking on their feet and dealing with last-second emergencies. Think of that scene in the movie *Broadcast News* when actress Joan Cusack has sixty seconds to get the vital information to the anchor and is sliding under desks and doing other stunts at top speed to get it to him in time for the evening news.

4. Turn off your call-waiting.

This is a must to avoid the clicking interruption during a phone interview. A host will get irritated by your lack of preparation and professionalism if he has to endure any sound lapses. With most phone companies, you can turn off call-waiting by dialing *70 before you place a call. Some systems also allow you to turn off call-waiting if someone calls you. Check the front of your White Pages for specific instructions.

5. Turn off your radio.

When you are doing a phoner, you must turn off your radio. The feedback and echo will disturb you, the audience, and the producer alike.

6. Make sure you are in a quiet place.

Dogs woofing, children yowling, teapots whistling, papers shuffling, and any other tiny little sounds will all come through loud and clear on the radio. They are distracting to the host and audience. Getting your environment in order, in advance, will give the impression that you are professional and will allow the audience to concentrate on your message.

7. Prepare a first-aid kit for your voice.

Keep a glass of hot or room-temperature water nearby so you can keep your vocal cords lubricated. Chamomile tea with honey is excellent as well. Keep some cough drops handy for any moment of scratchiness, along with a box of tissues for the inopportune sneeze or sniffle.

8. Be prepared to stay later.

If you are an excellent guest, producers will sometimes give you more time than you are allotted and bump the following guest. If the next guest cancels, always offer to stay and fill that time.

HOT TIP!

BOOK YOURSELF INTO THE FIRST HALF OF A SHOW.

In the event that the next guest is a no-show, you will get an extra segment.

---

9. Give your best.

An in-demand guest is prompt, prepared, pleasant, lively, humorous, entertaining, informative, involved, eager to help, and goes with the flow. There will always be some circumstance in your life that you think prevents you from being your "best." You didn't get a good night's sleep, your child was sick, you didn't get the raise you'd hoped for, a loved one has cancer, you are crabby for no good reason. . . . And I ask you to still give your 100 percent-plus, focused "best," whatever that is, right now during that show. For the duration of the show stay focused on this moment and this moment only.

During the show: five shortcuts to being a polished guest

1. Stand up and smile.

Invest in a headset and telephone cord that allows you free movement during a phone interview. You can use your hands to gesture and make points as if you were in front of a live audience. By using your whole body as an expressive tool, your animation will carry through to your voice. Oh, yes, and smile. We've all heard about telemarketers who do this, and it really works.

2. Use that mute button.

For any body-function sounds that threaten to erupt, push that mute button. This includes anything that emits from either end of your torso.

3. Assume you are on the air.

Once the host begins talking to you, assume you are live. One client had already chatted away five minutes of a ten-minute interview before she realized that *was* the interview. There was no introduction, nothing. She actually asked the host, "Are we live?" Since she wasn't introduced, it was her job to let the audience know who she was and why she was there.

You will need to work that information into the conversation at the right time if the host doesn't do it. Not all hosts are this lax. In the exciting pace of radio things are easily forgotten—by both parties. Many hosts are highly professional and are used to handling all kinds of daily crises. Understand that occasionally that means leaving out some minor details—which are major details to you.

4. Expect that your microphone is always on.

Sometimes you must be silent (not one peep) even during commercials. Usually the producer or host will alert you, but don't assume. Watch or listen for his lead.

5. Realize that your audience can change at any moment.

People tune in and turn off constantly during the program. Remember what Ira Glass said about the best guests being the ones who can get to their epiphanies in forty-five seconds. You don't want the host to interrupt you just before you get to the climax of your story. Please, if you are interrupted, maintain your sense of humor! This is not the end of the world as we know it, for goodness' sake. When someone tunes in for the first time, keep them from spinning that dial by saying something riveting.

Five professional secrets to make the content of your interview a classic

1. Personalize your presentation.

Listen to the host for cues as to how he addresses his audience. He may tell you about the weather, mention what has happened in their town, allude to a recent guest, or refer to a past show. When you link your information to what is personal and relevant to your audience, they will connect with you as one of them. If you are really ambitious, you can get on the Internet and scan the local newspaper to see what is happening in their area that might have relevance to your subject matter.

While this is a more subtle way to relate to your host and audience, it often makes the difference between having people feel like you understand them and not. If the show is syndicated, you can make your focus more national in scope by connecting an example or two to topical news.

2. Create vivid word pictures using all the senses.

Dean of the Graduate School of Journalism, University of California, Berkeley, and Chinese scholar Orville Schell told this resonant story on the radio: "In 1926 when a protest against Japan reached the gate of Heavenly Peace, the warlord then in power fired in the crowd, killing fifty people, wounding one hundred, and the square was bathed in blood. China's most famous writer, Lu Hsun, said a striking line: 'Lies written in ink will never disguise truth written in blood.' " In less than twenty-five seconds Schell gave his audience a picture of a political climate visually, aurally, and emotionally.

Radio is an ideal medium for storytelling. Your listeners are tuned into the purity of your voice. They don't have any other distraction, so they actually focus in on your words, tone, and expression.

HOT TIP!

PUT A RED DOT ON YOUR WATCH WITH THE WORD "UH" OR "UM" CROSSED OUT.

Speech coach Dorothy Sarnoff recommends this red-dot approach to remind you to stop these distracting intruders. She swears by it.

While your audience hangs on every word, they can get hung up on every "uh" or "um," so work to eliminate any nonwords from your conversation.

HOT TIP!

TALK STORIES TO KIDS.

To give your voice more expression and variety, try telling stories to children without a book. If you don't have a child, borrow one from a mother who will kiss you for the time off, and test your tongue. Children respond so well to unbridled silliness and rude sounds that you will have a heap of fun while lubricating your imagination. Then translate that talent to your more adult stories.

---

3. Project your image through your voice.

"On the radio one is just a voice, the idea of a human presence. In life I am such a specific person compared to that," says Ira Glass, the host of the award-winning National Public Radio show *This American Life*. "You get these weird random comments, like I met this woman who was absolutely convinced that I was a short, bald, heavyset Jewish man like with a cigar in his fifties. Which I am not. Then you think, 'What am I projecting that says bald, short . . . ?' People will often forgive you and your voice if you tell them stories full of insight, meaning, and pleasure. They'll associate those good feelings with you."

Invitation

Find out what people think you look like from your voice. Decide if it is something you can live with or would rather change, if possible.

4. Tell stories, stories, stories.

People remember stories. If there is one thing and one thing only you learn from being on radio, it is to tell stories.

5. Let your tone do the telling.

Tone tells how you feel about who you are—whether you are defensive, comfortable, nervous, or snotty. The other day I became mesmerized listening to a radio interview with actor John Cusack. He was all lazy, rumpled bedcovers and long gazes. There was something in his voice that let me know he was, as the French say, *"bien dans sa peau"*—comfortable in his own skin. What was it? He was both thoughtful and forthcoming. He took his own time and didn't try to mirror or match his interviewer's style or pacing in any way. Many presentation coaches recommend you mirror your interviewer in order to gain rapport, but to a degree I disagree. Keep your own rhythm. You might need to speed it up a tad because of the fast pace of the medium, but increase it only to *your* top speed. Anything more throws you off kilter.

Since tone can be subtle, recording yourself is important. Try first recording yourself when you are in a conversation on the phone with a good friend you really enjoy. In contrast, call your parents or someone else who can push your buttons. Get on a sore subject. Then listen to the two conversations back-to-back. Hear the defensiveness in your tone? Sometimes defensiveness comes out in volume and pitch registering as a sharp edge, whining, gruffness, impatience, subservient smallness, or sarcasm.

As you probably know from personal experience, when you get an apology from a customer service representative unaccompanied by a sympathetic attitude, you are unlikely to feel satisfied with the result— even if you get what you asked for.

Your audience is looking for a good customer service attitude when listening to you on the radio. Since tone reflects your internal response, when you feel yourself tensing up or getting defensive, pause, take a breath, and release on the feeling in that moment—consciously let it go before you respond.

Six keys to entertaining your audience while persuading them to buy

1. Quote from your book, business, product, or cause.

Tag the pages of your book or materials and rank them in priority. Give the audience a tasty bite of what it would be like to indulge in the banquet of your services or to buy your book or product. Think of it as an auditory sample that your audience can take home with them.

2. Say the name of your book, business, product, or cause.

Weave the name of your book, business, product, or cause into the conversation at least three time so it sounds like it is a necessary part of the sentence.

3. Lead a panel discussion.

When you are introduced, don't just say, "Thank you" or "Good morning," lead with a sentence that will spark the discussion. Often the host will then either come back and ask you the first question or refer to your comment to get the conversation percolating.

4. Tantalize your audience.

Right as the host says he's going to break for a commercial, take five seconds to say what you are going to talk about next. Use key words like, "When we return, I will tell your audience the biggest mistake to avoid (or the one thing they should never leave the house without, or the secret to speaking a mesmerizing message in thirty seconds)."

HOT TIP!

GET YOUR AUDIENCE INVOLVED.

People learn easily through the experience of getting involved in an activity. Speaker and author Joe Sabah, who has booked himself on 639 talk shows (and sold over $357,000 worth of books by phone), says, "Get your listeners involved. For example, before the last commercial break I ask them to get pencil and paper to write down the three tips I guarantee will turn every job interview into a job offer. Then they have pencil and paper ready when I later give out my 800 number."

By alerting your audience to the importance of your information, they are better prepared to hear what you have to say. You don't want them to miss it in some throwaway phrase.

HOT TIP!

CREATE A CONTEST.

Contests keep listeners interested, especially when they can call in for something free. There is a certain level of excitement when lots of people want one thing. Look at what happens at those department store sales where you hear that two otherwise well-behaved women tear a garment in two in a tussle for the bargain, ruining the thing for both of them. Really now!

---

5. Establish urgency to sell your product.

Promise your audience something and then deliver it. Give a special deal that has a limited time offer for listeners. Another way to establish urgency is to tell people what they are losing by not having your product or service or joining your cause. These are embedded marketing messages that spur people to action. Practice until you say them naturally.

6. End with a call to action or reaction.

There are two types of closes for your message—a *demand for action* or *a demand for reaction*. Which are you trying to elicit?

Seven top-notch ways to end your interview on a positive note

1. Manage listener call-ins.

Create a personal connection. Repeat each call-in person's name. If the host hasn't asked, you can. This serves three purposes: It will give you a sense of the person to anchor them in time, it brings that person's attention to you, and you establish a personal touch.

2. Repeat and clarify the question.

Sometimes callers' questions aren't clear even to themselves. Repeat what you understand the question to be by quickly summarizing it so the rest of the listeners comprehend it. Then answer it swiftly by addressing the core. This way you will answer what the caller, and your audience, really want to know.

3. Maintain your equanimity.

"If you listen to radio talk shows, you know that anything goes—and the first thing to go is civility," said former radio announcer Sam Ewing. While some shows make it a point to exclude civility, you can be a beloved, sought-after guest on any type of show by maintaining yours. One of my clients, who has been meditating for over twenty years, and also teaches meditation, says that her media tour was the most challenging roller-coaster ride of her life.

If you don't have a meditation practice or spiritual discipline that will help you develop a solid sense of self, I invite you to explore that possibility. If you are not drawn to anything remotely spiritual in nature, learning some breathing techniques will help you develop equanimity. Yoga, tai chi, or Qi Gong classes can give you a good start. Aristotle said, "We become what we repeatedly do. Excellence, then, is *not* an act but a habit!"

4. Empathize.

Let the caller know that you respect and can relate to his question. Even if you have heard it a hundred times, remember this person hasn't heard your answer.

Please honor the people who have made the effort to give you *their* time and attention. Practice some one-word or one-sentence answers from your material or wisdom to illustrate a point. Humorous answers are satisfying even if they don't address the question directly. At the moment people are amused, they forgive you almost anything because they're having a good time.

5. Speak in English.

What internationally syndicated technology columnist Larry Magid's listeners love most about him is his ability to turn the most complicated technological terms and ideas into plain, understandable English. Larry is a master at taking techno-nerd jargon and turning it into easy-to-understand words. He's also a master at taking callers' technical questions that are unintelligible to the average ear and repeating them so that nontechies will understand. Yes, it is your job to make sure everyone knows what you and your audience is talking about.

6. Corral those ramblers.

When a rambler has gone on a tad too long, San Francisco public radio broadcast station KQED's *Forum* host, Michael Krasny, is famous for getting them to the point by saying, "So what is your question?" You can follow his lead even if your host has taken a momentary nap. Give your host a chance to handle the caller first, but when someone has stepped over your patience line, reel them back to the here and now. A nice way to do this is to jump in with a karate-chop "Good!" then answer the question. When they continue to ask long-winded questions after you have answered the first one, interrupt with a polite "Thanks for calling. Who is next?"

7. Stay calm when you are attacked.

Did you know that producers are coached to take the most belligerent callers first? At top radio stations they are trained to reject up to 50 percent of call-ins. Valerie Geller, president of Geller Media International, a broadcast consulting firm, advises producers to prioritize the sequence of callers by the strength of their disagreement. She coaches producers to accept callers who express "vehement and vivacious disagreement" first. Your producer's favorite call-ins might be your worst nightmare! But it doesn't have to be that way. Count on the fact that controversy creates excitement and can be a godsend.

Four proven techniques to extend your coverage after the interview

1. Set another date.

There is nothing like setting another date while you are in-studio after you have finished a fantastic interview. Have your pitch ready for what you will discuss for the next show's topics.

This is also a good time to offer yourself to fill in in an emergency when other guests don't show up. You can leave the producer your pitch letter, which should have "911 emergency calls welcome" featured prominently on it, with all of your contact information. Let him know that you will make yourself available whenever possible, in all those wee hours. He'll be eternally grateful and you will get some unscheduled airtime. Captain Bob said he got over fifty extra interviews this way! If you are doing a phoner, ask to be connected back to the producer. He will likely want to wait a few months to have you back, so ask to schedule time three months out plus.

2. Give your audience a way to reach you.

Be sure to leave all of your contact information with the main switchboard as well as with the producer. Many times people who have heard the program have missed the information about how to contact you and call back later that day, or even weeks or months afterward! Call the receptionist and ask to have your number kept on the phone list for a few months for those callers who might have missed it.

3. Reconnect.

Follow up with a postcard thank-you note that includes the topics you can cover the next time. Include all your contact information again.

4. Ride a roll.

You might find that once you begin to do radio interviews, you get on a roll where the momentum carries you forward. It is often easier to do several interviews in a day, every day for a week, than it is to do one interview for fifteen minutes every two weeks. Plan time into your schedule to ride the roll. Psychiatrist Peter D. Kramer, author of the book *Listening to Prozac,* said he did one interview a day for two years. He credits his persistence as one of the top factors that catapulted his book to the best-seller list. That is commitment.

~ ~ ~ ~

CHAPTER 12

Get Booked on Oprah and Other Top TV Talk Shows

Oprah is considered by many the most powerful woman in America for making celebrities out of mere mortals. Most people's mantra is, "I want to get on *Oprah.*" Oprah is seen as a savior, someone who will change your life.

I know many people who have gotten on *Oprah.* For most, their appearance made less than a blip on the radar screen of their success. Others, well, I admit it, received showers of gold, fawning fans waving peacock feathers, thinner thighs, washboard abs, a book that took off on the best-seller list, and perhaps a truck that delivered a million dollars to their doorstep.

There is something that getting on *Oprah* can give you—credibility. When you gush that you were on *Oprah,* you may find a crowd around you as if you had changed water into wine. No doubt a few people will be bearing a crown of thorns, but for the most part you will get ample adulation. You can confidently leverage this point when seeking new business or getting on other national talk shows.

Here are sixteen ways you can begin:

1. Get booked on local shows first.

Think globally; act locally. It is great to be ambitious—I applaud you for it. But before jumping into national television and into the laps of viewers from the Carolinas to California, you need to get some practical TV experience. Jim Lehrer of PBS's *News Hour* compares being on TV to practicing the piano. He says it takes repetition, practice, repetition, practice. By getting practice on local shows first, you will be able to fine-tune your sound bites before you go for the big time. You will have the chance to discover organically what works and what doesn't work, in smaller venues where your risk for public embarrassment is minimized.

Publicity is built one article, one interview, at a time. Since everything you do has a cumulative effect, you can experiment first with finding what works best for you in less intimidating circumstances. Tallulah Bankhead said, "Working on television is like being shot out of a cannon. They cram you all up with rehearsals, then someone lights a fuse and—*bang*—there you are in someone's living room." Being fully prepared for when you burst through that cannon makes for a softer landing in the public's living room.

2. Tape and watch the shows.

Record two to four weeks of all the talk shows that interest you. Notice which producers (listed on the credits at the end) are responsible for each particular type of segment.

Send a producer information only after you are sure of whom you'd like to approach and why. Mention his previously produced shows and state clearly why you think the producer would be interested in your proposal. Send your media package to more than one producer at the same time if you are not sure for whom it would work best.

⌒ Invitation ⌒

Write down the titles, topics, and segments of the shows so that you can decipher which producer likes what kind of information.

Producer's Name	Show Name	Type of Topic	Show Segment
_____	_____	_____	_____
_____	_____	_____	_____
_____	_____	_____	_____
_____	_____	_____	_____

3. Ask yourself if your subject matter will truly change the lives of others.

Has what you have done already influenced people's lives in a significant way? Be specific and dramatic. If you are not life-changing, are you apoplectically appealing? Are you so entertaining that crowds gather around you even when you are down for a nap? Producers are looking for people who can make a stellar show. Can you?

⁓ *Invitation* ⁓

- Make a list and collect examples that illustrate your impact.

- Send only the relevant excerpts of letters from people who have written to or about you.

- Send photos if they speak louder than words. *Oprah*'s producers are always under pressure and stress. Make it easy for them to want you.

- Don't send them a packet recounting your life story. Keep focused and send only the most arresting material.

4. Assess your own skills realistically.

Take inventory of what you have to offer. Lisa Menna is one of a handful of female professional corporate magicians. She's known for incorporating business into her magic to make complex points understandable and memorable. By the time she contacted me, she had already been on CNN and *Good Morning America* and had been written up in *Inc.* magazine. The *Inc.* article alone brought her greater visibility and more prestigious high-paying clients in the business world. Menna now earns $60,000 for a three-day trade show.

Given her past success she believed that her next step was to perform her unique sleight-of-*foot* trick on Jay Leno and David Letterman. Menna was clear on the number of things already going for her. She had established a strong market niche, she was a highly paid expert in her field, and she had an unusual angle. What are the skills for which you are known?

While you don't need to shoot an apple off the head of your boss to get attention, you do need to know a few things before you attempt to make contact with top talk show personnel. Are you credible, authoritative, believable? Are you lively, funny, quick-witted, humorous, good-natured? Can you say what you want to convey compellingly in ten to twenty seconds? Can you say what you need to say simply? If you use jargon, complicated language, or drone on and on, you won't get airplay.

If you know you have something important to say but can't seem to say it quickly, you may just need practice. If you know that you are not going to win any prizes for your oratory skills, can you *do* something that captivates an audience instantly? Menna, for example, won't need to say much, since most of the audience's focus will be on her feet. Magic is a visual medium that lends itself nicely to TV, but she'll still need to be quick with her quips to keep her tricks light and lively.

WARNING! **KNOW THE THREE TIMES YOU SHOULD REFUSE TO BE ON *OPRAH* OR ANY OTHER TALK SHOW.**

1. The angle the producers propose is not congruent with your expertise.

2. You will be positioned in an uncomplimentary way.

3. They want you to air your dirty laundry.

---

5. Put together one segment or the whole show.

Create a theme. Collect people, statistics, stories, associations, businesses—whatever it takes to create a cohesive, compelling hour. If that is too much work for your time or interest, concentrate on developing your one segment in detail.

Prepare several angles for your show segment. Have a number of ideas motoring in your mind in the event a producer is slightly interested but not sold. Think of several ways you can present your topic. Sometimes an idea just takes a little tweaking to go from being okay to outstanding.

6. Act like you are the director of your own movie.

TV is primarily a visual medium. Words are secondary to movement and expression. Line up the whole cast and direct what will happen. Explain how you envision each of these characters or group of characters fitting into the plot.

Create your own visual aids and effects. This can be anything from products to a list of the how-to points you will cover that go up on the screen as you are talking. You don't actually have to do all of this yourself. You simply need to explain your vision. But if you have something that you know is a showstopper, include it.

7. Explore Oprah's Web site.

Oprah's Web site, *http://www.oprah.com*, has as much information as you will ever need to get on the show. There you can review her entire wish list of subjects. She even makes it easy for you with a link called "Be on the Show." With the touch of a key you can send an e-mail that will reach her producers instantly. The thought of Oprah being just a byte away is quite delicious, but don't lose your manners just because the food is almost within reach.

Make your topic relevant in a short paragraph and you will receive a response as quickly as you can say, "Hallelujah." Using the efficiency of technology, make yourself even more indispensable. Try this: Review the shows for the upcoming week on the Web site. If you see a segment that is perfect for you, jot off an e-mail stating why you should be included. Often, at the last minute, guests cancel or are canceled. The show's focus may shift and make the guest irrelevant, or a change in Oprah's schedule won't permit the guest to attend. Producers must then scramble to fill the empty slot. It is helpful to let the producers know that you'd be glad to hop a red-eye at a moment's notice to be a part of their show.

8. Identify your theme.

There are four main categories of Oprah's show:

1. Controversy.

2. Relationships.

3. Personal triumph.

4. Makeovers.

With these themes the possibility for high-intensity emotion is magnified. Controversy promises spicy dialogue and dangerous outcomes. Relationships touch on matters of the heart and sometimes elicit tears and laughter. Personal triumph often exposes unexpected feelings, which include surprise, joy, and tears, all easily understood on TV. Makeovers visibly show the difference before and after some sort of self-improvement or empowerment event or program.

Once you have figured out in which category you belong, let the producer know why your story is a match for his needs.

9. Create a three- to five-minute video of yourself that shows you are spectacular.

These "clips," or short commercials, are examples from local TV shows, talks, seminars, or classes you have led. They don't need to be professionally produced, but they do need to prove that you will be a lively, well-spoken, or humorous guest and that you don't look like the Loch Ness monster.

10. Choose *Oprah first.*

Remember, *Oprah* needs to be number one. If you have already been on with Sally, Jerry, Jenny, Maury, or Ricki, you are not going to be cavorting with Oprah.

11. Know the three things not to pitch.

According to Laurie Fried, former producer for *Oprah,* these are the absolute no-goes:

1. Hate.

2. Satanism.

3. Nudism or strippers.

If you have a spectacular idea for any of these topics, send it to Sally, Jerry, Jenny, Maury, or Ricki.

12. Remember, the moment you open your mouth, you are auditioning.

Keep your list of points by the phone so you will be ready when a producer calls or when you call a producer (much more likely). You will already have practiced reading them so that they sound natural and inviting. Your talk with a producer is a conversation. Allow the producer to ask questions before you unload everything you know about life on him.

13. Don't bug the producers.

Send your information first. Producers want to see everything in writing. Wait at least two weeks before you call. Then state your fifteen-second pitch and ask only what they think. Most of the time they won't take or return your call. Don't get discouraged, get creative. They typically send rejection letters out a month or so after they've reviewed your proposal. Even if you have gotten yours, don't give up.

Consider this a test of your perseverance and ingenuity. Come up with another six angles that are more provocative than the first. I say six because your subject may be of interest, but you may not have found exactly the right twist. By proposing a number of different ideas you demonstrate that you have given some thought to your subject matter and that you have a certain amount of realism.

14. Deliver what you promise.

If your idea is accepted (praise the Lord!), contribute ideas to shaping your segment. Help make your time on TV as remarkable and creative as you can. You want Oprah and your audience to remember you positively for the next hundred years or more.

15. Clarify how you will be positioned.

There are three ways you can be on *Oprah*. In order of importance, they are as

1. A guest.

2. An expert.

3. An audience participant.

As a guest you are the main feature and get to sit in the good chairs near Oprah. The focus of the segment is on your subject, area of expertise, or book. As an expert you sit in the front row of the audience and are introduced with your pertinent information. You are invited to comment on the material presented. As an audience participant, you will be called on to comment as yourself, an in-house viewer of the show.

The last way you may appear on the show is to have your book selected for Oprah's book club. Authors consider this *the* most important way to be chosen, since it nearly guarantees that your book will become a best-seller and make you rich and famous. Oprah chooses mainly fiction books with highly charged themes that deal with personal issues and intense challenges.

16. Keep your perspective.

Being on *Oprah* or national television is not like making history. Most of the time it doesn't make a career or a life either. "Not everything that counts can be counted," said Albert Einstein. Continue doing good work and touching others with your kindness and you will become known and loved—with or without Oprah, Sally, Jerry, Jenny, Maury, or Ricki.

17. Always give more than expected.

Note that this is the seventeenth step, when you were promised sixteen. Going out of your way even a speck is always a lovely surprise.

CHAPTER 13

Prepare for a TV Interview

Benjamin Disraeli said, "Success is the child of audacity." You have started your audacity training by getting booked on a talk or news show. Now—as you are preparing to face the public—the details can be daunting.

Once you arrive in the studio of a major TV station, you will find it is like peeking behind the curtain of the Great Wizard of Oz. All of the glitz you are used to seeing in your living room looks a bit tawdry behind the scenes. You will find yourself tippy-toeing over cables like you are in a telephone-switching facility. Expect people running around hooked to wires and then sticking devices up your shirt readying you for sound. And then there are all the cameras zooming in and out controlled electronically or by people whose bodies are only partially visible to the human eye. You have entered Hollywood through the back door—where glamour isn't natural, it's manufactured.

Before the show

Be realistic
Don't let the expectations of family and friends balloon your hopes. Often they have bought into your dream and sometimes have more exaggerated expectations than you do!

Ask for what you want

One of my clients has a limp. She didn't want to be put in the position of walking to her chair while the cameras were rolling and asked me what she should do. I told her to request that she be seated when the show begins. "What if they don't agree to my request?" I suggested that she briefly explain her reason for wanting to be seated and then state why it would be to the producer's advantage. In this case it would waste valuable airtime.

WARNING! **DON'T SAY YES BY ACQUIESCING.**

You have the right to say no. Setting limits is a way of saying no. There are lots of ways to do it. One way is to continue to insist, without blaming or becoming defensive, on having your way. Use the short, sweet, and repeat method until you are granted your wish.

Practice in front of a camera

Research shows that people alter their behavior on camera. One client who looked perfectly normal during media-coaching suddenly became a twitching mass of odd body movements—squinching up her shoulders and tilting her head from one side to the other—when I turned on the camera. Get comfortable with the idea of being in front of the camera so that you can ignore it when you are actually being filmed. As many cameras are now electronically controlled, keeping your attention on the host is your best strategy to appearing and being natural and engaged.

Make sure that you are "blurbable"

Have your sound bites ready and finely honed so that you can deliver them no matter what questions you are asked. Feel free to tuck your notes behind your chair so you can review them during commercial breaks. Just the security of knowing they are there can help you relax.

Take a friend along for moral support

If you are in a foreign city, even a distant cousin, a friend of a friend, your mother's third-grade teacher, or your kindergarten crush can bring solace when things are strange and new.

Bring visual props

Speaker, author, humorist, and firefighter "Captain Bob" Smith has two passions: "One is putting *out* flames and the other is putting *fire* back into relationships by helping couples communicate." Captain Bob brought his firefighter's helmet and a timer for his appearance on Barbara Walters's *The View,* to illustrate his five-point system for maintaining a hot relationship. He held up his timer when he told his audience, "You have to give men a time limit when you want to talk about an important relationship issue. Fifteen minutes maximum. We need to know there will be an end to the discussion!"

Let the producer know how you plan to use the prop ahead of time. He needs to give his cameraman a heads-up. During the show you also need to direct the cameraman to your object by pointing to it or holding it up to cue him for a close-up. Visual props add liveliness and help your viewers remember your points.

Dress to please the camera

The camera can be a fickle friend with its own eccentricities: There are a few absolute rules you need to know about dressing for TV that have something to do with the lighting and sets, and everything to do with how the camera "sees" you. They are:

- Wear your glasses if you can't see without them, but not the ones that darken in glare or bright light, which literally make you look "shady."

- No white shirts, solid black, tomato red, stripes, checks, plaids, herringbone, or small patterns, which threaten to give viewers eyestrain because of their "wavering" effect.

- No logos or printed slogans, which viewers will try to read.

- Avoid also bulky clothes that bunch up. TV already adds ten pounds, and thick clothing will make you cry when you see the replay.

- Some studies show that blue is rated the most pleasing color. The jewel tones, or deep tones, like purple, pink, deep reds, oranges, yellow, magentas, greens, and blues work well for women. Pastels are pleasing, too. Suits in blue, gray, and navy work well.

- A lower neckline lengthens the neck and is typically more flattering than a high one.

- If you choose to wear jewelry, you will want the camera to focus on your upper body, so chunkier necklaces and earrings are better than tiny trinkets, which serve more to distract than to locate the eye to your face. However, avoid bright metallic accessories such as bracelets, nose rings, and watches, which can cause flashes of light, or "flares," in the camera lens. Anything that might make clinking or other distracting sounds is also out.

- Most people look better in a jacket (with pants), though sometimes a long-sleeved dress can work. Absolutely no sleeveless shirts or dresses, as you risk having your arms appear as ham hocks that take over the screen like some planetary orb.

- Remember, you are not practicing for Sharon Stone's part in *Basic Instinct*. Wear pants or a dress or skirt long enough so the camera doesn't get a glimpse of something the audience is not supposed to see.

Once you are dressed, do all your fussing, smoothing, tucking, and twisting in the green room before you appear on camera. If your clothes are constricting you in any way, then you may want to consider changing into something that lets you breathe more easily in every sense of the word.

WARNING!
HOW YOU LOOK CAN AND WILL BE USED AGAINST YOU.

It's a sad fact that women's status is in looks, men's in money. That means you must look extra good. Male newscasters like Sam Donaldson can get away with having hair swooped down like a swallow's nest. No woman newscaster could. She'd be lambasted in a minute. You must take care with your appearance so you won't be judged harshly for it. I know it is a pain in the rear, but you will be glad when people focus on your message and not your makeup. Don't give anyone anything about your appearance to criticize and you will be given more leeway with your ideas.

Wear clothes to express how you feel inside

"Know first who you are; and then adorn yourself accordingly," said Epictetus. Your personal expression is the outgrowth of what you feel inside. Some people, like Tom Wolfe, always clad in his white suit, and Hillary Clinton and her six black pant suits, use clothes to define themselves as a "brand." If being a "brand" is important to you, then you might need only one outfit, one color, or one look.

Wear clothes that have a personal resonance for you. Not only do they make you feel and look good, but they are your second skin. Clothes are the flesh you choose to show the world who you are. They show the rest of us in a second how comfortable you are with yourself.

Choose attire that helps give you confidence. The famous harpsichordist Wanda Landowska wore the same red dress every time she played Bach's *Goldberg Variations* at a concert. What a great way to reinforce success and comfort at the same time!

Hire your own makeup artist and hairstylist

Makeup is crucial to making you look alive on TV. Don't assume that the show's hair and makeup person is available to you. Even if they are, the producers may want you to look "natural," which on television means looking like you were unearthed from the crypt. You must prevent shine at all cost. And shine you will, under those hot lights. You don't want the host to be able to see his reflection in your forehead or your nose. Always bring a powder compact with you to touch up those inevitable glossy spots. Much as you may resist the idea, creating glamour is a necessary part of being positively perceived on television. Save the natural look for when you are in your pajamas watching *Oprah*. You will have plenty of time for that later.

Since hiring a private makeup artist frequently can break the bank, you can go to your favorite cosmetics counter of a department store and have their makeup artist create your face. Ask for gobbed-on TV makeup. Otherwise your features could fade away like the Cheshire cat. Notice what the artist does so you can make yourself up the next time. Then buy something as a courtesy.

Another option you have when you are on a tight time frame is to pay to schedule an appointment at a makeup counter. This way you are guaranteed timely attention. Or go one notch better. Hire a makeup artist to teach you how to do your face and hair professionally. Many artists will also take you shopping to buy the best products for you, or they'll give you some great finds from their own personal stash. You will quickly become self-sufficient. Knowing that you can make your face camera-ready will reduce your anxiety when you are in a crunch.

Record history

Ask friends and family to set up their VCRs to tape this momentous event.

Request a copy of your tape from the studio

An original copy from the studio equipment is of much higher quality than one from a home VCR.

The countdown—in the green room immediately before appearing on the show

Adjust your attitude

Dorothy Sarnoff, who media-coaches everyone from diplomats to newscasters, has a lovely exercise she calls "the Sarnoff Attitude Adjuster," which encapsulates a way to project your well-intentioned mind-set simply and easily. It is: "I am glad I am here. I am glad you are here. I care about you. I know that I know."

These four simple phrases show respect for you, your audience, your knowledge, and your experience. By thinking and believing these phrases you will automatically convey them.

The matching cadence and rhythm of this "mantra" make it especially powerful. Sarnoff recommends you say this to yourself right before you go on the air or give a presentation, to prevent negative thoughts from entering your mind.

Breathe to relax

We're all breathing all the time, even if we don't notice it. Most of the time we notice breathing either when we can't do it enough or are doing it too much. John F. Kennedy mentioned that "the time to repair the roof is when the sun is shining." The time to become aware of how you breathe is before you set foot in front of a TV camera, while you are doing it without noticing. I will show you some media-coaching secrets to snorting, puffing, panting, and breathing your way to camera-ready calm.

TENSION RELEASE EXERCISE

This is a fast, therapeutic way to ease stored-up anxiety, which tends to accumulate right before an appearance.

Most of us hold tension in the jaw and neck. The principle works through resistance. As you use your muscles to resist an area that holds pain or tension, your body finds another neuro pathway to the brain. The creation of a new pathway results in relief.

So let's start from the top and move down:

- Jaw:
  Stand up. Breathe in and clench your teeth together for five seconds. Breathe out for five seconds as you release. You should feel a little whoosh of energy each time, lessening as you continue. Repeat three times.

- Shoulders:
  Squeeze your shoulders up to your ears, breathing in while

keeping your chin and head level. Pull your shoulders back down toward the floor, breathing out as you release. Repeat three times.

- Buttocks:
The next place we harbor a lot of energy is in our buttocks. So squeeze in those buttocks while breathing in and breathing out; release. Repeat three times.

- Full body:
After you have finished the main tension-holding areas, squeeze every muscle in your body at once, breathing in. Hold your breath for five seconds and release while breathing out.
Imagine all your tension whooshing out your hands, your feet, and the top of your head.

Gather your energy

This next exercise will get your chi, or energy, moving quickly. It is an easy yoga technique that movie stars love because it makes them glow radiantly. It has been dubbed the breathing secret of the stars.

- Breath of fire:
Sit in a chair with your hands on your knees and feet on the floor.

Take in a short breath through your nose and push it out fast as if you were blowing your nose into a Kleenex forcing the air out in a big puff (keep a Kleenex nearby just in case you give yourself a little rain shower). Your stomach should pouch out with your in-breath.

Speed it up so you are breathing continuously. Take an *in*-breath, force a sharp *out*-breath. You should be able to see your stomach move in and out right above your lower belly.

Try doing this for thirty seconds to a minute at a time and notice the effects. I find that doing this first before doing relaxation breathing (which you will learn next) helps me be both energized and relaxed. So I give off a calm yet bright inner glow. Now for the calming exercise.

Calm down

Shallow breathing is derived from an ancient yogic technique and is effective for both severe and mild anxiety.

- The meditative breath:
    Start by sitting in a chair with your feet flat on the floor.

    In the beginning put one hand on your belly and the other on your chest so you can feel your chest staying still as you gently pouch out your stomach as you take your first breath.

    Count to five as you slowly breathe in through your nose and hold your breath for three seconds. Release your breath slowly through your nose as you count to five while still not moving your chest.

    Continue for at least ten times.

    Notice that you are beginning to calm down. As you become practiced at this, you will no longer need to place your hands on your belly or chest. If you are particularly nervous, you can begin doing this on the way to your interview and continue it up until the moment you are on the air. No deep breaths here. Keep your intake of air to a minimum.

Be productive

Review your notes. Stretch your face. Pinch your cheeks. Move around to get your blood going. Above all, keep breathing. Waiting behind the scenes can be a long process.

Take care of yourself while you are waiting

Make sure you don't get too hungry or thirsty. Sometimes a studio provides refreshments, but don't count on it. At times like this it is a good idea to bring your own water and comfort food—snacks that make you feel cozy and loved and prevent you from evaporating. Forgo messy spaghetti, burritos, or sandwiches of hunky meat. Avoid anything that threatens to get lodged in your teeth or may adorn your clothes. You don't want that close-up to reveal what you had for lunch.

Showtime! Let your body do the talking

Ninety-three percent of the information viewers receive from you on TV is nonverbal! On TV your body is talking, telling the audience what you think about yourself and your subject at every moment with your conscious and unconscious "language." Even if someone can't articulate it, they know when something is off. And they also know immediately if they like, trust, respect, and believe you. To make your "manner" as natural as possible and be an engaging guest, let your body do the talking when you are not.

Connect with your eyes

Most people who interview you will be focusing on your eyes. Audiences take in your whole gestalt—body, face, clothes—and then settle in and look into your eyes. It is very important to maintain eye contact. While it is natural for people to look away, up or down, to the right or left, when accessing memories after they've been asked a question, train yourself not to do it. On television it can translate to dishonesty, nervousness, or hesitancy. To most of us this feels strange and alarmingly intimate. So if you absolutely need to break the connection occasionally, look down into your lap.

I was media-coaching an executive director of a large company when she protested against maintaining consistent eye contact. "It seems fake and insincere," she said. "I have experienced people doing it and it feels unnatural, like they're trying to be overly chummy and interested." That may be true in person, but on TV it is essential to practice not taking your eyes off the interviewer—even when you are listening. It is a way to convey that you are truly interested in another person.

HOT TIP!

PLANT YOUR MESSAGE IN THE EYES
OF YOUR HOST.

President John F. Kennedy is said to have used a method called "planting." When talking to someone, he would look first at one eye, then the other, as if he were leaving his message in the earth of your eyes. People read this as sincere and committed.

Don't expect your host to be gracious

Even if you are connecting with your eyes, your host may not respond with a warm fuzzy feeling. He has a lot of other things on his mind besides your comfort or desire to connect. Maintain your own equanimity no matter what happens. Many hosts save their energy so they can exude warmth and light up the camera once they are on the air.

Don't act like a deer caught in headlights when you are introduced

Recently, Oprah introduced the director of Curse University (or some such place), an institute for the banning of swear words. The camera cut nicely to him, while he acted like the deer. There was a long pause that Oprah expected him to fill. He might have made some insightful comment like, "By the time a child is five years old, he knows at least three cuss words. Most parents don't want their children to swear." That took less than ten seconds.

Introduce yourself with a stellar sound bite

Prepare an opening statement so that when you are introduced and the camera cuts to you, you won't be frozen, slack-mouthed, or bobbing your head like one of those toys on a low-rider's dashboard. This is a judgment call on your part. Sometimes it is not the right time to say something. Sometimes it is. Part of becoming comfortable with television is developing a good sense of timing. Unless you are a natural, this comes with practice—another reason why it is important to start with smaller TV stations and move up as you gain experience.

HOT TIP!

SAY SOMETHING FASCINATING FAST.

On TV put your most important information up front, whether in your introduction bio or the first line you speak. Get attention quickly. Your very first utterance sets the tone for all the information you plan to deliver. Say something that instantly brings focus to your most important message.

Talk like it tastes good

Former British prime minister Harold Macmillan said, "Know exactly what you want to say—have no idea how you are going to say it." Memorizing your points and then regurgitating them verbatim will sound like you are reading a rehearsed speech. It is a bit ironic, but practicing will make you more natural.

Because the rhythms of television are so different from the way we naturally speak, it is like learning another highly condensed language pattern. In this condensed form of speech you will want to develop a new naturalness that matches your conversational way of speaking. It should sound like a good chat between friends—you and the host in lively dialogue. We want the delicious *flavor* of you, not the line-by-line recipe.

Keep movement to a minimum

A group of experienced speakers in one of my media-coaching classes were astounded when they saw the difference between one another in person and on video. I requested that they keep their eyes on the TV monitor after they observed the interviewee for a few minutes in person. What looked perfectly natural in person looked awkward on the screen. Hand and body movements are exaggerated, sometimes comically so.

It is important to stay still, keeping your hands folded in your lap and your feet on the floor. To maintain an erect posture sit slightly forward in your chair. This will keep you from slouching or looking sloppy. Folding your hands keeps you from the temptation of fluttering them about like a bird. You don't know how much of your body the camera catches, so use your hands only if you are illustrating something visual and they contribute to the description.

WARNING!   **OWN YOUR SPACE.**

Watch a confident man at a meeting. He'll sprawl out and take as much space as possible. Women tend to squinch in and try to be accommodating or polite. Elizabeth Aries, a professor of psychology at Amherst College, found that people who display open body posture are more likely to persuade their listeners to their point of view than those who pull in their limbs and hold themselves close. If you can keep your hands still, use the armrests to expand your personal space.

⌒ *Invitation* ⌒

1. The next time you are at the movies, put your elbows on both armrests to see how it feels.

2. On an airplane, claim your armrests before your neighbor does. If he has already occupied them, ask that you get a turn. Notice if you feel uncomfortable or selfish. Once you feel satisfied that you can hold your own, try spreading yourself out more during a meeting or your next media interview.

Use your face to show your heart

There is an African proverb that states, "All that is in the heart is written in the face." To use your face to reflect what is in your heart, try these suggestions:

- *Open your face like a buttercup.*
  Allow your natural expression to blossom while staying neutral and pleasant.

- *Keep your eyes on the prize.*
  Make what speaking expert Lee Glickstein calls "soft" eyes while listening or speaking with your host. Soft eyes are neutral yet interested eyes that show that you are present and available. Maintain eye contact, especially when you are asked a difficult question.

- *Express yourself naturally.*
  When you speak of something joyful, allow yourself to show that joy on your face. When speaking about something difficult, disagreeable, or serious, don't smile. Your expression, whether joyful, serious, or sad, should follow your words and meaning. Otherwise you risk shattering your congruity.

Research shows that the 80 muscles of the face are capable of making more than 7,000 different facial expressions! Out of the 7,000 there are 5 of them that come across poorly on TV. They are

1. *Frowning as you think.*
   Frowning can be read as anger or disagreement.

2. *Looking away.*
   Not holding eye contact can be perceived as not being straight-forward.

3. *Smiling too much.*
   If you smile too much, people don't believe that you are sincere. They may also view you as submissive or weak.

 **DON'T OVERSMILE.**

Women tend to smile too much in an effort to be liked. Instead of smiling, wear a look of animation and approval. How? Imagine you like your host (hopefully you do) and are interested in what he has to say. Your face will give the message that you are open and alert.

---

4. *Blinking.*
   Blinking too fast or too often, or intermittently fast, can be interpreted as lying. Actor Michael Caine said that one way he developed his persona, as a man in the top-dog position in some of his best-known films, was not to blink. In situations where he stared at another man, the person who blinked first was less powerful than the one who maintained his steady stare.

5. *Lizard lip licking or the tongue flick.*
   Licking is considered a sign of nervousness or of lying. Best case, it is seen as distasteful.

Refine your naturalness by using the camera as your mirror.

Engage and interact

Remember you have been invited on a show to have a conversation and share your knowledge, not to spew out your points like an automaton. Fire captain Bob Smith bantered with two of the hosts on *The View* like he was a guest in their living room. The segment producer e-mailed him this message after the show: "You were an awesome guest! We can't wait to get you back." The hosts want to have fun, too. Make their job easy by doing your part to bring a light touch to your subject whenever possible, even when the subject is a serious one. I am not saying to downplay the gravity of your subject if it is indeed grave, but rather advising you not to take yourself too seriously either.

Talk show hosts are looking for three things from you. They want you to be

1. Genuine.

2. Fascinating.

3. Informative.

The number-one quality they want is for you to be genuine. The two others follow closely. In *The New Yorker*, Kenneth Tynan quoted Robert Blake's experience as a guest on the *Tonight Show*:

> You better be good or they'll go to the commercial after two minutes. The producer, all the federales, are sitting like six feet away from that couch and they're right on top of you, man, just watching you. And when they go to a break, they get on the phone. They talk upstairs. They talk to Christ, who knows? They talk all over the place about how this person is going over, how that person is going over. They whisper in John's ear. John gets on the phone and he talks. And you are sittin' there watching, thinking, "What are they gunna hang somebody?" Then when the camera comes back again John will either ask you something else or he'll say, "Our next guest is . . ."

HOT TIP!

REMEMBER YOU ARE NOT THE STAR.

Never make the mistake of thinking that you are the main attraction. Oprah, and Oprah only, is the star (and all other hosts of their own talk shows). Behaving accordingly means one thing: Don't try to take the lead by ignoring her comments, questions, or asides and just plowing ahead and hogging airtime. You will alienate both her and the audience. I have seen guests do this many times, and although Oprah is a master at keeping her cool, it is still clear that it irks her.

Expect that your segment may be cut or changed at the last minute

You never know what will happen with an audience plant, with other guests, or with the audience's interaction with the host. A woman who was an expert in calming upset customers was invited on *Oprah* to discuss her knowledge. In the green room, she overheard Oprah announcing that she would be refereeing a mother-daughter rift, even though Oprah and the expert had discussed a completely different angle.

The expert was never updated, nor did she agree to the change. Though Oprah doesn't allow contact between guests in this kind of situation, the expert speedily found the mother-daughter team in another green room, established rapport, and conducted a fast interview with them. Her quick thinking allowed her to come off as credible. She became an excellent example of the Danish proverb "Life is not holding a good hand, life is playing a poor hand well." Expect the unexpected and you won't be disappointed.

WARNING!   ### DON'T WASTE VALUABLE AIRTIME BEING EXTRA NICE.

Women often want to make nice and to keep harmony in group or social situations. I watched a very experienced speaker waste precious on-air minutes trying to be nice to the other guests by waiting to see if they had something to say first before she offered her suggestions. Be polite, but let everyone take care of himself. This isn't the time to play mom. Speak up or someone else will get your airtime.

Remember your manners

Thank your host personally at the end of the show for the opportunity to have been invited on as a guest.

After the show—leveraging your success

Write a thank-you note

Details like this are what help make you memorable. I know I mentioned this one before. It is so important, it bears repeating. When I did media placements as a publicist, I'd always send out a stack of handwritten postcard thank-you notes to all the hosts, producers, and journalists who had interviewed my clients. Many told me what a rare pleasure it was to receive such a note.

Putting this small gesture in your routine can be a way to relax and reflect on your experience. I would write notes on preaddressed postcards on planes, at events, while waiting for a client, in bed right before sleep. They become a sort of meditation done in between the many passing moments, a focusing on the breath, the pen, recalling a conversation, a closing.

Send in your video to get booked on other high-profile national shows

After editing your video to show you in the best light, immediately contact other national talk shows and use the leverage from this appearance to get booked on those shows. Pitch angles that are appropriate for their audiences—not the same exact thing you did on *Oprah* or your last talk show. Producers can see right away from your performance whether you are an appropriate guest for their show or not.

Let those producers know about any significant results to your business or any other changes related to your initial TV appearance.

Use your results to get invited back on a show

Keep the producers of the show you were just on abreast of your dramatic results as well. They may want to have you back. This gives them a sense of how well received you were by the public, as well as of the interest there was in your product, personality, or business. Also, be sensitive to the fact that many of the top shows compete, so come up with a fresh angle that will help boost their ratings.

If you do all of the above with grace and liveliness, you may even get invited back a second or third time as a guest. Wouldn't that be a pleasure?

CHAPTER 14

Use the Internet to Get Known

Today you don't even need to leave your house to become recognized and loved by the public and the media, though it might do you good to sniff the outside air and remember what a real kiss on the cheek feels like. If you are in the mood for connectivity without having to reach out and touch someone, this is the chapter for you. I will tell you how your name can circle the globe while you relax in the privacy of your own home. I once heard a freelance writer say that to let her body know she was making the transition from bedroom to office, even though they were one and the same, she took off her slippers and put on her shoes. You don't even need to do that.

There are lots of ways to connect with success. You can do it from your home or your office or on the road. Even when people can't see or hear you, it is still possible to create a "voice" that they'll want to cozy up to. You can teach a teleclass, start a newsletter, write for on-line magazines, do virtual chats and on-line interviews. You can even be on Internet radio. You can make your Web site your home-away-from-home that includes all the information you used to send people in a big fat package with lots of licked-on stamps.

Now you can take that time and do some publicity that will pay for a baby-sitter so you can get away a bit more often. Or if you just want to baby yourself, you can take a well-deserved trip to the spa. All this virtual effort to generate press can help make or break your career. But you will need to know how to develop a vital virtual personal presence in the vastness of Cyberspace. You may be just a few keystrokes away. . . .

Let technology be your publicist

The object of doing publicity on the Web is to have it working when you are not. You can get your name to travel the world while you are asleep or reading some nice book made of paper in your favorite chair with a child or a kitten on your lap. Once you set a few things in motion, you can spend your precious time with your family and friends sharing a meal or a story. Let technology do you the favor of keeping your name in front of millions of people who want to know about whatever you are selling. Here is how:

Join a listserve

Sally Richards has over 15,000 names on her Rolodex! The thing is packed with people she files by their first names. How did this rotund resource get to be so huge? Sally is a connector. A self-described geek girl who spends one-third of her time on-line, one-third going to networking events in Silicon Valley, and the other third writing about everything she learns. All Sally's columns in the technology, venture capital, and start-up fields landed her a hard-copy column in *Newsweek* writing about venture capital, plus contracts to write six books.

Sally thinks getting on a listserve is a great way to connect. A listserve is a group of people with a common interest who answer and ask each other questions. Those e-mails are sent to a spot in Cyberspace, then downloaded (as one long continuous "list") into your e-mail box. Listservers are segmented into all different topics, from poodles to publicity. You find the ones that pertain to your particular interest or what you are promoting and begin to participate in a discussion group with others of like mind. Visit Web-based search engines like *http://www.liszt.com* and *http://www.dejanews.com* for relevant lists.

Sally says she feels a loyalty to the people on her lists, "more like a sorority," than disembodied voices in the ether. She gets to know people's personalities through the tone and content of their e-mail by keeping up with the list daily.

Essentially a listserve is an ongoing networking opportunity where you get and give help regularly. You are "publicizing" yourself, making a name among your peers consistently. You begin using the principles discussed in chapter 9 ("Become Mediagenic") of being liked, trusted, respected, and supported in a community without geographic borders.

"It only takes a few minutes to network every day once you get it set up," Sally says. She helped Nolan Bushnell, the founder of Atari, build strategic alliances for his new start-up by introducing him with an e-mail to a venture capitalist. Now he's written the foreword to her book, *.com Success!* "Give and receive" is the listserve motto.

Buy your name

What is in a name? Your name is your reputation. It stands for something. Amnesty International stands for action against injustice. Habitat for Humanity means homes for the homeless. *Sell Yourself Without Selling Your Soul* means marketing with integrity and spirit. A name is what you stand for and who you are. That is why Sally recommends you buy your name on the Internet—before someone else does. Even if your Web site URL is already registered in the name of the identity or company you are promoting, it is important to buy your birth name. That way even if you don't have a business card or a business name, you can tell people your name and they can contact you via your Web site.

Sally, who gives a lot of public talks at conferences, says that people often don't remember the name of your business, but they'll remember your name. Make it easy for someone to find you wherever they are and no matter how bad a memory they have. Name recognition equals more publicity, which equals greater trust. Go to *http://www.network solutions.com* and buy your name.

HOT TIP!

BUY YOUR MISSPELLED NAME.

If your name or the name of your business is frequently misspelled, you will want to buy the mistaken name. Just today a company e-mailed my sweetie, Brett, wanting to buy a domain name he had purchased for a dot-com he consulted with, who ended up not using that moniker. The name was close enough to the calling company's name for them to know they could lose a significant amount of business if they didn't own it.

———————

Syndicate your articles

Syndicates are places where other "publications" can buy your material from one source and use it for a set fee. Newspapers all over the country do it. When you see the little credit at the bottom or top of a story in your local newspaper that says UPI or Reuters or the *Wall Street Journal*, these articles have been bought and reprinted with permission.

Typically the "author" either has a monthly agreement for a flat fee or is paid by the number of times the content is bought. Some writers choose to self-syndicate in the traditional realm of hard copy because they make more money that way. Bigger syndicates like the *Los Angeles Times* have a distribution system that typically covers a wider number of publications than you could access on your own. It is up to you how much time you want to spend versus using the efficacy of a system already in place.

You can start to make your Web site publicity central by letting people know what you have available. iSyndicate is one of the major purveyors of content. The catch is that your material has to be accepted by them before they'll offer it to others. In a way they are screening you just like a good journalist would and then offering your content to the people willing to pay for it. So your material must be at a level where you can prove that you are an expert, or that you're someone who is successful in your field or who has something of value to share that others are willing to buy.

The more people who buy your content to put on their Web sites, the easier it is to get noticed by the press. It is all about perception. They begin to see your name and information in strategic places all over the Internet and they begin to view you as an active resource who has insider information they might use. Dan Janal, author of *Dan Janal's Guide to Marketing on the Internet,* speaker, and Internet expert, says that getting syndicated is one way you can begin to "appear everywhere on the Web at once" with a magician's omnipresence.

Self-syndicate

On-line you can self-syndicate by offering your articles to other people's Web sites. There are thousands of e-zines and newsletters you can be a part of that are "out there" floating around. If you are like me, you don't want to unearth them one by one. You would rather be hiking the Huckleberry Trail, where you can actually eat the delicious berries right off the bush, than hunting down these sites hidden away on their own twisty trails: I have listed a few in the resource guide so you don't have to hunt.

Another way to self-syndicate is to post articles to your specific core audience. Dan posts articles on I-PR Digest.com, a moderate twice-weekly discussion for public relations professionals, because he teaches classes to PR professionals as well as marketing and branding on the Internet. He says he often meets people at conventions who ask him, eyes wide with admiration, how he does it all. The truth is, he doesn't. He recycles.

HOT TIP!

RECYCLE, RECYCLE, THEN RECYCLE AGAIN.

Dan has some systems in place that create the perception he is everywhere at once. He writes articles for two companies that pay him. Then after a certain amount of time he is free to use those articles as he wishes. So he's already done the work and been paid, and now he can either circulate those articles for free or sell them elsewhere.

Since most Web sites don't pay, Dan looks for where he's going to get the kind of visibility that will bring him in more speaking gigs, attract new clients, get him interviewed in more publications, or put him in front of editors who will hire him to write. He also reuses the material by putting it on his Web site and in his monthly newsletter. "That's how I write my books," he says.

Write a newsletter or e-zine

That is why I suggest you have a newsletter. Even if you are not planning to write a book, a monthly newsletter can give you access to people all over the world interested in absorbing your knowledge. Since it is by request only—the highest level of permission possible—you know your audience wants to hear what you have to say. A newsletter is great for a reporter to see because it is proof you can write, which is somehow equivalent to proof that you can think.

It is also a great way to give back. One of the most popular personal coaches in America, Cheryl Richardson, writes a free weekly newsletter and also gives free monthly teleclasses for anyone who wants to attend. Hundreds of people from all over the world ring in by phone to listen to her advice and learn how to balance their lives. What a great thing! Reward people who are loyal to you even if they don't buy anything. Loyalty comes in many forms, not just out of the pocketbook. Your readers may pass on your newsletter to their friends. They may call you five or ten years from now to hire you, but even if they don't, so what? You are enriching their lives, and hopefully that makes you feel good in some way.

There are some samples of a couple of free newsletters that I subscribe to on pages 252–263. I learn as much from the content as from the style and manner each person uses to pass on information and entice me to buy their products or services. The two I have chosen will give you some great ideas to get going.

- Joe Vitale:

    Vitale's newsletter always makes me want to snap into action. I learn more from his newsletter every month about marketing, publicity, and copywriting than I do anywhere else on the Web. His Web site is also one of my favorite destinations. I like his ethics and slight spiritual slant, too.

- Joan Stewart:

    Joan was a newspaper editor and reporter for twenty-two years. She gives much sincere advice from that perspective. Her tips are both practical and sound. I especially like that she's extremely generous in featuring people and their ideas in her newsletter. Her good ethics come through.

You will note that the styles of newsletters are as various as the authors' voices. Each person's personality is stamped on their content. I know I can count on consistent tone, pacing, and subject matter from these newsletters. They each have their own template, which includes the order in which they deliver information, their personal writing style and tone, and something they're selling or an offer of some kind.

SAMPLE E-ZINE OR NEWSLETTER

From: "Joe Vitale" <jgvitale@ix.netcom.com>
To: "Joe Vitale" <joe@mrfire.com>
Subject: April '00 "News You Can Use!" from Joe Vitale
Date: Sat, 1 Apr 2000 20: 19:01-0600
X-Priority: 3

Want to learn 405 ways to increase your business? Want to turn yourself into a magnet that attracts the perfect clients to you? Want to know 800 ways to gain publicity? Want to find out if your marketing is working? Keep reading!

You are receiving this because you either asked to be on The Copy Writing Profit Center's exclusive announcements list at http://www.mrfire.com, or you are a personal friend of mine. If you don't want to receive these monthly mes- sages, just send a polite note to me at remove@mrfire.com, and I'll take your name off my list. BTW, your e-mail address will never be sold or given to anyone by me. Finally, feel free to forward the following to your friends. Thanks!—Joe

* Is your Internet marketing working or not? Do you know for sure or do you just feel lucky? To learn the answer to this question and to get a free trial tool that will auto- matically track all of your e-promotions for you, visit http://www.roibot.com/w.cgi?R620_ROIbot. Since testing is the only way to find out what works in marketing, it behooves you to use this free new service to discover what is REALLY working—or not!

* Is your website designed to get MAXIMUM results? Web designers and marketers simply aren't trained in the psy- chology of selling, so despite their best efforts and your expenses, the answer almost certainly is "NO." Statistics are overwhelming: Over 98% of surfers are frustrated with the sites they visit. What that means is that if you spend more money to increase your traffic, the only thing that may

happen is more frustrated people who will never come back. Ron Klein is an expert in website usability as well as in powerful ways to increase traffic to your business, whether online or off. Plus he's offering a special deal just for my readers. He's willing to examine your website and offer ways to improve it. Contact him for fees at 914-243-7285 or e-mail him at ron_klein@msn.com.

* "Daily Strategic Attraction Tip" is an e-mailed newsletter packed with inspiring tips to help you and your business become irresistible magnets that naturally, easily, and automatically attract the perfect clients to you. Stacey Hall, my friend and a synchronicity marketer, practices the principles of "strategic attraction" and explains how you can do it, too, in her daily e-newsletter. The mission of these tips is to provide a daily inspirational reminder that we each have the power to attract to us anything we desire. Or said another way, successful marketing programs are based on the universal principle that like attracts like. This is truly Spiritual Marketing. To subscribe, send e-mail to stacey hall@perfectclient.com.

* Did you know that there is an "invisible path" to success? Sounds strange but there is a link between you and everyone else on the planet. If you want to get better results, use that link to place ads with the universe. I know this may seem wispy, but this method has been used to build Fortune 500 companies, help a computer store jump from $90 million to $350 million in sales, help a software company leap from $1.27 million to $10.6 million in sales, help pack seminar rooms, and much more. Get free details, a five-lesson introduction to the method, and information on an audiotape package at http://www.buildbiztips.com/t.cgi/105588.

* My e-book, "Hypnotic Writing," has made me more than $10,000 in less than 8 weeks! (Visit www.hypnoticwriting.com for the sales pitch.) You can do this, too. To learn how, get the e-book (of course!) called "eBook Secrets: How to Write And Sell Your Own Profitable eBook On The Web, Using Free and Nearly-Free Programs." Click on http://www.e-books. to/mrfire to get the scoop.

* If the whole concept of your being a magnet and attracting everything into your life on an unseen level confuses you or spooks you, then run and get a copy of "Excuse Me, Your Life Is Waiting," a brand-new work by Lynn Grabhorn. It's a wonderful book explaining how to intentionally cre-

ate the life you want. Get it at www.amazon.com or at www.hrpub.com.

* If you're at all interested in publicity and public relations-type marketing, then turn off your phone and prepare to spend HOURS at the following website. From public relations to marketing, business communications to Internet PR, there are 23 PR-related subject categories, and 800+ direct links (and growing!) at http://publicrelations.about.com. Whew!

* There's no reason why you can't increase your business simply because proven ways to do so are FREE at places like The Idea Site for Business online, now with 405 marketing ideas that can help your business grow. Visit http://www.ideasiteforbusiness.com/ideas.htm.

* Slow traffic at your website? Here are two proven ways to increase it, compiled by Jim Daniels, who has more info at http://www.bizweb2000.com.

1. Send press releases regularly. To generate interest in your products or services, why not tell the people who can tell thousands more—the press! You can do this online by using any of these free news release services:

http://www.comitatusgroup.com/pr/index.htm
http://www.m2.com/M2_PressWIRE/index.html
http://www.PRweb.com
http://www.webaware.co.uk/netset/text/

2. Submit articles. I've written lots about the power of submitting articles to ezine editors within your target market. You can now automate the submission process completely, thanks to the following websites:

http://216.147.104.180/articles/submit.shtml
http://www.ezinearticles.com/dd_url.htm
http://www.web-source.net/articlesub.htm

* What happens when you're committed to a goal, when your mental, physical, emotional and spiritual energies are aligned? You're "in the zone" or "in the flow." Nothing is impossible. Outrageous results are the norm. What keeps you from being like that? Sometimes the goal isn't clear. Sometimes, "stuff" gets in the way. That's where a coach can help. Cindy Reinhardt, a Master Certified Coach, is a

catalyst for change, results, growth. She coaches clients to clarify what they are committed to, to discover and remove what's in the way, and to align their decisions and actions to accomplish what they most want. You can reach Cindy via email at cindy@successzone.com or by phone at 1-800-349-0024. Or visit her website at www.successzone.com. I've known her for years. I also know that one single person giving you support is enough to help you accomplish by-god miracles. Take Mark Twain's advice (below) and shun non-supporters and attract supporters. Cindy can help.

I'm on my way back to Australia later this month. Don't look for a newsletter from me in May, as I'll still be down-under giving a seminar in Melbourne and making more audiotapes with my friend Winston Marsh, as well as drinking wine and chasing wombats.

Meanwhile, create a truly wonderful day for yourself—EVERY day!

"Keep away from people who try to belittle your ambitions. Small people aways do that, but the really great make you feel that you, too, can become great."—Mark Twain.

Stay ablaze!
P. T. Joe
****
Joe "Mr. Fire!" Vitale—Author of way too many books to list here

So go see my truly amazing giant website at http://www.mrfire.com Email: joe@mrfire.com * Ph: (281) 999-1110 * FAX: (281) 999-1313

BESTSELLER—"Power of Outrageous Marketing!" Nightingale-Conant

SAMPLE E-ZINE OR NEWSLETTER

```
Date: Tue, 13 Mar 2001 09:08:52 -0600
To: "Susan Harrow" <harrowcom@wco.com>
From: mail-list@publicityhound.com
Subject: Publicity Tips/Meet an Editor
```

```
              The Publicity Hound's
                 Tips of the Week
              Issue 24 — March 13, 2001
                Publisher: Joan Stewart
             JStewart@PublicityHound.com
             http://www.PublicityHound.com
                (C) The Publicity Hound

                Circulation: 2,566
```

"Tips, Tricks and Tools
for Free Publicity"

You are receiving this because you signed up for it at The
Publicity Hound web site at http://www.publicityhound.com,
or you asked to be on the list.

Please forward this e-zine to anyone you know who needs free
publicity to establish their credibility, enhance their
reputation, position themselves as an employer of choice,
sell more products and services, or promote a favorite cause
or issue.

PRIVACY STATEMENT: The Publicity Hound will not distribute
your address to anyone. Period. Promise.

****
Special Offer to Celebrate St. Patrick's Day: Instead of
just wearin' green, how about saving some with this special offer? Buy any six Publicity Hound special reports
and get FREE one of my two audio tapes called "Kick Up a
Media Storm" or "Brand Your Business and Make Profits
Explode." I'll even throw in two of my new "Magic Phrases
to Use with the Media" notepads so you don't miss an
opportunity to show the media you're looking out for their

interests. This package is worth $71.95. Yours for only $42. You save $29.95! Offer good only until Saturday night at midnight, when St. Patrick's Day is over. Order my special reports at http://www.publicityhound.com/cgi/shopping cart.cgi?reports. You will be billed only for the reports. In the comments box, please let me know which tape you want.

****

In This Issue

---

1. Meet an Editor

2. Why You Must Communicate During a Crisis

3. How to Pitch an Idea to Rosie

4. Oprah's Book Club

5. Tips for Pitching Women's Magazines

6. Irresistible Story Angles

---

1. Meet an Editor

Your local newspaper seems to be covering every organization in town but yours. Your news releases get no more than a scant few lines. The last time you called the paper to suggest a photo idea, a photographer barked "We're on deadline!" and hung up on you.

Welcome to the rough-and-tumble world of publicity. Rather than just stew about it, do what smart organizations do. Pick up the phone, call one of the editors and ask for a meeting. Instead of making it sound like a gripe session, borrow this line: "We realize what an important role The Daily Tattler plays in our community, and we want to know about all the ways we can help your staff do its job." That'll get their attention.

Rather than making them come to you, offer to visit the newspaper. Ask for 15 minutes of their time. Go alone or take no more than a few people with you. Take your media kit and several story ideas. Ask if you can also have a brief tour of the newsroom. You'll be amazed at how much you learn. Ask about deadlines. Ask to meet specific reporters who cover your beat. You can even ask if the newspaper lets visitors like you sit in on their daily planning meetings. It's a wonderful way to learn about how editors choose stories for that day's paper and start building what could be a valuable relationship.

If you can't meet with an editor, call a reporter instead. "18 Ways to Schmooze with Reporters" is a step-by-step guide to meeting reporters, whether it's over lunch or at their office. See Back Issue 2 of The Publicity Hound subscription newsletter at

http://www.publicityhound.com/cgi/shoppingcart.cgi?back issue

---

2. Why You Must Communicate During a Crisis

It's easy to blame the media for negative reporting. But the real blame lies with the companies that do nothing to control the flow of information, particularly when the news is bad. How a company responds often drives what the media reports. For more, check out this article at

http://www.mediainsider.com/tradeTalk/archives/article.cfm?ID=193

---

3. How to Pitch an Idea to Rosie

You don't have to pitch a major league star to score a hit on "The Rosie O'Donnell Show."

In fact, the show's producers are as drawn to stories from the trenches of everyday life as they are to tales of the Tinsel Town set, says editorial spokeswoman Laura Mandel. "We do a lot of lifestyle coverage; it's not all about celebrities."

FOCUS: Rosie O'Donnell is a nationally syndicated show that airs weekday afternoons (actual times vary). Styled after a late-night talk show format, its primary focus is on celebrity interviews. However, Rosie also gives airtime to child-friendly products, books, CDs, grassroots organizations and a slew of other lifestyle-related topics—from cooking to crepe paper crafts.

APPROACH: When she's not shmoozing with the stars, Rosie likes to talk to salt-of-the-earth types with amusing or amazing anecdotes to share. Remember that affinity in your pitch. "We highlight people from all walks of life who represent true life," says Mandel.

PITCHABLE PORTIONS: There are three specific, regular Rosie segments that may be prime for your pitch:

* Hometown Heroes—This segment highlights ordinary people who do extraordinary things.

* Craft Corner—As its name implies, this is an arts and crafts segment. Sometimes celebs participate, but often it just features regular people with fabulous ideas.

* Super Kids—Sort of the kid's version of Hometown Heroes, this segment puts the spotlight on a kid (usually a teen, Mandel says) who has overcome some personal obstacle to be successful at school or in their community.

AUTHOR OPPS: The show usually conducts one or two author interviews every week, so opps exist for new books. Here again, Rosie often goes for the unknown, but inspired—so pitch that unique author with an unusual yarn. For example, last season Rosie interviewed a teen mystery novelist.

PITCH: Mail or fax your brief pitches to The Rosie O'Donnell Show, Attn.: Human Interest Dept., 30 Rockefeller Plaza, Ste. 800 E., New York, NY 10012; (212) 506-3200; fax: (212) 506-3249, www.rosieo.com.

If you want to receive the unabridged article "Rosie O'Donnell Fancies Fun Folks with Fortitude and Fame," you can receive it FREE by calling 1-800-959-1059. In this same free issue of Lifestyle Media Relations Reporter, Bulldog Reporter's newsletter on PR placement in consumer media, you'll also receive concise articles on:

* USA Today's Vergano's voracious appetite for health research

* Key contacts at USA Today: beat chart

* Pitching A&E stories with a "me" angle to Mademoiselle

* Wall Street Journal's Golden's interest in global education stories

* Expedia Travel's ecstasy over E-travel news

* How to wow Heart & Soul magazine with an African-American angle

* Plus dozens of media news and contact-list updates.

Pick up the phone and call 1-800-959-1059—they'll send you this free issue of Lifestyle Media Relations Reporter, plus start your no-obligation 3-issue trial subscription. (You'll also save $100 if you decide to continue your subscription. If not, there's no risk—just cancel—you'll owe nothing.) Please mention code 13LE. Deadline for this offer is Tuesday, March 20, at 5 p.m. Pacific time.

Copyright 2001 Infocom Group. Reprinted with permission.

---

4. Oprah's Book Club

So you're trying like mad to get your new book mentioned by Oprah?

Phone calls, pitch letters, e-mails and other forms of badgering are useless. Those tactics could be doing you more harm than good.

Only Oprah chooses the books she wants to feature. Not even her army of producers can try to steer her toward a particular book they like. I read in an online discussion forum for publishers that authors who pitch their books for her book club are automatically blacklisted. I doubt the producers would go through all that trouble, but I thought I'd save you the cost of postage and long-distance calls just in case.

To all you authors on this list: If you know something I don't know about Oprah's book club, send it this way and I'll share it.

In the meantime, I learned the tip above from the audio tape "How to Get on Oprah and Other Talk Shows." It's $29.95 and available through SpeakerNet News at

http://www.kenb.com/speakernetnews/tsemorder.html. Scroll down to the third box.

---

5. Tips for Pitching Women's Magazines

If you want to know which hot topics catch the attention of editors and readers at the major women's magazines like Family Circle and Redbook, a good place to start is by reading the letters to the editor. They are often a tip-off to the types of story ideas that play well to that audience. That's one of the many suggestions found in this article at the Media Insider web site. It summarizes advice from the editors at Family Circle, Redbook, Ladies' Home Journal and Real Simple magazines, who spoke at a recent "Meet the Media" luncheon series, sponsored by the Publicity Club of New York.

The editors also suggest becoming familiar with each publication before pitching and observing how products are integrated into magazine coverage. There's a lot in the beauty, fashion and home sections, for instance. More tips are at

http://www.mediainsider.com/newsBreak/archives/article.cfm?ID=239

---

6. Irresistible Story Angles

The media love statistics. In fact, if you can tie your pitch to a statistic from the U.S. Census Bureau, or any other official report, you sometimes stand a better chance of being covered because statistics help frame your story, or put it into context. I recommend using statistics when sending a pitch letter.

That's one of the many tips I'll share during my one-hour tele-seminar March 21 called "Irresistible Story Angles the Media Will LOVE (and other secrets for catching their attention)" at 7 PM Eastern Time, sponsored by SpeakerNet News. Cost is $25. Everyone who signs up will get a free copy of The Publicity Hound newsletter, a $10 value. Can't make it? The tape will be available after the seminar. To register, visit

http://www.kenb.com/speakernetnews/tsemorder.html

***Spots are filling up fast for my one-hour tele-seminar called "Sizzling Story Ideas the Media Will LOVE" Wednesday, March 21, from 7 to 8 PM EST, sponsored by SpeakerNet News, the popular newsletter for speakers and presenters. As a former newspaper editor and reporter, I've accepted and rejected thousands of story ideas. I'll show you the secrets of what the media really want and how to capture their attention.

BONUS: Everyone who signs up for this seminar will receive a free issue of my print newsletter The Publicity Hound, a $10 value, and detailed handouts. Cost is only $25. To register, visit

http://www.kenb.com/speakernetnews/tsemorder.html

Can't make it? Tapes will be available after the seminar.

If you like these tips, please pass them on to your friends, clients and colleagues. If you REALLY like them, subscribe to The Publicity Hound, my 8-page print newsletter published six times a year. Great stuff. Three or four notches above what you read here. And lots of media contacts. If you want to test-drive it first, check out the sample issue which can be accessed from my home page at

http://www.PublicityHound.com

Call 262-284-7451 to subscribe, or send a check for $49.95 (inside the U.S.) or $59.95 (outside the U.S.) to The Publicity Hound, 3930 Highway O, Saukville, WI 53080. Or pay by credit card at my web site at

http://www.PublicityHound.com

To subscribe to The Publicity Hound Tips of the Week, visit http://www.PublicityHound.com and receive free by autoresponder the handy list "89 Reasons to Send a News Release."

To UNSUBSCRIBE and make The Hound really sad, please reply to mail-list@publicityhound.com with UNSUBSCRIBE in the subject. (Have you ever seen a hound cry? Not a pleasant sight.)

Joan Stewart
a.k.a. The Publicity Hound
3930 Highway O
Saukville, WI 53080-1330
U.S.A.

(262) 284-7451, Fax (262) 284-1737

Ten Things That Popular and Profitable Newsletters Have in Common That Make Them Work

You can apply them right now when you create yours.

1. *They're short.*

   Making it a quick read maintains the interest of busy people.

2. *They hold to a consistent format.*

   Keeping your structure constant gives people a sense of security and confidence. If you are going to change something, you need to let your readers know—or they'll let you know how they feel about it.

3. *They have links.*

   Providing links to longer-length articles or Web sites gives your audience the choice to read more detailed material on a topic of particular interest quickly.

4. *They draw you to their Web site.*

Giving a teaser for something new, free, or exciting to purchase—that readers can get only from your Web site—makes them eager to visit.

5. *They provide useful information.*

Imparting knowledge positions you to become a valued resource for your readers, who then look forward to learning from you.

6. *They highlight the success of others.*

Giving your readers the opportunity to hear about people like yourself who are succeeding makes them feel like they can succeed as well. Generate examples that show how clients, friends, and customers have used your techniques or products, and show your readers how they can do the same.

7. *They cross-promote.*

Offering to cross-promote with people opens opportunities for more subscribers or to sell your services or products.

8. *They offer products, services, or classes.*

Suggesting new things to potential clients or customers allows you to continue to deepen their relationship with you. They can expand their knowledge by buying your books or products, using your services, or attending your talks. You make more money, so you can enlarge your product lines or business or take more time off.

9. *They guarantee subscribers that their names will never be sold or given away.*

Ensuring privacy to your subscriber base gains their confidence and trust in your ethics.

10. *They give their subscriber base a way to unsubscribe.*

Continuing to ensure that your readership is by permission only is an essential condition of an ongoing relationship.

The advantages of a newsletter are numerous. They can give you a pulse on what people want, or create more content for your Web site. You can use your newsletter to conduct a survey and then publish the results on your Web site. It can help you write a book. The mega-best-selling *Chicken Soup for the Soul* series of books collected the stories of people who submitted them for a fee and for free. They were all "written" that way.

HOT TIP!

ARCHIVE YOUR NEWSLETTERS BY SUCCINCT TITLES ON YOUR WEB SITE SO YOUR READERS AND REPORTERS CAN ACCESS THEM.

Well-written newsletters are essentially tip sheets that a reporter can excerpt for information or quotes. If the title of your newsletter isn't enticing and descriptive of the content, create a one-line teaser so a reporter scanning your site will be able to open the link based on a hint of the information. Also, put a disclaimer that states anyone who uses your content must credit you with all of your contact information.

Write a regular column

I remember one of my very first clients wanted to be on the popular National Public radio show Terry Gross's *Fresh Air.* I talked weekly with Gross's producer discussing different angles. Though my client didn't fit the profile of her typical guest, the producer kept inviting me to call. For months nothing I suggested was quite right. Then she hit upon an idea. "Why don't I take a look at some of his columns to see if I can figure out an angle?" All of his articles were archived by topic on-line, so she could scan them easily.

Even if you don't have a regular column somewhere, your newsletters serve as your columns for reporters to peruse in search of a story idea or content. You can always send them to your newsletters when you know your information fits the topic of their story. And give them full permission to use your information as theirs as if it were a press release. In return you need to negotiate that your name and URL get mentioned in the article *before* you agree to any usage.

Post your press release

There is a service that is changing the face of public relations today. It is called Profnet and it works like this: Journalists post requests for stories they're looking for and you respond with the appropriate information. What a concept! Find the person who has the need and fill it instead of sending out hundreds of pieces of paper to unknown people who are sorry you found them.

Before Profnet, the traditional model was: You post your press release on a professional "newswire" service. A wide audience of media people daily scour it for story ideas. The service gets sent out to journalists and producers who subscribe to it for the express purpose of looking for leads. You wait for a response, bite your nails, and eat too much cake.

Put away the cake—with Profnet the tables are turned.

There is one caveat: Before you contact these reporters, please, please, please take extra care to make sure your information is truly relevant. The biggest complaint reporters have is that people—the public and publicists alike—send them useless materials that are sorely off base. Again and again, in articles, digests, and listserves, reporters rail that their time is wasted and requests are ignored. Do you want to know why reporters and producers get huffy? Imagine dealing with hundreds of irrelevant press materials *daily!* That said, you have the chance to become a cherished resource to these people, who will make your calls a priority once they know they can count on the credibility of you and your information.

Here is how the system works: When you sign up for the service, you get an e-mail three times a day. You stay on the lookout for stories to which you can contribute. With Profnet the journalist lets you know how he wants to be contacted, what he's looking for, and his deadline. He is delighted that you have responded because he *needs* you and he needs you for his story *now,* not in a week or a month or sometime in the distant future that may never arrive. You have answered his little prayer. And his response back to you is instantaneous. If you fit the request, you could receive a call within five minutes!

Dan Janal has had this experience a number of times. "Reporters don't care if you work for a Fortune 500 company," he says. "If they need an expert and you can show them you are one, that is all they care about." And another thing, it eliminates groveling. "Both of us are coming from a position of strength," explains Dan. "We can see each other as professionals." In fact, Dan, in collaboration with Profnet, has developed a program for enterpreneurs and small businesspeople. (See Resources for contact information.)

Now, it may sound like I am dissing the traditional newswire services—I am not. They have their place. It is just not first place. They have value especially if you are not the kind of person who is going to attach yourself to the computer like an umbilical cord. They have built a reputation for delivering ideas to the press on a regular basis, so they are "invited" into the reporter's "in box." Typically you don't get the same courtesy. If you have a reputable publicist, he will have the keys to the gated golden kingdom. The way to be given those keys is to become a credible and reliable source whenever possible— especially in a crunch. So make it your practice to be available as often as you can and always volunteer to be called at the last minute, anytime.

Niche your way up

There is a saying that a niche will make you rich. Instead of trying to be everything to everyone, get to know your niche. Just like you defined your niche when you developed the database for your hard-copy press materials, you do the same for soft copy. By specializing in one area and going more deeply into it, you will begin to be recognized for your savvy.

A reporter at *http://www.forbes.com* interviewed a lawyer regarding pre- and postnuptial agreements. Though the lawyer's specialty was real-estate planning, she had recently begun doing more pre- and post-nuptials for dot-com millionaires. She had already begun concentrating more fully on this aspect of her business. Since it was such a hot topic in the news, she seriously considered focusing even more attention on it. Without abandoning her core real-estate planning practice, she honed in on a vertical market within her area of expertise that helped plump up her knowledge and her press exponentially.

You might consider spending some time developing one aspect of your business that you enjoy and that is more newsworthy than the rest. Follow your interests, and notice where your business is taking you, then let the press know you are available to share your knowledge with them.

Teach a teleclass

What is a teleclass? Put briefly, it is a class conducted by telephone over a phone bridge that holds from ten to hundreds of people in a virtual "meeting room." The teleclasses of today are promoted through newsletters, seminar-finder sites, and sites that specialize in putting on teleclasses. Before you can list your class on a teleclass site, you must take a class on how to become a teleclass leader.

These sites offer both free and for-fee classes, one time only and in series. To understand how to run them efficiently and effectively, the people who run those sites also suggest you take a number of classes from different teachers first, before you give one yourself. From attending dozens and leading a few, I have found it is quite an art running a virtual class of people with only their voices, the phone keypad, and silences as a guide.

Expert teleclass leader and personal coach Nancy Gerber (she's my personal coach) suggests "developing one or two 'signature' programs that provide lots of content and value in a very short time frame."

Another benefit to teaching a teleclass, states Gerber, is that potential clients can get an experience of you with an investment of only about $29 (one session) to $250 (four sessions).

HOT TIP!

CONTRIBUTE A TIP TO THEIR WEB SITE.

If you are not ready to teach a class, you can still participate at teleclass.com (go directly to *http://www.topten.org/*) by contributing what they call a "Knowledge Nugget," consisting of a quote or tidbit of advice in your field. They give you the category to choose from and you supply the information. Your nugget may be included in one of their DailyCast broadcasts, which reach thousands of readers by e-mail. By the time you are ready to teach, your name will have begun to be familiar to those people who receive their DailyCast broadcasts. If you already have a class, submit a top-ten list, a quote, and other short bits for consideration as a way to publicize your

class. They give ample room in their "About the Submitter" area to supply your Web site, e-mail address, and title.

The advantages of teaching a teleclass are not only about the number of people who take the classes, but also about all the people who see what you do. The teleclass sites send out a regular listing of current courses to subscribers to keep them updated. Your class description, credentials, and picture is given space on their site.

In essence you are being seen by thousands, sometimes millions, of people every day, in places that give you credibility by upholding the high standards of an educational "institution." Most allow you to give your Web site address as well, so your potential students can check you out more thoroughly before deciding on a class. These sites are the colleges of the Internet; you are the regular professor or visiting expert to whom people all over the world can come to absorb what you know.

Chug along in a chat room

Chat rooms are like town meetings or little neighborhood papers that come out free and find themselves on your doorstep. They are sort of the orphans of the Internet. We all know that they are out there, but few people visit. But these little village meetings can serve as a powerful town crier that is heard from one small local community to the next.

A chat is an informal "talk" between you and the public in a virtual room. Anyone who wants to know about your product or service writes you questions that you answer as they appear on your computer screen. Your chat is set up well in advance of your appearance so the sponsor of the venue can publicize it and attract as many participants as possible. In some ways it is similar to a live radio show except that instead of being able to finish typing what you are saying, another person's question might jump in midsentence and interrupt your answer to the last person's question. Sometimes your "conversations" are controlled by a moderator to be more orderly, but other sites let things roll.

Most of these venues have a host, a moderator, or both, so they keep a tight rein on the visitors lest they become wild, unruly, or just plain off base. When you are out in the whole wide world, the expression of human nature comes in all its varied, mostly marvelous forms. The moderators are present to make the room a pleasant place for you to share your knowledge and expertise.

The disadvantage of doing a chat is that typically only a few stragglers show up, and of those people, several ask rather off-the-course questions. You spend a lot of time at your keyboard typing away at hyperspeed trying to cover a few points. At the same time you're trying to work in what you're trying to sell.

Dan Janal says he doesn't seek chats out but always accepts an invitation that is extended as part of his overall publicity outreach. "It takes a lot of time, and you don't often see immediate results," he says, but he still chooses not to abandon them altogether. Steve O'Keefe, author of Publicity on the Internet, who has set up over 300 chats for over 100 authors in the last five years, notes that the advantages of a chat are in the pre- and postpublicity announcements rather than in the actual chat itself.

For example, *USA Today,* which reaches millions of people, may mention your "tour" in their Cyber listings. MSNBC, which counts over a million users a month, may give you a mention as well. And Compuserve "publishes" a *What Is New* newsletter announcement that is seen by 150,000 people. That all adds up to several million "viewers" who may have noticed that you have a product or service for sale. It also gives producers and reporters a chance to see that you are getting around Cyberspace.

Prepare all your documents ahead of time (see below) to make it simple and easy to be a chat guest. Develop a number of themes based on your work, with corresponding excerpts. When a chat site requests to post them free for its members, e-mail them ASAP. In the event you're selling a book, establish ahead of time that a "Buy the Book" button linked to the on-line bookstore affiliated with the site is in prominent view of your visitors. In short, put chats into your publicity mix to gain extensive on-line publicity in prestigious places all over the Internet.

PREPARATION FOR YOUR CYBER CHAT TOUR

You will need much the same materials you already have prepped for your press kit in an abbreviated electronic format to send along. Here are the specifics:

1. **E-mail your bio.**

    You have already created a short and long version. This short bio is really a mini. Two sentences for the short. Two paragraphs for the long.

2. **Supply your introduction.**

    Your introduction should be two paragraphs max. Give the moderator or host permission to edit it as he sees fit.

3. **Attach your photo.**

    A color head shot that has been scanned and properly prepped in Photoshop and saved as a JPEG or GIF file (image) is the most desirable. You will want the caption embedded in the file to include your name, the name/title of your product, service, or book, and the photo credit.

4. **State your topic or theme.**

    You will need to narrow your theme down to a provocative and compelling line. Ask a question or pose an unlikely juxtaposition of ideas such as: "Does it really make sense to downsize your life?" or "Get rich with free newsletters." Prepare a number of topics for different audiences, then match your excerpts with your topics.

5. **Excerpt your book, feature article, or tip sheet.**

    The excerpt is used to promote your show in advance. It will be posted so viewers can access it for weeks, months, sometimes years, on various places on the Internet. The format should look similar to a tip sheet, with main headings or points followed by a few sentences. Remember to tell everyone how to order. Save this in both ASCII text and HTML (Web page) formats.

6. Write your ten questions.

To save yourself some time and effort you can modify the ten questions you prepared for radio to fit your theme. Be specific and direct. The goal of your questions is to inspire your audience to participate by asking questions: Just like an on-air talk show, the host wants to stimulate his audience's interest so they'll stay logged on and "listening."

7. Ask permission to contact your participants.

Clear, ahead of time, with the moderator that you can give out your Web site URL and offer something free to participants. You want to let them know what is available without being pushy. One supposed on-line publicity expert proudly said he asked for a transcript of the session and frantically jotted down the e-mail addresses of all the people who participated and then harvested those who "lurked" to send them an offer to use his services later. I don't advise you to surreptitiously gather names in order to solicit people. Asking permission to contact people develops a much more honest relationship.

8. Zip or stuff your file.

After you are fully prepared with all of the above materials, you can respond calmly to any requests. Save all of your documents in one stuffed (Mac) or zipped (Windows) file so the host can open them without a hassle.

9. Book yourself on a show.

O'Keefe recommends pitching the person who books guests by e-mail first. In that e-mail ask for a phone number, or you may risk playing endless e-mail tag. As time on the Internet is of the essence, call back ASAP to secure a mutually agreeable chat date and time. The most coveted time slot is eight to eleven P.M. EST, so try for a time within those hours for maximum attendance.

10. **Send in your materials immediately.**

As soon as you send in your materials, follow up to ensure everything is posted well in advance of the venue date. Treat your follow-up accordingly, as this is the *real* publicity opportunity to have your name appear in multiple places at once all over prestigious and prominent Internet sites.

11. **Zap a thank-you card.**

Send a personalized electronic thank-you card to your host immediately after completing your chat.

Plug into your values

I have been thinking about being connected. How do I plug my values into the vast electronic world of the Internet? One of the most important questions I continue to ask myself is "Am I promoting community versus consumerism?" This might not be an important question for you, but even so, it's important to know what is. This question is part of my desire to be a conduit that helps women connect with each other, with men, with the media, the public, and their community.

The Internet has eliminated so many boundaries between countries, people, and beliefs. It's a powerful connecting tool to help us choose our communities and how we would like to be represented among them. Begin to think about which "communities" you want to connect with. Review your personal and professional interests to see if there is any overlap. Then seek out those sites that support your interests and you will find your global community.

PART VII

Keep and Sustain
Media Interest

CHAPTER 15

Discover the Publicity Secrets of Celebrity Stars

There's a publicity myth that is bigger than any best-seller, any box office blockbuster, and any classic that has stood the test of time. The biggest publicity myth is this: "Instant" success happens overnight. A passage in *A Course in Miracles* says, "Only infinite patience produces immediate results."

What you don't see in a celebrity's rise to stardom are the rumpled sheets of failed auditions, and the tired eyes of vulnerability. The celebrity stars are the people who have weathered the hard times in order to shine more brightly. I have chosen the ones who have found ways to develop skills to survive and thrive in a world where pumpkins turn to royal coaches and then back again.

Secret 1. Never turn down an opportunity

Actor James Woods had a mission. He wanted to work with director Martin Scorsese. At the time, Scorsese was directing the movie *Casino*. Though typically agents don't want their clients to call directors themselves, Woods's agent knew Scorsese relished direct contact. She advised Woods to leave Scorsese a personal message even though all the major roles were taken. Woods called Scorsese and left a message on his answering machine that said, "Any part, anytime, anywhere, any price." It happened that that very same night, the director was lying in bed watching the movie *Citizen Cohn* and asked his then girlfriend what she thought about James Woods for the part of Lester Diamond. Right after that conversation he listened to Woods's message. He offered Woods the role even though he was afraid that he would be insulted by the bit part.

Woods gleefully accepted. He said he had more fun as the character Lester Diamond than in almost any other role he had played. There is often no way of predicting where something will lead, no matter how small or insignificant it may seem at the time. Make it a point to say yes when opportunity finds you. You never know who is watching, listening, or reading.

Secret 2. Stand up for a cause

Christopher Reeve, who played the role of Superman, has brought international attention to the paralyzed populace. He is still the embodiment of superhuman powers in his determination to relearn to walk. He has become an eloquent speaker and an image of courageous perseverance for our nation.

At a concert in Oakland's historic Paramount Theater, singer Natalie Merchant devoted a song to Julia Butterfly Hill. Not only was she connecting with her local audience (the news marked Julia's one-year anniversary living in a tree protesting deforestation), but she was showing us what was meaningful to her.

Demonstrate to the world what is important to you by dedicating a part of your pocketbook or time to support a worthy organization. When you make it your business to get involved with issues that are already meaningful in your life, it becomes easy to find a place for your services within your community.

Do some thinking about what is important to you. After you are active in a charity, write a press release about it. Explain why this particular cause is meaningful to you. That way your good deeds will become synonymous with important issues.

Secret 3. Arrest the audience with the invisible

The public's fascination with Sharon Stone's private parts in the movie *Basic Instinct* launched her career, even though we never actually saw her "flower" in that famous interrogation scene. While your privates might not cause quite the same stir as Stone's, what you don't show can be titillating. Sometimes you want to titillate if that is your thing. Typically though, intrigue is created through actions or words by hinting. Film critic David Thompson wrote of Catherine Deneuve in the movie *Belle de Jour,* "Deneuve is a fantastic actress, her beauty a receptacle for any imagination, perhaps the greatest cool blond for ever hinting at intonations of depravity." Notice he didn't say for *being* depraved. Deneuve's power came from a performance full of nuance.

Refuse to talk about your sex life. Keep the private parts of your life private. For that matter, keep your privates private. Perhaps titillate with a peek into your personal depravities if you must, but don't spell them out for us. Boundaries are a good thing, and so is imagination. An aura of mystery and respect will surround you when you are elusively charming, and the public will clamor for more. Let people speculate. Enjoy it. Allow enticement to be a preview for your next big entrance.

Secret 4. Don't let a body part upstage your talent

Susan Sarandon said, "For years I was more famous for my boobs than for my talent. [But] it is very hard to be naked in a scene and not be upstaged by your nipples. People don't even hear what you are saying for the first thirty seconds if you are standing there nude."

You don't want to reveal your nipples if you'd rather people noticed your insights. Make sure you are not doing anything to distract the public from your point.

Secret 5. Toot your own horn . . . lightly

The object of publicity is to invite others to man the vehicle that sounds the gorgeous rhythms of your life. Think of yourself as providing the license to drive your best qualities forward. There is an art to giving a well-timed beep on your own behalf. Horn-tooting is a delicate business. Too loud and you bring out the fight in people. Too soft and you risk not being heard.

There are ways you can rise to an occasion without putting yourself on high. Thanking others for helping you become great is one way you can gracefully get in a toot or two without people holding their hands over their ears. Steven Spielberg did this with his 1999 Oscar acceptance speech for the movie *Saving Private Ryan*. He thanked his dad and war veterans with sincerity. Graciousness was reflected right back on him.

Leave it to others to shout out your glory. Include these "glory statements" in your press kit. One way to disseminate compliments is through the mouths of your clients. Such compliments include specific benefits or clearly delineate the payoffs of your service. In a press release for a company-sponsored day of rejuvenation at Architects & Heroes, a hair salon and art gallery, I quoted Valerie Durantini of Esprit, who said, "We're out in the public eye all the time. A lot of people at Esprit thought that Architects & Heroes would mirror our philosophy and fit with our thought process at Esprit—simple and clean, a fresh look. Everyone is energized now after this event. They look alive and modern." Built into that statement are several bottom-line benefits to both the clients and the corporation. And it doesn't sound like bragging at all.

Consciously or unconsciously reviewers and other media people are influenced by reading about concrete results. Your positive press will leave an important impression.

Secret 6. Give good copy

People whose ideas are ready-to-quote get more airtime and print space than those whose comments need editing. Writer Dorothy Parker was a goddess of good copy. She could be counted on to say things like "Wit has truth in it; wise-cracking is simply calisthenics with words." You can get a sense if you are giving good copy by observing your interviewer. If you're being interviewed by phone, listen for computer keyboard clicking.

I was sitting with a client at a banquette in a trendy restaurant a few months ago as she was being interviewed by a journalist. I had told her to watch when he scribbled furiously and when his pen was idle. My advice was to elaborate on the subject when she saw scribbling. Note-taking means he's getting information he can use. Curb your conversation when he's idle. Journalists don't try to remember scintillating information. They only write down pertinent statements, stories, and facts that they may be able to incorporate into their piece. At one point during the meeting he actually said, "Great sound bite!" and used it in his widely read newspaper column.

Lawyer and ethicist Lori B. Andrews started on the right foot by titling her book about the issues of reproductive technology *The Clone Age*. In a radio interview she discussed the emerging controversy of "procreation without permission." In a number of cases, wives and parents were collecting the sperm of their dead or comatose husbands/sons so they could have children and grandchildren. Given the circumstances, they didn't have the explicit consent of the men. Andrews said, "[Those] men might feel differently about being a daddy after death." That is a statement that commands attention.

Giving good copy takes practice if it doesn't come naturally to you. The easy formula is this: Quotable quips are always short, one to three lines. They are often funny, gutsy, controversial, shocking, and to the point, and sometimes include innuendo.

Secret 7. Turn your faults into trademark touches

According to Ann Reinking, Bob Fosse's director, choreographer, and longtime companion, "Fosse didn't like his hands, so he put gloves on [his dancers]. He was going bald, so he put hats [on them]. He was turned in instead of turned out, so he made all the steps slightly turned in and sometimes pigeon-toed." In essence, he turned a dance vocabulary based on his shortcomings into spectacular stage performances.

Your unique faults can give you an inside edge to understanding the audience to which you are marketing. San Francisco–based keynote speaker and author Susan RoAne said she included an open letter to her first-grade teacher in her third book, *What Do I Say Next? A Guide to Making Conversation*. This was the teacher who would not double-promote her because of her constant chatting with classmates. "Now I get paid big bucks to talk," Susan says.

Kelli Fox, the mastermind behind *astrology.com,* the most popular astrology site on the Internet, is impatient. She likes to get things done fast without any fuss. The people who use the Internet have come to expect immediate results as well, so Kelli uses a system to get personal astrological charts to her clients instantly. A perfect match. Within seconds of placing an order, a detailed dose of destiny is downloaded to her customers.

Besides speed, Kelli's popularity comes from a no-nonsense attitude about astrology, which she says is "a guide, not a god." Over 250,000 people a day visit the site to receive her insightful guidance. Kelli has been spotlighted on E! The Entertainment Channel, Net-Cafe, *Daybreak, Donny and Marie*, and other programs catering to the Internet and Generation Xers. Her quick wit makes her a respected guest on TV talk shows, where speed is of the essence in getting your point across.

Do an assessment of your ill-mannered ways. Your shortcomings are the greatest teachers you will ever have. If they have not yet metamorphosed into commendable career assets, reflect on how they can.

Secret 8. Be a nice guy/gal

Write a letter to your mother. Tom Hanks does. On a typewriter. Keynote speaker Susan RoAne says she always asks the Author Escort Service drivers, "Who are the celebrities who treat you well?" Hanks's name came up consistently. He not only plays nice guys, he is one.

Author Carol Adrienne is one of my dream clients. She has what I call a big "yes I can" muscle. She exercises it on a regular basis, so it has become a mighty muscle. When we developed a strategic publicity plan for her book *The Purpose of Your Life,* I asked Carol to collect all the articles she had written. The next day they arrived at my door. Anything I asked Carol to do, she did easily and eagerly. Being "nice" is doing what needs to be done with a smile, as soon as or before it is asked. . . . Carol has the "just do whatever it takes" attitude. Producers appreciate that. Colleagues appreciate that. Bosses appreciate that.

How can you be a nice guy or gal? When your clients or customers ask you for something, do it immediately with pleasure. Think of media people as your clients. Make their requests your first priority. Do their bidding with eagerness (even if it means going far out of your way).

Secret 9. Speak out for those who don't have a voice

Singer and rape-awareness activist Tori Amos cofounded the rape, abuse, and incest national network (RAINN), a nonprofit organization based in Washington, D.C. RAINN is one of the few, if not the only, national hot line services for survivors of sexual assault. Over 4,000 victims called the hot line in its first thirty days. Amos has brought visibility and awareness to the cause by writing songs, recording ads, and donating concert revenues.

To make a difference you don't have to sing, dance, or dig into your pockets. Get active. Become a spokesperson and help give voice to those who can't do it for themselves. Use your know-how for doing what you do best.

Dana May Casperson, a manners and etiquette expert, taught inner-city kids the correct way to use their utensils at posh restaurants throughout the country. The restaurants volunteered their services and edibles for the sake of education and etiquette. The *Chicago Tribune* wrote that Casperson's wisdom gave the kids much more than a lesson in bread and butter. The local TV evening news picked up the story. Some children said that they had always felt like society outsiders but now, manners in hand, felt included. Others were excited to go home and teach their parents their new skills.

Heartfelt giving within your own community or in the larger world attracts immediate attention of the news media for two reasons: First, community-conscious acts bring notice to underrated issues that concern society. Second, stories about social saviors counter the negative news that threatens to overwhelm us.

Secret 10. Offer love in the face of hate

This, of course, is the work of a lifetime. The Dalai Lama continues to say that the Chinese are not his enemy, despite the fact that they have tortured his people and banned him from his Tibetan homeland. When asked about his current life in exile, he replied, "Sometimes I think this Dalai Lama is the hardest life of all—but of course it is the most interesting."

When you begin your publicity plan, it can feel like taking your heart in hand and tossing it freely to a pack of hungry wolves. Know that among the snapping jaws there also exist warm muzzles. Seek them out. There is a saying, "As long as you can be irritated, something will irritate you." There will be the inevitable criticisms of you and your work. Your facial tics or thick ankles will come under scrutiny. Most likely you will have people peeking under your skirt trying to find that inevitable flaw (or private part). My mother always told me to wear good underwear. I still think it is very good advice.

CHAPTER 16

Study the Publicity Secrets of Spiritual Masters

Eternal wealth comes from practicing publicity with heart. Heart means coming from the center of your self. Heart means that you do everything in accordance with your own internal barometer. "Having a heart," "heartfelt," "hearty," means that you are in complete alignment with your principles, what you believe, how you think, act, and behave. You are in harmony with yourself and the world around you to the extent that is possible for you in this moment.

Eternal wealth isn't a static state. Eternal wealth is the foundation within yourself that you can call on to give you what you need to keep developing your kindness, generosity, and good spirit. If you are taken with the glitz and glamour that publicity can offer, this chapter serves to balance your desire for something gilded with common sense and common good. With spiritual masters as our guides I will show you how your foibles, fears, friends, and a big mouth will lead you deeper into discovering what it is you really need to know to make your life an act of giving.

Secret 1. Refuse to be silenced

Ma Jaya calls herself a "Jewish Hindu woman who loves Christ." Before it was hip to die or work with the dying, Ma Jaya was doing it. I recall musing over her words months after I interviewed her for a show of her paintings that I was publicizing, an exhibition called "Faces of the Mother." She called being present to share a person's death an incredible privilege.

Ma is not some silent little nun who spends her days sitting around meditating in a cave. She's an outspoken advocate of those who don't have the fortitude to fight for themselves. "Wha'd you expect, some quiet little holy woman?" she asked me when I talked to her. Well, kinda. . . . What I remember most from our conversation was her fierce need for compassion and her insistence that everyone be loved. She practiced this by hugging the grossly ill and kissing the brows of people who were sick and hard to look at.

When she was at the Parliament of World Religions event in Chicago some ten years ago or so, everyone was ignoring one issue that was uppermost in Ma's mind—that gay people were excluded from being loved and accepted by the Catholic Church. This hypocrisy made Ma a furious bull. She refused to be silenced. She jostled her way to the Pope and asked in a loud voice if he would just hug one adult person with AIDS. "It would change the world if he did. People would follow his example of compassion," said Ma. But he wouldn't agree to do it. Ma is a noisy unrelenting voice for the acceptance and love of all human beings.

Certainly we all have times when we not only don't feel loved, but feel attacked. It was so sad to me that a woman I media-coached for two hours decided that she was being "raped" by the media and so chose not to continue her publicity campaign. We had begun with the questions she feared because that was her first focus, but her family circumstances made it impossible to proceed. Because she felt unprepared and attacked, she gave up a scheduled CNN show and called off the TV part of her tour altogether. She ran to her therapist after each interview. If it is too much, it is too much, I understand that. But if you choose, you can use the experience to uncover all the sorrowful places in yourself. If you can bear it, there is much joy, relief, all kinds of emotions that accompany publicity, and that sorrowful part is just part of the range.

When I teach a media-coaching class, I ask students, "When should you refuse to be interviewed?" The answer? "Never." By refusing to be interviewed you choose to silence yourself. I don't believe you should be silenced if there is something you want to say. Women in particular need to refuse to be silenced. If we can't say what we want to say alone, let's get a group of voices to make sure we are heard.

Insist on your right to be heard like a mother protecting her child. There is nothing more fierce. And remember to do it with compassion, fierce compassion, like Ma, like a mother. Publicity is the chance to have your voice heard. You choose the subject, the time, and the place. If you take your place, your seat, or your stand with courage, compassion, and a newsworthy angle, the media will make a space for you.

Secret 2. Make your connections from warm hand to warm hand

Zen Master Shunryu Suzuki, author of *Zen Mind, Beginner's Mind*, who founded the first Buddhist monastery in the Western Hemisphere, said Buddhism is always best passed on "from warm hand to warm hand." The same is true of expanding your network. I ask every person who works with me to make a list of all the people who might be willing to help them in their publicity or promotional campaign. This includes friends, neighbors, relatives, colleagues, competitors, workout buddies, classmates, alumni, people whose services you use (doctors, printers), corporations, organizations, clubs, charities, writers, journalists, authors, people who know influential people, and image makers (people who influence others).

To help sell her niece's first book, *Living Happily Ever After,* Laurie Wagner's aunt Marlene invited all of her friends to a gala celebration at her house in Los Angeles. She knew that the hundreds of people she invited would be interested in finding out about the secrets of staying together from couples married thirty years or more. She helped Laurie sell over 160 books! A number of people bought more than one to give as gifts. Well-connected Aunt Marlene also invited a reporter from the *Los Angeles Times,* who wrote a glowing piece about the event. In her elegant invitations Aunt Marlene also did some savvy marketing. She gave people who couldn't attend the party the opportunity to prepurchase books and have them shipped. Sixty books were presold to those supporters of Laurie and her project. Laurie says, "My aunt would host a party for any book I had written, even if it was on rodents." *Living Happily,* which promised everlasting love, probably had more of a draw.

HOT TIP!

ASK YOUR FRIENDS AND BUSINESS ASSOCIATES FOR HELP.

Many people are waiting for the chance to help you. Allow them to. "Help" is one of the most underused words in our vocabulary. You'd be surprised how flattered and eager people are to help you.

You might ease into it with, "I am looking to expand my business. Is there any way you can think of to help?" This gives them the opportunity to use their imagination fully.

Celebrations and special occasions throughout the year are prime times for promotion because parties put people in a good mood, which makes them open to meeting strangers.

Feminist Susan Faludi, author of *Backlash,* said of my good friend writer and cartoonist John Grimes, "[His] delightful cartoons prove you *can* be a feminist *and* have a wonderful sense of humor." I describe him as "a man without a swagger." I have such fun introducing him like that. The statement creates curiosity, and a conversation is born. At my fortieth birthday party, my sweetheart, Brett, and I created name tags for each person that included a one-word description of them. With this tag, all the people who didn't know one another had a way to begin a conversation. That is all a publicity campaign is. The beginning of a conversation with you and "the public," who are really just a bunch of people a lot like you.

Invitation

Have your friends introduce you to anyone who might help you further your career and vice versa. Ask them to start with the phrase "I thought you two would like to meet each other because you have _____ in common." This sets up an immediate rapport between you and the stranger and you don't have to search for a mutual interest. Then, before they depart, have your friends tell your new acquaintance something extraordinary about you.

Network for friends. Allow all of your friends to take you by the hand and join your hands to others. Find other warm hands by holding them, or holding them through the hands of others, and your circle of prosperity will continue to grow.

Secret 3. Run toward your fears

There is a legend about the feisty and provocative Tibetan spiritual master Chogyam Trungpa. One hot and dusty day as he approached the gates of the monastery, a vicious dog began running toward him with dripping fangs. Instead of trying to escape, Trungpa ran at the dog, growling and snapping. The dog put his tail between his legs and ran from Trungpa howling. Most of us make a mad dash away from our fears when we catch a glimpse of them. But what if you ran toward these large, looming, fang-dripping beasts? When you run at your fears, they often put their tail between their legs and gallop off in the other direction.

Goethe said, "Whatever you can do or dream you can, begin it. Boldness has genius, power, and magic in it. Begin it now." You can begin a good boldness practice in your personal life that you can carry on in your publicity campaign. If you can't run toward your fears, then jog alongside them for a while. Decide right now that you will do one bold act to counteract a fear that will help move you forward on your publicity path. I am not talking about something outrageous (unless you are up for that). I am telling you to say, do, or write something you have been meaning to get to.

Run toward your fears. If you get really bold, you can ask for publicity opportunities that address all of them. Wouldn't that make friends of the vicious beasts?

Secret 4. Do what is right for you

The only one who can decide what is right for you is you. When you doubt that what you are doing, saying, being, is the right thing, listen to the words of one of my favorite teachers, Martin Luther King.

Explaining his then-unpopular position against the Vietnam War, King wrote, "On some positions, Cowardice asks the question, 'Is it safe?' . . . Expediency asks the question, 'Is it politic?' And Vanity comes along and asks the question, 'Is it popular?' But Conscience asks the question, 'Is it right?' And there comes a time when one must take a position that is neither safe, nor politic, nor popular, but he must do it because Conscience tells him it is right."

Who are we to judge? When I study someone's presence, actions, words, I learn from them what I can and decide what is right for me, not what is right for them.

To avoid the hidden heartbreaks of marketing and publicity, ask yourself what is right for you. You may get your panties in a twist if you see your competitor getting that juicy place sitting across from Katie Couric or Matt Lauer on NBC's *Today* show while you are at home doing the dishes. You will have many temptations, to be sure, each more succulent than the last, inviting you to behave badly. We all have to ask ourselves what price we're willing to pay for what we want. If you can continually bring yourself back to this one question, the direction of your marketing and publicity plan will move you to your genuine path. Is it right for you?

Secret 5. Stop looking for your eagle feather

Are you hoping that the power and prestige that comes from being recognized will give you your eagle feather? My friend Jacob, a screenwriter, just told me over dinner last week that waiting for money to change your life is a mistake. His screenplays are always on the edge of being bought by some huge Hollywood studio. He's been waiting for his big break for almost fifteen years now and it has held him back from relationships, health, and happiness. Until this year he believed that women weren't attracted to poor writers over forty who didn't own a car.

Over the past several years he's been evaluating his psychological barriers and even doing a bit of meditation. It has finally had an effect. As we speak, he's dating three women and he has a well-paid gig writing a script. For him this is a major shift. If you are in a holding pattern at this moment circling your own success, stop.

Instead of focusing on yourself, sit your big dreaming butt down and make a list of all the ways your product, personality, or service can benefit others. There may be some bodaciously bad beliefs lodged in your unconscious mind, but I am no shrink, so let's put those aside for a minute. Let's see what you can do for others rather than what they can do for you. Before we even get to your publicity goals, have you considered your family and friends? Can you make some time in your day for the most important people in your life? Try telling each of them something you'd like them to know about how much they mean to you.

In her course called "The Energy of Money," Maria Nemeth, Ph.D., said that a study showed that given the choice between knowing that their children loved them or knowing that they had done a good job, parents would choose the latter. I took her advice to heart. This year after our Passover celebration I told my parents they had done a good job raising me and my brothers. At first they stared at me. Then they both guffawed in embarrassed pleasure. The next day my mother called and told me it made her feel really good to hear those words.

Can you stop looking for money, power, prestige, whatever the eagle feather is for you, and just go on doing your work in the world? Publicity is doing good and then telling others about it. But I think the real work begins when you no longer have the need to be the town crier for your own deeds. Others automatically pick up the trumpet and call your name out to everyone they know. You just may find that your eagle feather is attached to your very own wings.

⁓ *Invitation* ⁓

To help you prepare for making your goals happen, ask yourself the following questions:

1. What was your original vision when you began your business, book, project, or idea?

2. How will people feel using your (or your company's) product or service?

3. What do you want them to come away with?

I am always surprised by the answers my clients give me when I ask them what was most meaningful about our brainstorming sessions. Rarely does the information I thought essential turn out to be what was most critical to them. Try it yourself and see what you find.

HOT TIP!

ASK YOUR CUSTOMERS AND CLIENTS WHY THEY CHOSE TO USE YOU.

From this information, list the ten hottest selling points of you and your business. You can begin to see in black-and-white what makes you unique. You can use this information when you create new press materials.

PART VIII

Integrate Publicity into Your Life

CHAPTER 17

Speak for Free or a Fee

We all talk. When people hear you on the radio or TV, they get a taste of what you have to offer for an average of two to ten minutes. When they have the chance to experience you talking for one to three hours, they realize that they have much more to learn from you. In a sense they get a richer experience of what you have to offer. Because they're excited about their new knowledge or experiences, they tell friends and family about it and the word about you spreads organically. The natural progression of learning dictates that those people will then buy your books, tapes, or products, or hire you or your business for the services that you provide.

Even better than that, if a company has hired you to speak to their business, they will buy your products to give to their employees, and your influence will deepen dramatically. When you teach what you know in a class, workshop, lecture, seminar, speech, or panel discussion for organizations, companies, or adult learning centers, you automatically have a reason for getting media coverage. Combining speaking engagements with all the other publicity you have chosen to do increases exponentially the impact of your plan.

How to get publicity from speaking engagements

Invite journalists to attend your talk

To encourage local journalists to come to my San Francisco Learning Annex class, I sent out an e-mail press release. (See it in chapter 4.) The purpose of the press release was to give journalists the opportunity to cover the students attending my course. I knew that many of these students had worthy news stories, but they didn't know how to get press coverage for their talents. That was why they were taking my class.

Journalists from prestigious publications like Salon.com and *Fast Company* attended. Another journalist from the *San Francisco Chronicle* couldn't make the date, but asked if I'd give him information on anyone who was media worthy.

The result? The *Chronicle* reporter wrote about a number of my students in one column and wrote a snippet about my class in another. Salon.com did a feature article on me and the course itself. An editor from Simon & Schuster called to see if I planned to write a book on the topic of my class. Some journalists will come to your class, even if not specifically invited, if it ties into a topic that they're covering. Listing your class in the free Sunday Datebook lecture listings (most newspapers have a version of this section) can attract both students and journalists.

Send an announcement to the press before your events

Local producers and journalists are always scanning the news for ideas. If you do a good job of tying in your announcement to some newsworthy event, or have a creative angle, you give press people a reason to call.

Send an announcement to the press after your event

After your talk is over, you can still get coverage in national professional organizations to which you belong. Simply write a one-page tip sheet for their newsletter about your event as it relates to their interests. You can also send an announcement to your hometown newspaper or your alumni newsletter, where people who know you may be interested in your activities.

My publicity organization regularly summarizes the guest lecturers in their monthly newsletter. Every month or so my publicist, Leslie Rossman, submits updates from her list for key media contacts. Her list is invaluable to those who don't have the phone glued to their ears as regularly as Leslie. As a consequence almost everyone in the media community knows her name. Is there information you can give to one of the organizations you belong to?

PLAN YOUR TALK:
FOLLOW THIS COMMON TEMPLATE TO
STRUCTURE A TALK

1. **Opening introduction:**
   Open with an anecdote, a humorous or touching story, a joke, one charged potent word, an unusual fact, or a shocking statistic.

2. **Message statement:**
   Assert your theme or most important idea. Begin with the words "I believe," "I feel," "I think," "I have been thinking about."

3. **Background link:**
   Tell a story that illustrates your connection to the company, the subject, or the organization.

4. **Points:**
   List the main ideas you will cover during your speech.

5. **Point development:**
   Elaborate each point you have promised to cover (above).

6. **Preliminary conclusion:**
   Sum up the key points and relate them back to your opening.

7. **Climax:**
   Conclude with the most exciting moment of your talk.

8. **Question and answer (Q&A) period:**
   Take questions from the audience.

9. **Conclusion:**
   Wrap up with your final closing statements.

Employ seven tips to develop a smooth presentation

1. Write your own introduction.

You wrote your introduction for your radio or TV interviews and it's a good idea to do the same for a talk. Part of maintaining control of how you are perceived is to write out *exactly* how you'd like to be introduced.

2. Guarantee your subject matter is relevant to your audience.

"Your listeners won't care how much you know until they know how much you care," a sage anonymous person said. Find out in advance of any special interests, hopes, desires, of your audience so you can address them accordingly. Plan some of your stories around these special desires. All you are doing here is applying what you learned in angling your press material to a particular media market. Your talk in this case is part of your press kit, your knowledge. What matters most is to continually come back to the question, "How is this relevant to my audience?" The essential question to ask yourself is, "What do they want to know that will make a difference in their lives?"

3. Develop an outline as a guide for participants.

Your audience will appreciate a guide to your main points. Besides showing that you are organized, it gives them something to take away with all of your contact information. People tend to save and file information that they find useful and want to access later.

4. Keep it simple.

You don't need elaborate visual aids to keep the interest of an audience. The fewer technical things you have to worry about, the better. Most of the time the audience is so busy taking notes, they don't have time to watch a PowerPoint presentation. Plus you have to dim the lights, so you can't see people. To some, the low lights are a Pavlovian cue to catch a little shut-eye. Even if they're not dozing, you don't really want them focusing on your materials, you want their attention directed at and anchored on you.

5. Practice out loud.

Dorothy Sarnoff, an authority on speaking and speech, recommends that you practice your entire talk four times out loud. As you get comfortable hearing your own voice say what is important to you, your relaxation level rises and you don't hear your teeth chattering or knees knocking. You will just hear the audience listening.

6. Prepare an evaluation form.

Although many organizations provide an evaluation form, you will want to bring your own. Think about the comments you want to elicit that can help you improve the content, style, and presentation of the material. On mine I always include the question "What would you say if you were to recommend this course/talk to others?" I also ask permission to use their comments, names, and company information in my marketing and publicity materials by requesting their signature designating that I may do so.

With an evaluation you can examine how people perceive you and it can assist you in changing any negative perceptions. As you sift responses from the piles of testimonials, you will find the most sparkling ones to excerpt for other speaking and meeting planners to show you were well received.

7. Bring business cards.

Have your business cards out and available for any person who wants one before, during, and after your talk. You might want to put some on the back table in the area provided for speakers' materials. I like to have people come up to me personally and hand it to them directly.

Follow the ten secrets to delivering a presentation that ignites interest and spurs sales

1. Encourage audience interaction.

Do you know how long it takes for someone's attention to wander? Seven minutes. That is conservative given that psychologists say we're thinking about sex 97 percent of the time. In between all that thinking about candlelight, peacock feathers, and variations of the *Kama Sutra,* you are trying to squeeze in *your* information. What you have to say has to be mighty important.

Participation in your talk can take the form of an outline with your main topics or fill-in-the-blanks with a single word. In the case of larger groups you can ask rhetorical questions or questions that require a verbal response. Another way to encourage silent participation is to ask a question that signifies a transition in topic that participants answer automatically in their minds. Moving through your audience while making direct eye contact and addressing a few individuals will create a good feeling among everyone.

2. Involve your audience.

Alfred, Lord Tennyson, said, "Things seen are mightier than things heard." Studies show if you can involve all of a person's senses, the information is retained up to four times more than if only heard. People remember only 10 percent of what they read, 20 percent of the information they hear, 30 percent of what they both hear and see, but up to 80 percent of what they hear, see, and do. Every seven minutes do something that involves the audience, or they'll be thinking of something that does.

3. Market yourself *during* your talk.

Saving the marketing of your products or services for a break, or blatantly bragging about results you have produced, can be off-putting to your audience. Marketing yourself is a subtle affair that is more like being graced by the wisp of a feather than being hit with a brick. Position yourself as an expert gently in three ways through

1. Personal experience:

    Showing how your personal experience has shaped who you are today lets your audience see you as a full, rich person. Develop stories and anecdotes that show how your childhood or adolescent adventures contributed to the kind of person you are and why you do what you do. This serves to differentiate you from others and gives the audience a chance to connect their past with yours.

2. Knowledge or research:

Displaying that you have solid evidence to back your claims shows you've done your homework. You've spent time reading and keeping yourself updated in changes in your field. People are impressed by discipline and hard work.

3. Client and customer results:

Including examples relevant to your point about how you have helped clients or customers spotlights the results your clients have had working with you, and how they've experienced you, your product, or your service. Their success becomes your success. Show how you have solved difficult customer problems. Choose the stories that most of your audience can relate to on some level.

When you have done these three things, you will have exchanged more than money, you will have mingled your best blessings with your audience.

4. Illustrate a point by giving something away.

People love surprises and free gifts. Who doesn't? Incorporating a way to give away your product or service during your talk or at the beginning of a break creates excitement and interest. A number of years ago I attended a sold-out Steven Covey seminar. At one point the leader held up a tape set and promised to give it to the first person who answered his question correctly. All eyes were pinned on that tape. Suddenly, every one of us wanted it. If we couldn't get it for free, well, we'd just have to buy it. Relate your gift directly to a point you are making and people will remember you, your point, and the product better.

5. Offer to send something via e-mail.

People often respond to different methods to receive information. While some prefer the tangibility of a business card, others prefer the speed and accessibility of e-mail. Offer something like a tip sheet for free via e-mail.

6. Ask permission to contact your participants.

When you give talks to large groups, many publicists say you should ask for a participant database, explaining it is the easiest, most expedient way of finding out contact information. I prefer to have people's permission to contact them. I send around my own mailing list and ask that people who are interested sign up. I offer my on-line newsletter to that list, which states that I don't ever sell, trade, or give away their names to anyone. Don't we all get too many catalogs and invitations from people or companies who want to sell us a toe separator or a hunk of cheese? I don't want to be sending people information they have no interest in receiving. Rather I want *them* to invite *me* into their mailboxes and into their lives.

7. Underpromise and overdeliver.

Overpromising is like finding a gift certificate in your drawer and finding out it expired the day before. Promise only what you can deliver in the time you have to deliver it. Avoid the temptation to promise anything that you can't guarantee, such as anyone's future success if they follow your advice. Don't ever tell the audience how they are supposed to feel, or how fantastic what you are about to tell them is. Set their expectations early in a conversational way by telling them what to look forward to, but leave out a few extras you plan to cover. Then when you do give them those extras, they'll be thrilled.

8. End on time.

If you really want to please your audience, stay within the planned time frame. This is particularly important in a conference setting when every section is timed and there is no moderator regulating the Chatty Cathy types.

9. Plan your final impression.

Before you tell your audience your last point, have them fill out your evaluation and answer their questions. You can't control questions, that is the beauty of them. The Q&A portion of my talks is one of my favorite times and always renews my faith in the human imagination, though you can count on a few doozies. Since you can't predict the type of questions you'll get or the audience response, you can't regulate the last feeling that your audience carries with them either. You want your audience to leave on an upbeat note. By telling them your last point after the Q&A, you will be able to manage their last impression of you and your presentation.

10. **Finish with a flourish.**

"Great is the art of beginning; but greater is the art of ending," Henry Wadsworth Longfellow noted. I find it fascinating that many of my friends who have attended a significant number of both births and deaths say that of the two, death is more profound. From what I have observed in friends and family close to me, people do die how they've lived. How else could it be? All those experiences are reflected in the final beingness as a person nears their end.

In a way, your talk is a beginning, or birth, of a relationship with your audience. The end of your connection comes symbolically at the conclusion of your talk. You may never come into contact with any of these people again, so your parting is a crucial step in your relationship. What do you want them to remember? How do you want to be remembered?

HOT TIP!

END YOUR TALK LIKE A ROCK CONCERT.

Pete Townsend, the guitarist for the rock group the Who, was famous for smashing his guitar at the end of every concert. Why did he do it? He wanted to embody the whole energy of the concert in his one last act.

Do something that will inscribe itself on a person's memory physically, emotionally, spiritually, wholly. Leave them with a burning memory of you.

How to get started if you have never spoken

Partner sponsorship with local organizations

Dottie Walters, president of Walters International Speakers Bureau, one of the largest speakers bureaus in the world, recommends getting a sponsor to help get your speaking career started. Dottie tours the country presenting her class, "Speak and Grow Rich," to help new speakers get started.

Get in touch with your church, temple, library, nonprofit, museum, community school, or one of your professional or personal organizations. Dottie often recommends that the speaker share a percentage of the door (the money that you collect as an entrance fee) if you are the one who approaches an organization to sponsor you. They send an announcement to the people on their mailing list and you do the same. Of course, you will want to match your interests to the organization you have chosen to guarantee substantial attendance.

You might want to start out with a slightly lower amount than you think you can command, in favor of encouraging more people to attend. Find out if the organization you are partnering with sends out their own press releases. You will want to be involved in the process to maintain control over how you are positioned. This is really a nice option. By beginning with a sponsored talk, a small community venue will support your chosen organization, while you gain their goodwill. It also gives you a chance to get to know some more people within your local area, deepening the bonds you have within your community.

Sponsor a talk yourself

You take all the risk—and you keep all the profits. But if you don't have a name within the community already, I don't suggest this path. One way to begin is to contact your existing client base and give them several options to choose from, to get a sense of what your public wants.

Speaker Carol Adrienne invited people on her mailing list to attend a new weekend seminar for free in exchange for their feedback. Carol already had an extensive mailing list and a loyal client base, so this was an ideal way for her to beta test new material. It sold out. After her trial talk she took the suggestions of her audience and made some changes. She now plans to offer the class to corporations.

I remember hearing that the peripatetic motivational speaker Zig Ziglar will speak anywhere at no charge for a crowd of 1,000 because he knows he can sell at least $20,000 worth of products. If this is your first talk, you might want to offer it for free and publicize it extensively in the media. In time, like Carol and Zig, you will build a loyal following and be in a position to charge for both your knowledge and products.

Contact organizations to talk for free

Many professional organizations publicize their events to their members and sometimes to the local media. They count on you doing such an exquisite job at your talk that you will automatically get clients from their group. Talking for free lets you build your portfolio, get experience, and gather kudos to talk more for free until the day arrives when you can charge money to move your mouth.

HOT TIP!

RECORD YOURSELF EVERY TIME YOU TALK.
All you need is a Lavaliere microphone, a high-quality tape deck, and an extension cord. Your talks on tape can be your first products. Have them duplicated and sell them at the next talk you give. Publicity is about reaching people exponentially. An audiotape lets you expand your reach quickly.

Propose teaching a class at your local university extension or adult learning center
You will never get rich teaching here, but you will get experience. The honorarium is minuscule, but that is not the point. The catalog exposure alone makes it well worth your time. You also have the opportunity to sell your products to the attendees. In many major cities adult learning centers are fiercely competitive, as famous business people and authors use these venues for national tours. You will start out with seven to twenty people in your classes and in time may fill a lecture hall.

Another advantage to teaching in such centers is since many classes begin small, you will have the chance to try out new ideas and materials in a low-key environment with people who are motivated to learn. Once you are accepted to teach, the center's programming personnel will help write the catalog copy and select times suited to your subject matter.

To propose a course, first review the catalog to determine whether someone else is already teaching the subject you have in mind. Angle your class so it is unique to you and your ideas. Write a title and a short description (about 150 words) matching the style of the catalog you are pitching. Include a brief bio that lists your most prestigious credentials or qualifications *that relate directly to the subject you are proposing to teach.* Your best bet is to propose one three-hour class versus one that lasts an entire day.

WARNING!   **KEEP YOUR COPYRIGHT.**

Very important! If you are participating in a large event, don't sign away your copyright. Always, always, always keep your copyright. Many times these events are taped and the organization reserves the right to sell the tapes to their members. You can put a clause in your agreement allowing them to do so while you still keep the copyright to your talk (even if it is just ten minutes on a panel). You don't want anyone owning your material except you. Request that you receive a copy of their tape so you can sell it yourself. Make sure your agreement includes the right to do so. You will be happy you did when you want to repackage your ideas in some other format, or use your talk as a demo tape to get other speaking engagements at a later date.

Accept any invitations to speak to a corporation

Just as with public talks, you never know who might be a contact for you. There are a lot of talented people in corporations. Many of them start their own companies or move to a position where they can hire you as a speaker. Dan Janal taught a Dale Carnegie class in 1991 in the Silicon Valley. A woman who attended that class and is now in another position called him and hired him to speak to her organization for a sizable sum—nine years after initially hearing him speak!

Once you become a skilled speaker, corporate gigs can be quite lucrative. A number of years ago I negotiated a $50,000 corporate speaking engagement for one of my clients, who had a real way with words. In total he worked about twenty hours for that fee, which included the preparation and delivery of his talks. Accepting invitations to speak to corporate personnel gives you the chance to expand your connections. I believe that those people who really connect with you, and what you have to say, will make the effort to stay in contact. Follow the next few steps to make sure you make it an easy and effortless task.

Furthering your speaking career

Let your event sponsors know you are available as a speaker

The executive director of the San Francisco Learning Annex has called me several times to find out if I'd be interested in speaking to corporations who have requested her input on an appropriate speaker. The adult learning centers in your community have a vivid presence there. Industry leaders, corporations, journalists, and individuals use them as a resource when they're searching for a speaker. Let your event sponsor know that you are willing to talk to other organizations. Once you have done a good job for them, you stay in their minds as a good person to recommend.

Send your sponsor your great evaluations

After I teach a new class, I e-mail the program director a few (not the whole batch!) choice comments from participants. I select the ones that say something about my teaching style, the content, and what they learned. You will be able to stay fresh in the minds of your sponsors so they'll think of you when another opportunity comes. Occasional reminders of how your work helps people makes you stand out from others.

Get listed in the course catalog for the organization to which you are speaking

A catalog profiles your course and your qualifications—and sometimes even prints a photograph. With or without a photo, your status as a professional within your community is recognized by thousands, if not millions, of people. You are pictured in the catalog alongside famous speakers, businesspeople, and authors, so you're automatically elevated to their level of prestige. Potential students and clients get to know you by seeing your face and your skills month after month. They trust you because they feel like they know you.

Practice the three methods to grow your speaking business

1. Hone your speaking skill.

After you talk, you will want to keep on improving your skills. You may choose to join a Speaking Circle, the National Speakers Association, Toastmasters, or all three. They each have very different perspectives on the skills of speaking. All have regional and national conferences, where you can hear experienced speakers' advice on a wide range of topics. The National Speakers Association has free talks all year round given by members in their homes for anyone who wants to attend. You will be able to learn a tremendous amount by watching, listening, and absorbing the methods of many different types of speakers. I often take classes from, or go to, talks by experienced speakers just so I can watch how they handle a group, present their material, and sell themselves.

2. Hire a media or presentation coach.

One-on-one or group coaching can give you personalized instruction on everything from your presentation style to the content of your talk. You will be able to address technical as well as subtle areas of improvement with guidance from a perceptive coach.

3. Submit your demo video to a speakers bureau.

Once you have given enough talks to command a $2,000-per-speaking-engagement fee, you will be eligible to submit a request to be considered by bureaus. You may think I am joking, but that is what it takes. Most bureaus require you to have been paid at least $2,500 per engagement for a minimum of about thirty a year (they vary). They also request a substantial number of recommendation letters from these paid engagements. In-demand speakers such as celebrities, politicians, and forward-thinking businesspeople earn huge sums of money. At this time, comedian Jerry Seinfeld is noted to have the highest per-engagement fee of $600,000.

But before we jump ahead to the six-figure domain of the speaking superstars, you will need to begin with a consistent record of solid engagements. Dottie Walters, president and CEO of Walters International Speakers Bureau and author of *Speak and Grow Rich*, requires that "you have given at least 100 paid dates for fees of at least $2,000 per hour, on topics that are saleable to associations and corporations," before you approach her. In short, bureaus want a proven track record.

Will a bureau take you with less experience? If you can show that you have booked yourself with associations and corporations and have received glowing recommendations, you may get them to look at you. In any case you will need a professional demo video, a list of your topics, a client list, and recommendation letters, all in a professional-looking package. But don't send any materials until you are sure that a speakers bureau is an appropriate fit.

Once you qualify, the advantage of working with many bureaus is that they have significant connections that would take you years to cultivate and maintain. And to your benefit most bureaus are not exclusive. They work on straight commission, taking 25 to 30 percent of your fee and only charge you when they have closed a contract.

Many bureaus specialize (in sports figures, humorists, celebrities, business, etc.), so you'll want to find one that matches your area of expertise. They have a roster of speakers who fit different topic needs of corporations and associations that consistently hire speakers. They are looking to match your skills with a request for a particular topic. "One of the most important things is to match your market with your speaker," says Dottie, who specializes in business-topic speakers. "Once I am considering a speaker, I send them an information form to fill out and then make an appointment to speak with them personally on the phone. I want to hear their voice and language. I want to make sure they speak respectfully and can tell great stories." For a listing of all the speakers bureaus, contact Dottie Walters, who has compiled a comprehensive list.

For twenty-five dollars the International Speakers Bureau will review your demo tape for eligibility in their bureau. Take a look at their site at *http://www.ISBspeakers. com* for an idea of how speakers commanding respectable fees market themselves.

CHAPTER 18

Know What Matters Most

Stephen Covey says, "How different our lives are when we really know what is deeply important to us, and keeping that picture in mind, we manage ourselves each day to be and to do what really matters most."

When you know what is important, you can constantly check in on the marketing and publicity campaign you have mapped out for yourself by asking, "Does this support me in what matters most? Does my plan reflect my own standard of excellence internally and externally?" Once that happens, you automatically attract the people with whom you want to associate.

Create partnerships of passion

Like many artists or performers, women want to be passionate about their work. When they leave their corporate jobs, "most women either start a business totally unrelated to their previous jobs or turn a personal interest into a business pursuit," explains Linda K. Paresky, chair of the Committee of 200 Foundation. Women business owners (14 percent) are more likely than men (2 percent) to have turned a personal interest into a business pursuit.

When I started my marketing and public relations firm, I wanted every client to feel like a lover. I knew what it felt like to have great rapport with some of my clients in the sales position I had just quit. And I also knew how I felt as if a dead branch had broken off inside me when I didn't have that. With this in mind I *chose* my very first client. And have continued to do so ever since.

I first saw Nina Glaser's provocative black-and-white photographs in a magazine. Two years later I walked into an art gallery the day I decided to start my own company and was once again mesmerized by her work. I called her as soon as I got home and said, "I am a publicist and I want to represent you." We met and she became the first artist to become my client. When I contacted her, I never considered that she might not want to work with me. I knew I could get the kind of exposure she needed to raise her career to the next level and I felt passionate about her talent and vision.

Nina didn't have much money, so she paid me the only way she could—with photographs. I didn't know it at the time, but I was already beginning my business with a philosophy that continues to this day. I wasn't seeking Glaser's business, I was creating a partnership of passion. You, too, can choose to develop partnerships of passion with people, businesses, and the media that further your philosophy or goals by following the guidelines in this book.

Follow your gypsy spirit

When I was traveling in Israel, I learned that the gypsies there offer you three things when you are a guest in their home. A glass of water, a mug of coffee, and a cup of tea. First they give you water because it is what we are mostly made of—it represents the fact that things are fluid and moving. Then they serve you coffee, because life is often bitter. And lastly they bring you a cup of tea with a few cubes of sugar, for life has its sweet moments. You get their whole philosophy in one visit with three drinks.

Your gypsy spirit doesn't censor. Your gypsy spirit knows where the honey is and is willing to get stung to get it. Your gypsy spirit is a rose that blooms in the middle of the desert with no water in sight. Your gypsy spirit is long hair, long nights, and the moon showing you which direction to take.

Your gypsy spirit knows where to go and how to get there. It puts you on the move and asks you to pitch your tent wherever you are—no matter how harsh the weather, how impolite the company—and make yourself a hot cup of tea.

Making that call to Nina was listening to my gypsy spirit. I was moved by her work, so I picked up the phone. First this, then that, no hesitation. I didn't fret that she might think me daft for calling her out of the blue. I had a sense that we would meet in that place where gypsy spirits go, a great open expanse where things can happen with little more than a thought and one small step.

Andrea Siegel, textile artist and author of *Open and Clothed,* has this gypsy-spirit spunk. One Sunday morning she read an article by Trish Hall, who writes for the real-estate section of the *New York Times,* describing how real estate was unaffordable in Manhattan. Hall purported that all a home seeker could find were dank dungeon apartments with bathtubs in the kitchen for thousands of dollars. Andrea has a $600-a-month studio in Queens and thought, "She should do a story about me." Her next thought was, "This is Sunday; you don't have to write on Sunday," but she knew if she didn't go with the inspiration, and write a letter to Trish and "beat back the part of my personality that wanted to lie around and eat too much breakfast and feel sorry for myself," she wouldn't do it. "So before that inhibitory sensor started beeping, I put a stamp on the letter, ran to the post office, and the letter was gone. What works for me is when a project comes from joy."

A few days later Andrea got a call from the *New York Times* saying they wanted to send a reporter with a photographer over that same day to cover her. Of course, they talked about her book and the fact that she's a textile artist who makes projects to order. She put that article in her press kit and sent it to Terry Gross of NPR's prestigious show *Fresh Air,* who booked her.

The result? The book shot up to number seventy-nine on Amazon.com's best-seller list, and Amazon's subsequent order paid for the *entire* second (self-published) printing of the book. "I have been getting almost daily book orders for months," says Andrea. "The interview didn't result in more interviews, but resulted in my reaching people in Alaska, Utah, Georgia, etc., places and people I never could have reached otherwise. That was a huge gift. I love getting calls from obscure bookstores in Ohio and Colorado. The point is not that publicity causes more publicity; it's that I fulfill my responsibility to reach as many people as I can."

Following your gypsy spirit comes in all different forms. Writing a business letter on a Sunday when you "should" relax, jetting off an e-mail in the middle of the night, jumping on a plane when a distant land calls you. Follow your gypsy spirit wherever it takes you, to the *New York Times,* to the Internet, to a land of coconuts and perfumed air, to a place unknown, and you will find something that you didn't know before and be happier for it.

"Do with"

I believe that will and desire are far more important than talent or smarts. Knowing how to get what you want done counts for a lot. "Do with" is one of my favorite sayings. Use what you have available right now. It can be your talent, your expertise, the materials or people you have access to this very minute. Don't wait to change yourself or hold yourself back because you don't have the right resources or the right pencil. Spring into action.

I have seen the "Do with" principle in the thousands of salespeople I have interviewed as a consultant for a large corporation, and in my clients and students, who use what they have to its maximum. People with the "Do with" philosophy, those who have creativity or perseverance, often perform better than the best and brightest. "Do with." Make your plan, then act on it.

Enjoy the process

Enjoy the process of carrying out a marketing and publicity plan, because it is all process. My friend Cecile Moochnek is an excellent example of the joys of process. I remember walking into her art gallery for the first time. She stood at the top of the stairs, her bright blue eyes pleased. She invited me into her beautiful space, offered me a cup of oolong tea poured into two handmade green cups.

Every detail is important to Cecile. In her gallery you don't look at art, you have an experience. You don't see paintings, sculpture, or watercolors—you feel them. All that is seen and done in her presence is done so in the name of beauty. And that beauty is part of her process.

The process of walking on her polished wooden floors, the process of noticing the open space—the areas not filled with art that are themselves works of art, the serenity of her outdoor deck arranged just so, with a rock sculpture, greenery, and the bench her son built.

And then there is the process of the art itself that graces her walls and floors. Cecile delights in telling how an artist created his work, what he thought about, the materials he used, why it is meaningful for him, and why it can be for you, too. John Keats said, "If something is not beautiful, it is probably not true." As you follow the pathways toward publicizing your offering, it is as if you were entering a beautiful and true space defined by your own thoughts, actions, feelings, and what you choose to see. The process, the unfolding, is the thing itself.

Be a real somebody

In describing the theme of his film *The Talented Mr. Ripley,* the director Anthony Minghella said, "The film asks the question, 'Is it better to be a fake somebody than a real nobody?' At the heart of the film is a kind of debate about the cost of giving up on yourself."

We live in an age where the predominant message is that we must change or improve ourselves. What we say, who we are, how we smell, or the way we look isn't good enough. Is it better to be a fake somebody than a real nobody? I don't think so. We all know this, somewhere in ourselves. And we know that we must return home, make the journey back from all the places where we have lost ourselves along the way. Remembering who we are, where we came from, and where we are going is an essential part of creating a marketing and publicity plan with integrity and spirit.

Make of yourself a light

In our culture, presence often goes unacknowledged. Deepak Chopra calls to our attention that we're human *beings* not human *doings.* Yet it seems not to be so. We're all so busy doing that we often forget that our presence, our being, is sometimes all that is called for.

I was reminded of how important presence is several months ago when I walked into my acupuncturist's office to get a treatment for back pain. She sat talking to a boy of about fifteen who was animatedly telling her a story. I knew he was special. I immediately forgot the reason why I'd come, thinking only that I wanted to connect with him. But I didn't know how. I felt awkward and stood by the door.

Fortunately he knew what to do. He walked directly over to me, thrust out his hand, and said, "Hi! I'm Aaron." Then we started talking. But it really wasn't talking at all; he was gesturing and making sounds. I could make out only a few words, but we were communicating.

I think he had Down's syndrome. But he had much more than that. The phrase "Make of yourself a light" kept running through my mind. He was like a pure beam of warm gold. For days afterward I walked around in a lighted-up alive state from the pleasure of meeting him. Presence. Aaron was the full expression of who he was, and you are, too. We all are. It shows in whatever we do, whatever we say, and whatever we are. Make of yourself a light and you will be welcomed wherever you go.

~~~~ ~~~~ ~~~~ ~~~~

CHAPTER 19

Put Your Publicity Plan into Action!

A s you near the end of this book, I hope you feel energized and ready to put your plan into action. Reading it is not enough. You must *do* the things you've promised yourself. Now is the time to take inventory of all you've accomplished so far. Make a photocopy of the Invitation on pages 27–29 in chapter 2. For the next few minutes review your answers. Then answer the questions below and photocopy those. Put them side by side. You'll be able to see the total pattern of your desires and the kind of plan that works best for you.

Just seeing your ideas on the page, black-and-white on paper, is incentive enough to take the next step. Rainer Maria Rilke wrote, "Live your questions now, and perhaps even without knowing it, you will live along some distant day into your answers." Answer these questions as a way to move into your answers today.

1. My overall intention is:

_____

_____

_____

_____

2. The feeling I want to have while accomplishing my marketing and publicity plan is:

_____

_____

3. The way the plan will unfold will look like [describe it as if it were happening now—visually, kinesthetically, mentally]:

_____

_____

_____

_____

_____

This is actually a deceptively simple and valuable exercise called looking at your life "as if" you held the view of your future self in mind. If you continue to stay focused only on the vision of what you want, things will fall naturally into place.

WARNING! **DON'T THINK ABOUT WHAT YOU DON'T WANT.**

If you find yourself lapsing back into seeing what you don't want to happen, stop. Get the image of what you want in your mind. Remember the good _feelings_ you had when you saw yourself doing and being what you want.

4. In three months I see myself:

_____

_____

_____

_____

Congratulations! If there is anything at this point that you haven't done that you'd like to do, please, do it now. Take a quick review of the work you've done throughout the book. Write down the three most important things you want to remember.

1. _____

2. _____

3. _____

5. Write below anything that you want to accomplish in the near future.

Item _____Date to finish _____

Item _____Date to finish _____

Item _____Date to finish _____

Item _____Date to finish _____

Item _____Date to finish _____

To stay on track you might do something simple like my friend Laurie and I do. Every Monday we e-mail each other the list of what we want to accomplish that week. We chunk it into manageable little steps. The following Monday we e-mail the next list and talk on the phone for five minutes each to check in. During that conversation the first person tells what she's accomplished and what she hasn't. The other person gives her applause (kind words, etc.) for the things she's done and asks her how she is going to do the things that are left on the list. Then we switch. That's it. Call up a friend or colleague today and set up a weekly time to do this effortless and satisfying exercise.

CHAPTER 20

~~~ ~~~ ~~~

Prosper by Perseverance

Though things happen in their own time, many of us want "success" yesterday. Often, what we desire doesn't seem to come fast enough. Marketing and publicity plans take time to reap results—sometimes an hour, sometimes a year, or sometimes more. One of the things I love most about the process is that it's so mysterious the way one thing leads to another in some crazy pattern. As you incorporate the practices you have learned in this book into your life, you will find it easier and easier to accept that things will happen when they happen.

Jung said, "Sometimes the longest way is often the shortest way." And sometimes the shortest way is the shortest way. Or, as Suzuki Roshi said when he was asked to explain Buddhism in three words, "Not always so." In this last chapter we'll contemplate easy-to-implement ideas to incorporate marketing and publicity into your life on an ongoing basis, with no separation. We'll loosen up enough to accept that what appears to be is not always so.

Find the juiciness in failure and reward yourself for your achievements

Make lots of mistakes

"Mistakes are the portals of discovery," said James Joyce. Become a connoisseur of mistakes. Mistakes can provide hours of amusement and lead to new inventions. Often, when innovators talk about how they came up with some wild idea or product, it turns out it was through some unpredictable mishap. They fool around for so long that lots of things go awry. Some of those things trigger a new thought or are in and of themselves something useful. Medical researchers continually find that the potent side effects of certain drugs are useful in curing other illnesses—a surprising unintended effect.

A professor at Stanford says to reward success and failure equally and punish inactivity. He found that if students were punished for mistakes, they naturally made fewer of them. This in turn led to less imaginative solutions and fewer innovations. It's been said that the definition of an entrepreneur is someone who keeps on failing until he succeeds. Your marketing and publicity success depends on your ability to keep on failing until you don't. Consider this: If what you are doing doesn't work, it could be a complex combination of things. Use this checklist to sort out where you might be going wrong—and where you can try to make your next mistake.

❑ It is not the right time.
❑ It is not the right place.
❑ It is not the right medium.
❑ Your story isn't newsworthy.
❑ Your points are unclear.
❑ You are working the wrong angle.
❑ You have contacted the wrong person.
❑ You have contacted the wrong publication.
❑ You need a different approach.
❑ You are not the right person for this job.
❑ Your attitude could use adjusting.
❑ You need to give it a rest.

Do something different

Lily Tomlin said, "Insanity is doing the same thing over and over again and expecting a different result." If whatever you are doing isn't working, why not do something else! It may mean you need to reevaluate your goals or to change your strategy. It may be making a minuscule change, or it may mean making a gigantic one. In Kathy Myers's case it meant doing a little of both.

Kathy, marketing director for Conducent Technologies, hired a PR firm for $10,000 per month. Three months and $30,000 later, when Conducent still hadn't received any significant press, Kathy took the job of publicity into her own hands. Now when reporters are doing a story related to her industry, "they call two companies and we're one of the two." How did she do it?

First she began by revising and honing her releases every time she sent them out. She realized that when she sent out 100 e-mail releases and didn't get any responses, something was probably wrong with her pitch or subject line—not with the reporters. She also noticed that the release might not have been news-driven at all! After she examined her release for those three elements—right pitch, right subject headline, right news angle—she tried humor. The three elements plus humor finally got the attention she was seeking.

She found that she got the most responses when she was funny or self-deprecating. She titled one release "Former PR Queen Loses Her Crown." When that didn't get much of a response, the next week she escalated it to "Former PR Queen Jumps off Golden Gate Bridge." At that point, six out of the ten reporters she queried said, "You made me laugh. Okay, give me your pitch." Her sense of humor at her failure created an opening for listening. And now the most important reporters in her industry read her e-mail and respond.

Celebrate your success

Publicists send their clients weekly or monthly statements of all the press they've gathered. Since you are gathering your own media placements, keep them on a list in one place with all the relevant information. Whenever you have another idea, angle, pitch, call all the people on this list first. But before I get ahead of myself, and you of yourself, take a minute to celebrate your success.

Take your sweet time and review your list with a loved one over a delicious dinner. Bring all your articles mocked up attractively, along with the big box full of video- and audiotapes from the shows you have been on. Or treat yourself to something extra as a pat on the back to yourself: a trip to the museum to see a show you have not quite made time in your schedule for, new flowers or herbs to plant in the garden, whatever pleases you most. Rewarding yourself is an important part of the self-appreciation process. Enjoy!

Keep what matters most uppermost in your mind

Check in honestly with yourself

In the beginning of this book I said that you would learn to embody six things if you followed the *Sell Yourself Without Selling Your Soul* principles. They are

1. Be yourself.

2. Know your message.

3. Practice your points.

4. Remain true to yourself.

5. Become the message you want to give.

6. Persevere.

If, at this point, you don't feel you've yet fully experienced all six, please feel free to review the chapters that will guide you toward them.

You might also consider starting a Success Team or a Mastermind Group (a group of like-minded individuals in different or complementary professions who meet regularly to share ideas, encourage each other, and stay on track). Getting support and being held accountable are good balancing motivators.

Don't ever forget your public

I heard Willem Dafoe speaking with Roger Ebert at the Cannes Film Festival in 2000. When Ebert asked him if he minded doing publicity, Dafoe said something that made me shudder. Lamenting that he wasn't naturally glib, captivating, or clever-spoken, he bemoaned that he wasn't a particularly interesting person in an interview. Wait a minute. He's an actor, right? Why wouldn't he prepare for his publicity tour just like he would for a movie role? Doesn't he owe it to his audience, his movie producers, the studios who supported his films, to be just as fascinating in an interview as he is in his movies? I think so.

The public supports you. You give to and receive from them. They give to and receive from you in return. Don't disappoint by not holding up your end. Plan, prepare, and practice and you will find your audience waiting to find you fascinating.

Remember the small touches

No small touch is too small. Ann Maruhashi of Meyralights healing candles did a delightful thing. I ordered her candles over the phone and asked if I could send her a check right then. She said, "I'd like you to receive the candles before sending me anything." This small touch exemplified Ann's entire business philosophy, and now I rarely order candles from anyone else. What small touch will make your customers or the media give you their business again and again?

Step out

Forget safety!

Some of the best advice I have ever read for marketing and for life was from Rumi, the thirteenth-century Sufi mystic, in "A Spider Playing in the House." Rumi says:

> You must become ignorant of what you have been taught
> and be instead bewildered.
> Run from what is comfortable and profitable.
> Run, run, run!
> If you drink from those liqueurs,
> you will spill the springwater of your own life.
> Forget safety!
> Live where you fear to live.
> Be notorious!
> Destroy your reputation.
> You have tried prudent planning for long enough.
> From now on, be *mad!*

HOT TIP!

ABANDON YOUR COMFORT ZONE.

This is your time now to realize that there really are no walls to your comfort zone. What is a "zone" anyway? Is it an imaginary boundary that you have set for yourself with fear on one side and happiness on the other? Take Rumi's advice and do something *mad*. If not *mad*, then take the hand of *mad*'s little sister, *bold*, and do something dangerous.

Be bold and brazen

Who would buy a calendar of nude old ladies? Apparently quite a number of people. The ladies of Rylstone (England) have raised money by raising eyebrows. The eleven "ladies" began as "WI"—a pastoral women's service organization—when they got the idea to strip for charity. In the calendar they created, these fifty- to sixty-six-year-old pinups of various backgrounds are photographed in sepia (with yellow sunflowers in each portrait) painting, pouring tea, playing the piano, preserving, and more—posing in nothing but their good humor and a pair of pearls. Gutsy.

And for what? All royalties go to leukemia research, split between the Leukaemia Research Fund in the United Kingdom and the Leukemia and Lymphoma Society in the United States "Both groups are dedicated to finding cures for blood-related cancers, including leukemia, lymphoma, Hodgkin's disease, and myeloma."

The calendar is already a hit in Britain. *People* magazine called them "the U.K.'s hottest female ensemble since the Spice Girls," and *USA Today* said, "The women who rocked their nation are coming to America." Workman Publishing's original North American calendar and the ladies' 2000 British calendar have sold about 300,000 copies, raising almost $750,000 to fight leukemia.

There are so many wild ways to make a difference in the world. Find one that speaks to you. The ladies embodied what French writer Jean Cocteau defined as genius: "Knowing how far to go too far." How far are you willing to go to get what you want, to give what you have?

Hang on one minute longer

A Norwegian proverb claims that "heroism consists of hanging on one minute longer." When things seem bleak and nothing is moving forward fast enough, or seemingly at all, that is the time to keep hanging on. At the moment when you think you must give up on yourself or a project, consider it a signal to hang on one moment longer.

Persevere

Kat Albrecht is living proof of so many practices and principles outlined in this book. Kat is a "pet hunter" who searches for lost animals using high-tech tools and the skills of a homicide detective. (She was a police detective before she turned her time to cats, canines, and things that slither and crawl.) She came to my "Sell Yourself Without Selling Your Soul: How to Become a Media Sensation" class and took one thing I said to heart—never pass up an opportunity. She is a model of following one idea to its fruition and then expanding to include almost everything else I have covered here in this book.

Here is how Kat made herself a media sensation:

She sent a pitch letter to develop an educational television series for the Animal Planet channel. The director of development said their producer wasn't interested in that idea, but he wanted to know if they could develop a one-hour dramatic television series (budget $800,000 per episode) based upon her life (female cop–turned–pet detective). "My first thought was 'No' because my focus has been to educate pet owners in how to find their missing pets and not to have a fluffy TV show about my life. *But I remembered something you said* and that is 'Never pass up an opportunity.' So I didn't." Instead Kat insisted she have some creative control and be involved in the writing of the episodes.

A few weeks later one of her volunteers asked if she could call a tiny local paper in Half Moon Bay and ask them to come and do a story. That tiny article was read by a reporter from the *San Francisco Chronicle,* who wrote another article. The *Chronicle* article was read by a photographer for *People* magazine. *People* magazine ran a story. Since then Kat's been on CNN, *National Geographic Explorer, To Tell the Truth,* PBS, *Extra!,* the *Today* show, and more.

What is amazing about publicity is how fast one thing can lead to another. It is no accident. Kat has done a number of things right:

1. She's passionate about her work.

2. She's providing a service that no one else does.

3. She has a story that touches people's hearts.

4. She continues to contact her prime media people with fresh angles and ideas.

5. To get more coverage she leverages the press she has.

6. She's open, imaginative, and persistent.

7. On top of all that, her stories read like detective thrillers. Most of my days go at breakneck speed, but when I see Kat's e-mail, I give myself a little treat of reading her animal rescue sagas before I get back to business. I applaud Kat and her wild successes!

Persistence pays, as Kat's story illustrates. Or as author Annie Dillard said, "Perseverance leads to truth."

Leave a legacy

Exercise choice—define your heaven

Steven Covey calls making something of your life to enrich the lives of your family, friends, and community that keeps on going when you are gone "leaving a legacy." No one wants to be forgotten, no matter who they are. The question for you right here and right now is, "What is it really that you want to do here on earth?"

My friend Hector, who died of cancer at age thirty-three, never made that decision. Everyone loved Hector. He was the sweetest man, always getting his friends to talk, never wanting to talk about himself. But Hector didn't know what he wanted until he got cancer, and then the only thing he knew was that he wanted to live. Up to that point he couldn't even choose a restaurant without deferring to his wife, or his friends, or his colleagues. It wasn't that he didn't want to, he didn't even know what kind of food he liked best.

As his flesh melted from his bones and he got increasingly weaker, Hector still refused to acknowledge that he was going to die. Day after day as he began to drift into different states of consciousness, he reported a journey he took to four realms of heaven. He said that Buddha, Jesus, Krishna, and Allah invited him to visit their versions of the promised land. "Each was more beautiful than the next," he reported. "You can't imagine how fantastic these places are." Then, in turn, Buddha, Jesus, Krishna, and Allah asked him to choose his heaven. He refused. "I like it right here on earth," he told them. "I don't want to go. This is where I want to stay." Finally he made a choice. A few weeks later he died.

Don't wait until you are dying to make your choices. Exercise your choice muscle regularly to keep it flexed and sturdy. Camus said, "We are the sum of our choices." All those small and large choices you make every day are what define your heaven, from the food you eat to the words you speak. Once your heaven is defined, live it here on earth. Your children, your family, your friends, your colleagues, your community, and the world will remember you for it.

Peel your potatoes

In a cartoon of two men panning for gold in the mountains one said to the other, "Of course I hope to find gold. But my real goal is spiritual growth and inner peace." When the poet Joan Logghe won the National Endowment for the Arts award, she was asked by the *Santa Fe Reporter* to write an article titled "How I Won an NEA." Her statement in the article reflected her deep understanding of how fleeting fame, name, fortune, and kudos can be. She said simply, "Before enlightenment I peel potatoes. After enlightenment I peel potatoes. So it is with this blessing. Before the NEA, I write poetry; after the NEA, I write poetry."

Forget all that stuff and blow

Arthur Schopenhauer observed, "We forfeit three-fourths of ourselves to be like other people." Don't forfeit your original qualities. Practice being your best natural self. And I am not talking about in presentations for your company or the media—I am talking about to your friends, kids, lovers, parents. Then, when the time comes for you to be in front of an audience, this person who you are will show through, and we will all be glad for it. Dizzy (or was it Bird?), said something like, "Learn your scales, learn your chords, then forget all that stuff and blow."

Push the edge

I have talked a lot in this book about how you can prepare, plan, and practice for publicity so you can become spontaneous and free; how you can become recognized and loved for your God-given gifts; how you can help others to do their jobs while increasing your own abundance. In the end, though, the true measure of how good your PR has been shows up not on the front page of the *New York Times,* or on the cover of *Newsweek,* or on *Oprah,* but on your epitaph. Your epitaph tells you how you have lived your life and whom you have touched along the way.

Here is one epitaph for a person who was greatly loved by people of different nationalities and genders. When she died suddenly in a car accident right after her fiftieth birthday, people all over the world felt the loss. Hundreds of people gathered together to celebrate her life and acknowledge her death at a memorial service. Her name was Bambi Holmes. She chose her name when she was a kid and made sure that everyone called her by her chosen name instead of Michelle, the name she was given.

Though Bambi grew up and lived in Marin County, she considered herself a citizen of the world. She traveled through Europe, Africa, the Middle East, Indonesia, Mexico, and the United States, including all the bike trails of Mount Tam. Each journey filled her with wonder and confirmed her conviction that an open heart accompanied by an open mind was the most important passport a person could carry. Having recently returned from a raft trip down the Colorado River, she delighted in a motto a guide yelled as they ran Lava Falls: "If you are not living on the edge, you are taking up too much space."

Let's all go forth and live as close to the edge as we can.

Thank you for accompanying me on this journey. I wish you the best in giving us, the World, whatever it is you have to offer. Know that we are waiting.

RESOURCES

Introduction

In the following resource section I've collected an extensive list of people, products, books, organizations, newsletters, Web sites, and more that will save you time and money. I've also made it easy for you to contact marketing and publicity professionals and to buy the books and resources that you may need by going directly to my Web site: *http://www.publicitysecrets.com*

Over the past twelve years as a media coach and marketing strategist, I've crossed paths with many people who have knowledge and experience in marketing, publicity, and running a business that will be helpful to you. You'll also find links to many people I've mentioned in the book so you can contact them.

While I personally endorse some of the people here, there are many others whose services or products I have never used. Look for the Harrow Kiss of Approval for people and products I have personally used and/or endorse. As with any business decision, please decide for yourself whether the person or product listed will work for you. If you have a less than positive experience with anyone or anything on the list, please let me know and I will reconsider their status immediately. Conversely, if you find someone exceptional, I'd like to hear about that as well.

If you have suggestions for other resources, please send them to: *newslettereditor@prsecrets.com*.

Enjoy.

Marketing and Publicity Experts
Business and High Tech Publicists

Susan Harrow—Harrow Communications
510.419.0330
susanh@prsecrets.com
http://www.prsecrets.com
Specializes in media coaching and creating marketing strategies for executives, speakers, authors, and entrepreneurs. Clients include *iVillage, PlanetRx,* Pacific Bell Directory/The Yellow Pages, Random House, Doubleday, and many successful businesses and best-selling authors. Fees are determined on a project basis.

Kare Anderson—Say It Better Center
800.488.KARE (5273)
kareand@aol.com
http://www.sayitbetter.com
Speaks and coaches on how to communicate to become more credible, quotable, and attractive to clients. Clients include SAP, Olive Garden Restaurants, SONY, Council of State Governments, and Abbott Laboratories. See Web site for program descriptions, coaching arrangements, and related educational products.

Connie Connors—Connors Communications
212.807.7500
connie@connors.com
http://www.connors.com
Connors Communications is a strategic consumer PR and marketing agency specializing in the (emerging) consumer technology, entertainment, and education markets. They have offices in New York, San Francisco, Los Angeles, and London. Focus is on companies and products and minimum retainer commitment, either project or ongoing, is $25,000.

Dan Janal
Dan@Janal.com
http://www.danjanal.com
Dan is regarded as the leading expert in publicity, media relations, and crisis communications on the Internet. He was on the public relations team that launched America Online nearly twenty years ago. For over twenty years he has worked with companies to launch the first GPS navigational systems, as well as more than 100 hardware and software programs. Dan does a one-day customized consultation and hands-on seminar at your office for $10,000 (plus hotel/travel expenses). Call his private line at 952.380.1554 to schedule a day.

Deborah Kwan—Deborah Kwan Communications
415.586.4885
debkwan@earthlink.net
Specializes in food-related clients (gourmet food products, restaurants, cookbooks, and magazines) publishing, and fashion retail and design accounts. Clients include Scharffen Berger Chocolate Maker, Gastronomica, Kenneth Cole New York, American Eagle Outfitters, Montage restaurant, Chronicle Books, and ChefShop.com. Prefer six months minimum. Average $2,000+ per month. Project-based, retainer and/or hourly ($85–$100/hour) depending on the scope of work involved.

Suzanne Jackson—Cornerstone Communications
540.832.0583
sj@CornerstoneDelivers.com
http://www.cornerstonedelivers.com
Specializes in high-tech, commercial finance, art, and trade association clients. Clients include KnowledgeWorks, ScholarOne.com, Allegiant, Key Equipment Finance, The ProMarc Agency, Brady Photographics, and Equipment Leasing Association. Prefers three-month minimum. Average $3,500+ per month (about thirty hours) depending on scope of work and results desired.

Alyson Dutch—Brown and Dutch
2300 Los Flores Canyon
Malibu, CA 90265
310.456.7151
alyson@bdpr.com
http://www.bdpr.com
Clients include the *Lion King* and the Beach Boys. They specialize in Web-based consumer, and corporate businesses and special events. Minimum six months @ $6,000 per month.

Sally Douglas Arce
1185 Solano Avenue No. 136
Albany, CA 94706
510.525.9552
sdarce@jps.net
Sally Douglas Arce specializes in media relations and marketing. Clients served include health, public health, and affordable housing organizations; film companies; economic development projects; and more. By designing strategic media plans and implementing them, she works to improve short- and long-term visibility and marketability. Sally Douglas Arce also designs and implements book publicity and marketing campaigns.

Janine Warner Communications
305.883.7833
editor@janinewarner.com
http://www.janinewarner.com
Specializes in helping businesses expand into the U.S. Hispanic and Latin American markets with culturally appropriate and cost-effective strategies. Her experience includes directing the on-line operations for the *Miami Herald* and serving as Director of Latin American Operations for CNET. Prefers business development projects with a $2,500 minimum.

Jenai Lane—Zeal, Co.
jenai@respectus.com
http://Respectus.com
Zeal, Co. is a business consultancy firm that specializes in product concepting and developing, brand strategy, and promotions.

Diane de Castro—Offtime press.
41 Sutter Street, Suite 1763
San Francisco, CA 94104
Drdecastro@hotmail.com
http://www.marketingsenseconsulting.com

Mary Schnack—Schnack and Brody Communications, Inc.
270 Last Wagon Drive
Sedona, AZ 86336
520.204.9834 Mary Schnack
310.582.0085 Joanna Brody
ms@sedona.net
http://www.schnackandbrody.com
Specializes in crisis communications, writing, media management and promotion, and marketing.

Kathleen Archambeau—Archambeau Associates Marketing Results
1328 E. 38th Street
Oakland, CA 94602
510.336.3190
karchambea@aol.com
Specializes in high-tech strategic marketing; branding; positioning; and company, product, and service launches. Executive management training and coaching.

Book Publicists

Leslie Rossman—Open Book Publicity
510.658.7520
hiLeslie1@aol.com

Leslie's Partner: Emily Miles Terry (East Coast)
617.522.3206
eamiles@earthlink.net
Leslie is my publicist. Heart of gold and a mouth that's always in motion (which is what you want in a publicist). She's the best of the best. She usually works for publishers directly and rarely takes on fiction, though she will work on any subject that interests her from parenting to health, women's studies to African-American interest. "Must be provocative enough for me to pitch and get truly behind." Clients include dozens of best-selling authors including Sister Wendy Beckett, Shirley MacLaine, Ray Bradbury, Cherie Carter-Scott, Jonathan Kellerman, and the Dalai Lama.

Arielle Ford—The Ford Group
1250 Prospect Street, Suite Ocean 5
La Jolla, CA 92037
858.454.3314
fordgroup@aol.com
http://www.fordsisters.com
Arielle specializes in nonfiction books only. Her clients include best-selling authors Deepak Chopra, Wayne Dyer, Marianne Williamson, and Chicken Soup for the Soul. Minimum four months @ $6,000 per month.

Anita Halton—Anita Halton Associates
559 Alta Vista Way
Laguna Beach, CA 92651-4057
949.494.8564
ahapub@aol.com
Anita specializes in spirituality, religion, psychology, business, fiction, and mysteries. Her clients include best-selling authors Thomas Moore, James Redfield, Mimi Latt, and Rachel Resnick. Minimum 3 months @ $1,500 per month.

Isabella Michon
415.898.4838
impublicity@earthlink.net
Former TV and radio producer with twenty years' experience. Specialties
include health, spirituality, and lifestyle/feature topics. Clients include Deepak
Chopra, Melody Beattie, Robert Thurman, Mickey Hart, and Clive Barker.

Willy and Robyn Spizman—The Spizman Agency
770.953.0850
spizagency@aol.com
Specializes in aggressive author/book promotion and publishing companies
for first-time authors as well as seasoned literary giants. Clients include *New
York Times* best-selling author H. Jackson Brown, *300 Incredible Things to Do on
the Internet* book series (over 1.7 million sold), and Al and Laura Ries. Publicity can include: national speaking opportunities, developing next book angles,
and proposal writing. Fees are quoted upon request.

Annie Jennings—Annie Jennings PR
26 Wilshire Drive
Belle Mead, NJ 08502-5521
908.281.6201
annie@anniejenningspr.com
http://www.anniejenningspr.com
Works with authors and speakers. Has a pay-for-placement program. You only
pay for interviews you accept. National TV and print placements begin at
$1,500. Radio begins at $300.

Celia Rocks and Dottle DeHart—Rocks-DeHart Book Publicity
Riverview Office Building
811 Boyd Avenue, Suite 101
Pittsburgh, PA 15238
412.820.3004
http://www.CeliaRocks.com
CeliaRocks@aol.com
Rocks-DeHart specializes in business and consumer nonfiction. They have
publicized Michael Gerber and dozens of the *Dummies* books. Minimum three
months @ $3,000 per month.

Tammy Richards—Richards Public Relations
2526 Butterfield Drive
Ft. Worth, TX 76133
817.423.9400
trpr@concentric.net

Kate Bandos—KSB Promotions
616.676.0758
kate@ksbpromotions.com
http://www.ksbpromotions.com
General lifestyle books, travel, gardening, general health for the consumer. Clients include Meredith Books, Child Management, Inc., and Mile Oak Publishing, Inc. Fees are $500 and up, figured per element with a "cafeteria-style" price list.

Joyce Lynn
P.O. Box 682
Mill Valley, CA 94942
415.267.7620
joyce lynn@hotmail.com
Joyce Lynn, "the Pro-motion Doctor," works with authors with books in various stages of publication that need emergency care, short-term attention, or a well-tailored wellness program. Clients include authors published by major houses such as Crown, St. Martin's, Rowman & Littlefield, and small publishers like Wildcat Canyon and Winedale, as well as self-published writers. Retainer based on your needs.

Public Speaking and Media Coaches

Robert Dickman—First Voice
1122 Sixth Street #202
Santa Monica, CA 90403
310.394.8829
bob@first-voice.com
http://www.first-voice.com
Robert specializes in training for business in authentic communications. First Voice is a consulting firm dedicated to helping companies discover the compelling story of their products, services, and underlying technologies. Among his clients are Ford, Mattel, and The Limited. Fees are determined on a project basis.

Lee Glickstein—Speaking Circles International®
375 Marin Avenue
Mill Valley, CA 94941
415.381.8044
800.610.0169
info@speakingcircles.com
http://www.glickstein.com
Keynote speaker Lee Glickstein is founder of Speaking Circles International®.

"He is committed to working with people at all levels of speaking experience who want to be completely comfortable, fully authentic, and powerfully effective with groups." Clients include Chevron Corporation, Pacific Bell, Kaiser Permanente, Stanford University, and more. To join a speaking circle near you go to his Web site.

Natalie H. Rogers, M.S.W., C.S.W.—Talkpower Inc.
333 East 23rd Street, Suite 11B
New York, NY 10010
800.525.3718
212.684.1711
http://www.talkpowr.com

Sandra Miller—ICT Impact Communications Techniques
301 East 22nd Street 5R
New York, NY 10010
212.387.8939
ict1@webspan.net

Internet

Paul J. Krupin
800.457.8746
http://www.imediafax.com
Specializes in creating custom-targeted media lists for your specific audience. He has worked with major publicity houses and gets results. He can also help you write or edit a release. Minimum charge for a project is $25. You can create a targeted list of your top picks for a reasonable rate.

Red Dog Publicity
330 SW 43rd Street
PMB K-547
Renton, WA 98055
425.228.7131
Talion@ix.netcom.com
http://www.Talion.com
For those on a tight budget, programs start at $59 for two dozen phone pitches.

Publicity Products and Services
Books and Tapes

> *You Are the Message: Getting What You Want by Being Who You Are*
Roger Ailes and Jon Kraushar
Currency/Doubleday; ISBN: 0385265425 (September 1989)
Still the best book out there on managing your media appearances. Ailes is the media advisor to U.S. presidents, America's top executives, and celebrities. He is *the* authority on the subject. I read his book for the first time last year and wished I had read it earlier. His philosophy and mine are close kin. But he says it all so much more brilliantly and wisely. If you read nothing else about publicity, read this one.

> *Six Steps to Free Publicity: and Dozens of Other Ways to Win Free Media Attention for You or Your Business*
Marcia Yudkin
Plume; ISBN: 0452271924 (October 1994)
I've read a lot of books on publicity and marketing and this is the one I recommend. It's packed with information and a fast read.
http://www.yudkin.com

> *How to Get Your Point Across in 30 Seconds or Less*
Milo O. Frank
Reissue edition Washington Square Press; ISBN: 0671727524 (May 1991)
Learn to communicate powerfully fast. This slim book is as concise as the title. Frank makes his points walking his talk and teaches you to do the same.

> *Never Be Nervous Again* (Audiocassettes)
Dorothy Sarnoff
Simon and Schuster (Audio); ISBN: 0671794183 (October 1992)
http://www.dorothysarnoff.com

Mediasmart: How to Handle a Reporter by a Reporter
Dennis Stauffer
MinneApplePress; ISBN: 0964042908 (August 1994)

> *1001 Ways to Market Your Books*
John Kremer
Open Horizons; ISBN: 0912411481 (May 2000)
This one book would keep you busy for years publicizing your book. It's a gold mine of information. A must for any author.

Chases Calendar of Events
http://www.chases.com
Considered the premier reference calendar, Chases has produced this voluminous tome for forty years. A day-by-day directory of special days, weeks, and months of events, anniversaries, birthdays, and more. Over 12,000 ways to tie into a holiday or news event. Bonus: You can register your event for the next edition. $49.95.

Celebrate Today!
John Kremer
Open Horizons; ISBN 0912411449
http://www.bookmarket.com | 515.472.6130
A comprehensive resource book listing thousands of ideas about how to tie whatever you're promoting to an event or special day. Bonus: lots of helpful tips on publicity. $12.95 (includes shipping).

Tongue Fu!
Sam Horn
St Martin's Press; ISBN: 0312140541 (February 1996)

Dan Janal's Guide to Marketing on the Internet: Getting People to Visit, Buy and Become Customers for Life
Dan Janal
John Wiley and Sons; ISBN: 0471349763 (January 2000)

You Just Don't Understand
Deborah Tannen, Ph.D.
Ballantine Books; ISBN: 0345372050 (June 1991)

That's Not What I Meant: How Conversational Style Makes or Breaks Relationships
Deborah Tannen, Ph.D.
Ballantine Books; ISBN: 0345340906 (January 1991)

Talking from 9 to 5: Women and Men in the Workplace: Language, Sex, and Power
Deborah Tannen, Ph.D.
Ballantine Books; ISBN: 0380717832 (January 1991)
Smart, researched material on language showing how men and women communicate differently. If you want to learn to better understand what we say to each other really means, this book provides some fascinating insights into interpersonal relations.

EVEolution: The Eight Truths of Marketing to Women
Faith Popcorn and Lys Marigold
Hyperion; ISBN: 0786865237 (June 2000)
http://www.faithpopcorn.com

The Tipping Point
Malcolm Gladwell
Little, Brown and Company; ISBN: 0316316962 (February 2000)

Spin: How to Turn the Power of the Press to Your Advantage
Michael S. Sitrick and Allan J. Mayer
Regnery Pub; ISBN: 0895264110 (April 1998)

The Anatomy of Buzz: How to Create Word-of-Mouth Marketing
Emanuel Rosen
Doubleday; ISBN: 0385496672 (October 2000)

Publicity Stunt! Great Staged Events That Made the News
Candice Jacobson Fuhrman
Chronicle Books, 1989

Be Heard Now: Tap into Your Inner Speaker and Communicate with Ease
Lee Glickstein
Broadway Books; ISBN: 0767902602 (October 1998)
Speak authentically from the heart about any subject.

The New Talkpower: The Mind Body Way to Speak Without Fear
Natalie H. Rogers
Capital Books Inc.; ISBN: 189212324X (August 2000)
Learn to write a speech, use breathing to work with your fear, and perform under stressful conditions.

How to Get on Radio Talk Shows All Across America Without Leaving Your Home or Office
Joe Sabah
Self-published, Pacesetter Publications; ISBN: 0940923041 (February 1999)
P.O. Box 101975, Denver, CO 80250
http://www.joesabah.com | 800.945.2488

How to Work a Room: The Ultimate Guide to Savvy Socializing in Person and Online
Susan RoAne
Quill; ISBN: 0060957859 (December 2000)
http://www.susanroane.com | 415.461.3915
Susan RoAne is a keynote speaker and best-selling author.

The 7 Habits of Highly Effective People
Stephen R. Covey
Fireside; ISBN: 0671708635 (August 1990)

First Things First: To Live, to Love, to Learn, to Leave a Legacy
Stephen R. Covey, A. Roger Merrill, and Rebecca R. Merrill
Fireside; ISBN: 0684802031 (January 1996)

How to Say No Without Feeling Guilty: and Yes to More Time, More Joy, and What Matters Most to You
Patti Breitman and Connie Hatch
Bantam Doubleday Dell; ISBN: 076790379X (March 2000)
No-nonsense guide to saying all you want to say no to and making the room to say yes to all those things that really juice you. Indispensable.

The Gift of Fear: Survival Signals That Protect Us from Violence
Gavin de Becker
Little, Brown and Company; ISBN: 0316235024 (June 1997)
Strategies to stay safe. Read this before you begin your publicity campaign.

Risky Business: Protect Your Business from Being Stalked, Conned, or Black-mailed on the Web
Dan Janal
John Wiley and Sons; ISBN: 0471197068 (March 1998)

Dot.com Success! Surviving the Fallout and Consolidation
Sally Richards
Sybex; ISBN: 0782128513 (March 2001)

Ask Jeeves: How to Build a Successful .Com Business
Sally Richards
Osborne McGraw-Hill; ISBN: 0072126590 (January 2001)

Databases

Bradley Communications—Publicity Blitz Media Directory
For free info, call their fax-on-demand line 800.759.5294 and request document #301.
Nearly 20,000 editors and producers coded by the subjects they cover.
http://www.rtir.com/products.htm

The U.S. All Media E-Mail Directory
This source contains 11,000 magazines, 1,500 daily newspapers, 5,700 weekly newspapers, 400 news services and syndicates, 1,300 broadcast TV stations, 1,800 broadcast TV shows, 1,200 cable TV stations, 1,050 cable TV shows, 6,200 A.M. and F.M. radio stations, and more than 2,700 radio talk shows.
800.457.8746 | http://www.owt.com/dircon

Bacon's Newspaper/Magazine Directory and Bacon's Radio/TV/Cable Directory
http://www.bacons.com

PR Newswire
800.832.5522 | http://www.prnewswire.com

Gebbie Press
P.O. Box 1000
New Paltz, NY 12561
http://www.gebbieinc.com | 845.255.7560

Press Releases

Free Press Release Posting

Wireless Flash
Wireless Flash specializes in exclusive "off-edge pop culture news and entertainment content." Radio personalities use Wireless Flash to prep for their shows. Newspaper and magazine editors use it for a "column tip sheet and as original page content." Talk show producers rely on it to book guests. Special editions of Wireless Flash are used as content for Web sites.
P.O. Box 639111
San Diego, CA 92163-9111
http://www.flashnews.com | tel: 619.220.7191 | fax: 619.220.8590

http://www.comitatusgroup.com/pr/index.htm

http://www.PRweb.com

http://www.webaware.co.uk/netset/text

PRESS RELEASE DISTRIBUTION

PRleads
http://www.1shoppingcart.com/app/aftrack.asp?afid=20994
Dan Janal teamed up with Profnet to offer this great new service. Leads are emailed to you almost daily from reporters looking for experts, and you get instant publicity without writing a press release or managing a database. I got an interview with the BBC in less than two weeks, and a colleague of mine was contacted by *Business Week* magazine the day after he tested this service! Wow. A must.

Profnet.com—owned by prnewswire
http://www.profnet.com/makingmost.html
Please read this before you respond to a reporter.

http://www.prnewswire.com
For general news, post your press release at PR Newswire, which has a fax service available as well. The way their electronic service works is the media goes to the site to find newsworthy releases. So you need to wait for them to find you. Which is less direct than sending it to select media chosen specifically for their known interest in your content. $300 and up.

http://www.businesswire.com
Use this for business or financial news. They also have a fax service available. This works the same way as PR Newswire. $500 and up.

http://www.press-release-writing.com
Their basic distribution package goes to over 35,000 journalists and media outlets. Content is republished on leading Web sites and syndicated on leading distributors, including Bloomberg, COMTEX News Network, iSyndicate, and Screaming Media. $300 and up.

http://www.corporateNEWS.com
Try this for business-oriented news. They have a distribution list of over 30,000 traditional and on-line contacts. $295 and up.

http://www.partylinepublishing.com
Fifty-two weeks of this newsletter gives you more than 1,000 placement opportunities a year or nearly two dozen per week. $200/year.

http://www.internetwire.com
http://www.newsbureau.com
http://www.newsfeed.com

Resource Directories

Bradley Communications
Radio-TV Interview Report
800.989.1400 ×408
http://www.rtir.com
Consider "the bible" of the industry, this is the world's largest database of authors and experts. You pay to get listed as a resource to radio and TV producers. Expert copywriters write your ad. If you don't plan to do the research to send out your press materials to the appropriate people and you would rather draw journalists and producers to you through "advertising" in a respected resource book, this is for you. Bradley also has databases and other excellent publicity resources.

Yearbook of Experts, Authorities and Spokespersons
800.YEARBOOK
editor@yearbook.com
http://www.yearbook.com
One time per year 10,000 hard copies of yearbook are sent to journalists. The Web site gets 2 million hits a year.

Broadcast Interview Source
1.800.DAYBOOK (329.2665)
Fax: 202.342.5411
http://www.daybooknews.com—Interactive calender of events on the Web. Authors can post their appearances and releases.

http://www.daybook.com—Interactive. You can post events that you want journalists to see. Journalists go there to find new ideas.

http://www.Guestfinder.com
Regular memberships: one page for one year (twelve months) is $249. Special membership: For $349, you receive a twelve-month membership *plus* an ad in the "GreatGuests" newsletter that is faxed to 1,500-plus media professionals. You must be a member of NSA (National Speakers Association) or have proof that you're a professional speaker, and/or have your book listed in R. R. Bowker directory *Books in Print* to qualify.

http://www.cheappublicity.com

First two months are free. After that you'll pay $99 for six months. This site lists you (as an author, expert, or speaker) and gives you a link directly to your own Web site. They market their site to media outlets, organizations, and associations nationwide who can then access their site (and your name and link) for free via "ads." Use this as a supplement not a substitute to your ongoing marketing and publicity program.

http://www.biginterview.com

Statistics and Research

Statistics help you show that your ideas have substance. Being backed by influential institutions assists the credibility of your claims. To show specifics of how dramatic your discovery is, search these.

http://www.ceoexpress.com
Links to major media, government, search engines, and more. A fantastic resource for just about anything.

http://www.firstgov.gov
Facts on the federal government, links to state and local government sites, and more.

The Census Bureau
http://www.census.gov

http://www.halibot.com
Database of lots of useful information from tennis to toll-free numbers.

The Department of Health and Government Health Agencies
http://www.os.dhhs.gov

The Library of Congress Newspaper and Current Periodical Room
http://www.lcweb.loc.gov/global/ncp/ncp.html

Movie Web Sites

http://www.allmovie.com

http://www.imdb.com

http://www.Lexis-Nexis.com

News Sites

http://www.thestreet.com

http://public.wsj.com/home.html

Trend Watch: Trend Newsletter
http://www.imagitrends.com

Hoover's List of Lists
http://www.hoovers.com/company/lists best
The list ranks companies and people by size, sales, reputation, and many other criteria.

Organizations

Public Relations Society of America
212.995.2230

PMA (Publishers Marketing Association)
http://www.pma-online.org
PMAonline@aol.com
310.372.2732

The Northern California Book Publicity and Marketing Association
http://www.ncbpma.org

Newsletters

MY FAVORITES

These are ones I subscribe to. Go to their Web sites to subscribe:
http://www.I-PRdigest.com

http://www.audettemedia.com/subscribe.html | i-pr-join-request@list.audettemedia.com

http://www.PublicityHound.com

http://www.sayitbetter.com

http://www.antion.com

http://www.mrfire.com

http://www.yudkin.com

http://www.danjanal.com

http://www.larrychase.com

BOOK PUBLICITY

Publicist Annie Jennings
Annie Jennings PR Crash Course in Publicity.
Has a feature called "Media Alert" to e-mail you media opportunities, many of which are free. Send e-mail with "subscribe ezine" in subject line to: annie@anniejenningspr.com

Self-Publishing Guru Dan Poynter
Fantastic advice for any self-published or ambitious author.
http://www.ParaPub.com

NetRead
http://www.netread.com

ON-LINE PROMOTION

http://www.webadvantage.net

http://clickz.com

http://www.digitrends.net

http://www.marketingtips.com

http://www.promotion101.com

http://www.mediamap.com/webPR

sallyrichards.com
See her links for entrepreneurs.

Book Writing, Publishing, and Marketing

Promotion

GENERAL

The Jenkins Group
http://www.bookpublishing.com
Offers guidance for corporate marketing, book publishing, packaging, and marketing; and special sales channels to sell your books in blocks of hundreds or thousands to companies and nontraditional markets.

Book Marketing Update
http://www.bookmarket.com
JohnKremer@bookmarket.com
http://www.bookmarket.com/top101.html
800.784.4936
This one site will keep your marketing plan in motion for a very long time. Subscribe to Book Marketing Update. One of the most valuable services for marketing books yourself.

About Books Inc.
http://www.about-books.com
MarilynRoss@about-books.com
A full-service writing, self-publishing, and book marketing firm.

E-BOOKS

http://booklocker.com

http://www.fatbrain.com

http://www.wordsmith.com

http://www.mightywords.com

http://www.iuniverse.com

Writer's Resources

Book Writing Coaches

 Maggie Oman Shannon
Founder and principal of The New Story
415.970.0079
maggie@thenewstory.com
Achieve a creative dream from personal coaching on how to birth your projects, to editing, copywriting, or marketing services. Maggie, a former magazine editor and director of marketing who has successfully realized her own dream, will help you achieve yours.

 Jennifer Basye Sander
Proposal writer and book consultant
Big City Books Group
The author of many best-selling books herself, Jennifer helps authors with their proposals and to shape their book ideas into sure sellers.
916.791.2101
ginsander@hotmail.com
http://www.goalsandjewels.com

 Sam Horn—Action Seminars
703.456.0870
SamHornTongueFu@aol.com
http://www.samhorn.com
Specializes in one-on-one consulting for books at any stage of the process from a title, proposals, or a finished manuscript. She also conducts writers' retreats. Former executive director of the Maui Writers Conference and current emcee of the conference, Sam is also a top-rated speaker and best-selling author. Clients include Young Presidents Organization, Hewlett-Packard, and Holland America Cruise Lines. Private consulting $300/hour, presentations $4,500.

Directory of Literary Agents
http://www.writers.net/agents.html
None of these agents charge reading fees (considered disreputable). One caveat: Agents enter themselves into this database. Searchable by country or by genre (nonfiction, literary fiction, romance, science fiction, biography, etc).

Writer's Marketplace: Authorlink
http://www.authorlink.com—A Random House Affiliate Site
A marketplace where editors and agents buy and sell rights to unpublished

and published manuscripts, and screenplays. Covers industry news, information, and marketing services for editors, literary agents, and readers plus interviews with editors at major publishing houses.

💋 Guide to Magazine Guidelines
http://www.writersdigest.com/guidelines/index.htm

http://www.writemarkets.com

💋 *Writer's Digest* Magazine
http://www.writersdigest.com
Provides searchable guidelines for over 1,500 magazines. Includes editor's viewpoint. Great resources to sites of interest to all kinds of writers.

💋 101 Writer's Sites
http://www.writersdigest.com/101sites/media.html
A super source for media information and magazines and more.

Books on Writing and Publishing

💋 *The Shortest Distance Between You and a Published Book*
Susan Page
Broadway Books; ISBN: 0553061771 (June 1997)
The best guide to writing a book proposal the way the top agents want to see it. Susan gives you a quick tour through the publishing industry maze in good, plain English.

Write the Perfect Book Proposal: 10 Proposals That Sold and Why
Jeff Herman and Deborah M. Adams ·
John Wiley and Sons; ISBN: 0471575178 (March 1993)

💋 *Writer's Guide to Book Editors, Publishers, and Literary Agents, 2001–2002: Who They Are! What They Want! and How to Win Them Over*
Jeff Herman
Prima Publishing; ISBN: 0761522166 (July 2000)
Lists the names and specific areas of interest of thousands of editors at over 500 book publishing houses. Over 121 interviews with literary agents.

💋 *The Complete Idiot's Guide to Getting Published*
Sheree Bykofsky and Jennifer Basye Sander
Complete Idiot's Guides; Macmillan Distribution; ISBN: 0028639197
(July 2000)

Makes the mysterious processes of getting published understandable and enjoyable. Learn how to write book proposals, pitch ideas to agents and editors, and more. Essential if you're just getting started.

How to Write Irresistible Query Letters
Lisa Collier Cool
Writer's Digest Books; ISBN: 0898793912 (March 1990)
This is a book I've used since I began freelance writing ten years ago. All the information is still current and clear.

Bird by Bird
Anne Lamott
Anchor; ISBN: 0385480016 (October 1995)
Love her. One of my all-time favorite writing books. Anne balances pinprick humor with snidely compassionate remarks about the joys and sorrows of the writer's life. She puts me into hysterics on a regular basis. I wish she'd write more books on writing.

Writing Down the Bones: Freeing the Writer Within
Natalie Goldberg
Shambhala Publications; ISBN: 1570624240 (November 1998)
One of my all-time favorite books on writing. Even if you've never written a word, this book will help you get started.

Wild Mind: Living the Writer's Life
Natalie Goldberg
Bantam Books; ISBN: 0553347756 (November 1990)

The Artist's Way: A Spiritual Path to Higher Creativity
Julia Cameron
J P Tarcher; ISBN: 087476945 (July 1992)

Writing Classes

Joan Logghe
505.753.3174
jlogghe@espanola.com
Joan is one of the best writing teachers I've ever had. Wise, funny, and willing to go deep wherever her writing (or life) takes her. To book Joan as a speaker, workshop leader for writing groups, teachers, therapists, or students, contact her directly.

 **Ghost Ranch**

To go on a retreat and take a writing class with Joan in Georgia O'Keeffe country in the sacred desert, call Ghost Ranch in Abiquiu, New Mexico.
505.685.4333
http://www.newmexico-ghostranch.org
ghostranch@cybermesa.com
Ghost Ranch is a no-frills, semicamp-style environment. The grounds are spectacular. If you want a peaceful retreat for a bargain and the guidance of a special teacher, you won't be disappointed.

Laurie Wagner

On-line writing classes: http://www.writers.com
Laurie teaches personal essay writing by introducing students to "the volcanic marriage of real life and fiction, and inspires them to take risks with their writing by telling the truth."
http://www.word-wrangler.com
gurlfrend@word-wrangler.com
She's also available for personal writing coaching.

Laurie is one of the most honest writers I know. That's one of the things that makes a writer a "can't put it down" read. She sees right to the heart of what's right and what's wrong. And you can take her class on-line. Do it while you can before she becomes too popular! Her classes fill fast.

Cecile Moochnek

Cecile Moochnek Gallery
1809 D Fourth Street
Berkeley, CA 94710
510.549.1018
http://www.cecilemoochnek.com
art@cecilemoochnek.com
If you're ever in the area, I urge you to experience Cecile and her gallery. Cecile's wisdom encompasses the intimacies of both art and life. I never tire of hearing her talk about why a commonplace object or more formal work of art is beautiful. She's one of a kind! Cecile also teaches writing classes ("Taste Your Life Through Writing Practice") and brings the same astuteness to the writing process that she does to her love of art. See her Web stie for a schedule of classes.

Writer's Organizations

National Writer's Union
http://www.nwu.org

American Society of Journalists and Authors
http://www.asja.org

Writer's Guild
http://www.writersguild.com

Prosperity and Personal Growth

Tapes

**Sedona Training Associates**
60 Tortilla Drive
Sedona, AZ 86336
1.888.282.5656 (Orders only)
520.282.3522
http://www.sedona.com
info@sedona.com
Even if you've been meditating your whole life, these tapes *Freedom Now* and *Sedona Method* course can produce a profound shift. You can learn to let go of any uncomfortable feeling on the spot. It also works to get to the root of physical and emotional pain. These tapes are essential if you're getting ready to go on a media tour!

Sounds True
800.333.9185
http://www.soundstrue.com
"Audio, video and music for the inner life." This is one of my favorite companies. They epitomize beauty, integrity, and value. You'll find tapes on everything from work satisfaction to Sufism. They offer courses and cutting-edge thinking in religion, science, music, and more.

Books

Creating Money: Keys to Abundance
Sanaya Roman and Duane Packer
H J Kramer; ISBN: 091581109X (June 1988)
This is an old classic in its genre. Very hands-on. I credit this book with getting

me started in public relations. After I read it and did the exercises, I got my first client just as the rent check was due.

When Things Fall Apart: Heart Advice for Difficult Times
Pema Chodron
Shambhala Publications; ISBN: 1570621608 (January 1997)

The Wisdom of No Escape: and the Path of Loving-Kindness
Pema Chodron
Shambhala Publications; ISBN: 0877736324 (September 1991)
I love Pema Chodron's books. They are wise, kind, and just what I need to hear when times are tough. Distilled from her talks and teachings over many years, these slim books provide great guidance from a woman's spiritual perspective.

Clear Your Clutter with Feng Shui
Karen Kingston
Broadway Books; ISBN: 0767903595 (May 1999)
http://www.spaceclearing.com
info@spaceclearing.com
Clear out your home and office to make space for the new. This book will put you into action, so don't plan to do anything else for a week. I couldn't put it down, and then I couldn't stop throwing away old stuff that was holding me back.

Creating Sacred Space with Feng Shui: Learn the Art of Space Clearing and Bring New Energy into Your Life
Karen Kingston
Broadway Books; ISBN: 0553069160 (February 1997)

Organizing from the Inside Out: The Foolproof System for Organizing Your Home, Your Office and Your Life
Julie Morgenstern
Owl Books; ISBN: 0805056491 (September 1998)

Lit from Within: Tending Your Soul for Lifelong Beauty
Victoria Moran
HarperSanFrancisco; ISBN: 0062517333 (May 2001)
Moran shares her thoughtful observations and experience from her own life-long search for inner and outer beauty.

Creating a Charmed Life: Sensible, Spiritual Secrets Every Busy Woman Should Know
Victoria Moran
HarperSanFrancisco; ISBN: 0062515802 (May 1999)

Beloved national lecturer and workshop leader Victoria Moran shares her secrets and philosophy for discovering what is "right" about what you have and suggestions for finding the things you don't. Someone called it "an essential girlfriend gift." I agree.

The Purpose of Your Life: Finding Your Place in the World Using Synchronicity, Intuition, and Uncommon Sense
Carol Adrienne
Eagle Brook; ISBN: 0688166253 (April 1999)
A fantastic book for discovering your passion and doing your true work.

The Purpose of Your Life Experiential Guide: The Program to Help You Find Your Reason for Being
Carol Adrienne
Eagle Brook; ISBN: 0688167144 (September 1999)

Take Time for Your Life
Cheryl Richardson
Broadway Books; ISBN: 0767902076 (December 1999)

Don't Sabotage Your Success! Make Office Politics Work
Karen Ginsburg Wood
Enlightened Concepts Publishing; ISBN: 0970214308 (November 2000)
http://www.karenwood.com
Build professional intimacy and secure critical relationships while negotiating the corporate hierarchy with ease.

Journal to the Soul: The Art of Sacred Journal Keeping
Rose Offner
Gibbs Smith Publishers; ISBN: 0879057025 (November 1996)
roseoffner@aol.com
This book is so gorgeous that many women who bought it didn't want to mar it with their writing! The thoughtful blend of self-help, art, and storytelling leads you to your own insights.

Beyond Fear: Twelve Spiritual Keys to Racial Healing
Aeeshah Ababio Clottey and Kokomon Clottey
H J Kramer; ISBN: 0915811820 (February 1999)
Aeeshah and Kokomon run the Center for Attitudinal Healing. They work tirelessly to address racism in a way that makes sense. This is a seminal work that shows you how viewing anyone as "other" is a form of racism. Gifted storytellers, they share moving "incidents" that brought me to tears. They made me see the world in a different way.

Zen Mind, Beginner's Mind
Shunryu Suzuki
Weatherhill; ISBN: 0834800799 (March 1988)
Transcripts of lectures by this master on the essentials of beginner's mind being in the moment with no other thoughts or preconceived notions. I reread this book every year to remind myself to return to my "original" nature.

Crooked Cucumber: The Life and Zen Teaching of Shunryu Suzuki
David Chadwick
Bantam Doubleday Dell Publishers; ISBN: 0767901053 (February 2000)
Insightful and lively biography of one of the most beloved Zen masters of our time.

Shambhala: The Sacred Path of the Warrior
Chogyam Trungpa
Shambhala Publications; ISBN: 1570621284 (September 1995)
One of my all-time favorite books, which shows you how you can be brave, vulnerable, compassionate, funny, and feisty while creating paradise or Shambhala inside yourself.

An Autobiography: The Story of My Experiments with Truth
Mohandas Gandhi, Mahadev Desal (Translator)
Beacon Press; ISBN: 0807059099 (November 1993)

A Call to Conscience: The Landmark Speeches of Dr. Martin Luther King, Jr.
Clayborne Carson (Editor)
Warner Books; ISBN: 0446523992 (January 2001)

A Knock at Midnight: Inspiration from the Great Sermons of Reverend Martin Luther King, Jr.
Time Warner Audio Books; ISBN: 1570425728 (May 1998)

Other

Kelli Fox
http://www.astrology.com
Kelli's site is the number-one destination on the Internet for astrology. You can download your personal chart for free or order all types of charts. Check out the charts for career and business for some no-nonsense advice.

Rob Brezsny
http://www.freewillastrology.com
Updated every Tuesday, on this site you can read your horoscope free.
900.903.2500
Listen to your gorgeous truth-and-beauty horoscope averaging three minutes
in length. Well worth it just to hear Rob's voice expounding on your virtues
and possibilities.
If you have a 900# block on your phone or live in Canada, use your credit
card; call 877.873.4888 to purchase any amount of time.

Meyralights Candles: Candles of Illumination
Ann Maruhashi
4501 Interlake Avenue N. #4
Seattle, WA 98103-1812
info@meyralights.com
http://www.meyralights.com
206.633.1284
Remarkable scented or unscented candles that peel open like the petals of a
flower as they burn. Ann has a gift of infusing each one with her kind and loving nature. Strange as it may sound, you feel that from each of her candles.
Watch them closely and they'll show you where you are stuck or flowing by
how they burn.

Other Professional Services

Career and Business Advancement

CONSULTANTS

Management consulting, strategic planning and valuation
Brett Sharenow
Principal, Morris Associates
brett@morrisassoc.net
http://www.morrisassoc.net
Morris Associates is a savvy management consulting firm, helping their clients
create value by assisting with business strategy and business plan writing,
financial modeling, acquisition analysis, and both internal and external presentations. Clients include Verio, Pacific Telesis, Chevron, Siemens, Syntex,
and many others.

☙ *Life purpose workshop leader and consultant*
Carol Adrienne
The Spiral Path
510.527.2213
cadrienne@spiralpath.com
http://www.spiralpath.com
Carol is available for workshops on life purpose, keynote addresses for large and small groups, and book signings. A woman who walks her talk and helps you do the same.

Visit Carol's Web site for your personal numerology life chart, books, and tapes. Get a free thumbnail sketch description of your birthday number. Sign up for her newsletter on her Web site.

PERSONAL COACHES

☙ Rich Fettke
FETTKE Success Development
Speaker, success coach, and author of, *EXTREME SUCCESS: The 7-Part Program That Shows You How to Break the Old Rules and Succeed Without Struggle* (Simon & Schuster, 2002), ISBN: 0743229533.
800.200.COACH (2622)
Rich@Fettke.com
http://www.FETTKE.com
Rich Fettke helps people achieve a lot more, struggle a lot less, and have a lot more fun. He is a dynamic professional speaker and one of the country's top success coaches. Rich also has an inspiring two-cassette audiotape program entitled *FOCUS: A Guide to Clarity and Achievement.*

☙ Colleen Newlin
collette@sacredgoblet.com
Colleen is a gifted coach who helps people with major and minor hurdles. She is fully booked and only takes on new clients when current ones are ready to move on.

☙ Nancy Gerber, the 21st Century Communicator
President of SteppingStones
http://www.mindspring.com/~steppingstones
nancybq@steppingstones.com
Take a class from Nancy at http://www.teleclassinternational.com
E-mail Nancy now to get a free half-hour coaching session before you sign up for her weekly personal coaching service. That's how I got started with Nancy and have been working with her for two years. She's a gem.

Cheryl Richardson
http://www.cherylrichardson.com
Free monthly teleclasses on how to balance your life.
Sign up for her newsletter at her Web site for weekly assignments to keep your life in balance. Note: She no longer does one-on-one personal coaching.

CAREER COACH

Sepha Schiffman, President of Redwing Consulting
Sepha@mac.com
Sepha specializes in career transition, overcoming blocks, finding work you love. She's a sensitive listener who is able to elicit just what you need to work on most right now.

Speaking

TELECLASSES

http://www.teleclassinternatinal.com

http://www.teleclass4U.com

http://www.teleclass.com

SPEAKING ORGANIZATIONS AND SERVICES

Speaking Circles International®
415.381.8044
800.610.0169
http://www.speakingcircles.com
(See Lee Glickstein)

National Speakers Association
480.968.2552
http://www.nsaspeaker.org

Toastmasters
http://www.toastmasters.org
800.993.7732
949.858.8255

International Speakers Bureau, Inc.
214.744.3885 ×238
http://www.ISBspeakers.com
Suzanne M. Pharr, Research and Information Manager. $15 cassette on How to Work with Bureaus—"They Are on Another Call Right Now, Can I Put You into Voice Mail?" by Michelle Lemmons, ISB (International Speakers Bureau) president. They are one of the top three speakers bureaus in the country.

Walters International Speakers Bureau
Dottie Walters
Sharing Ideas Magazine
P.O. Box 398, Glendora, CA 91740
626.335.8069
http://www.walters-intl.com
call4spkr@aol.com
Please call at the end of the day and only after you've reviewed Dottie's requirements please. Pick up a Learning Annex or Adult Learning Center catalog for a course near you. Dottie also does personal consultations. She's a gold mine of information!

Geller Media International
Valerie Geller, President
212.580.3385
vgeller@aol.com
http://www.gellermedia.com
"Broadcast consulting firm specializing in New-Talk and personality radio."

Speaker Net News
http://www.speakernetnews.com
Ken Braly and Rebecca Morgan put together this e-zine full of valuable tips on speaking, advice for new and experienced speakers, and information about the speaking industry.

Great Speaking
http://www.antion.com/ezinesubscribe.htm
Filled with tips on presentation, speaking, and training, this ezine also gives you free speaking leads when available. Tom covers everything from marketing to using humor. This packed e-zine is a godsend for new and experienced speakers.

Tips on Speaking
http://www.abacon.com/pubspeak
An extensive site with lots of links on everything from assessing your audience to delivering your speech.

Taping and Duplicating Services & Equipment

V-Corp
800.826.7799 (V-Corp 99)
626.966.0412
vcorp99@aol.com
http://www.vcorp99.com
Video and audio cassette and CD duplication service. Minimum quantity 100.
Fast, efficient, accurate service. I use them. Ask for Irene Francisco.

J&R Music World and Computer World
http://www.jandr.com
800.221.8180
Recording and electronic equipment at great prices and excellent service.

Multimedia Publishing and Packaging, Inc.
800.982.8138
They package, replicate, and deliver CDs and tapes for John Gray, Dr. Laura,
and many others.

Internet

Syndicates

http://www.iSyndicate.com

http:/shwww.mastersyndicator.com
"Master Syndicator" software. For less than $150 you can get this software
installed, which automatically sends your syndicated piece to everyone who
has subscribed to it.

On-line Education

http://www.Uachieve.com
Great destination for business classes and information of all kinds.

http://www.MentorU.com

Web Design

Hot Studio, Inc.
steve@hotstudio.com
http://www.hotstudio.com

Hot Studio is a cross-media design studio based in San Francisco. Hot has completed successful design projects—in on-line and print media—for Charles Schwab, Sun Microsystems, *PCWorld,* Glide Church, and others.

Dean Sharenow

dean@killhenrysugar.com
http://www.killhenrysugar.com
Dean did my excellent site. He is a dream to work with and has a keen marketing sense (very unusual in Webmasters) and a design eye equipped for both beauty and efficiency. Go see for yourself at http://www.prsecrets.com.

Susan Pomeroy

Susan@susanpomeroy.com
http://www.susanpomeroy.com
Susan is an excellent Web designer and also a skilled writer. She has six years' experience designing corporate, small business, and personal Web sites. Her specialty is creating unique Web sites for creative (the profitably offbeat, artistic, or self-employed) professionals.

Dear Readers:

I'd love to hear from you. I welcome your ideas, thoughts, concepts, or whatever else inspires your gypsy spirit. There are many ways you can stay involved with me, especially if you have ideas about

- What was most meaningful for you.

- What you wished I'd covered (or covered more in-depth).

- Your own success stories.

- Strategies, tips, insights you'd like to share with others.

- Your favorite stories about publicity.

- People I should profile who are doing extraordinary work in their community and/or the world.

- What you'd like me to write about next.

Feel free to jot me a note and send it to *susan@publicitysecrets.com*. (Please include a self-addressed stamped envelope if you're writing in hard copy. Administrative stuff is my bane, so I'll really appreciate your thoughtfulness.)

You can also join my monthly newsletter: *Sell Yourself Without Selling Your Soul: 60 second Secrets,* and be a part of a community of people interested in marketing themselves with integrity and spirit. The newsletter offers

- Hot tips from my clients, friends, and subscribers.

- Web sites, quotes, and stories that will inspire and will help you grow your business.

- Bright ideas for the bold and brazen.

- Tips for the intrepid and the reluctant publicity seeker.

- Personal experiences and the mistakes I and others have made so you don't have to.

- Success stories from those who dared and lived to tell their tales.

If you want to subscribe, visit *http://ww.publicitysecrets.com* and you'll receive your free copy shortly. Your privacy is protected. I never sell, trade, or give away names, and you can unsubscribe anytime.

You can also order my audiotapes (many with other experts, too) or booklets to keep ideas alive to continue your publicity "roll." I've created a number of these tapes, which include more "insider" secrets, as companions to this book (not readings of the book). Go to *http://www.publicitysecrets.com* for e-books and more.

Here is a partial list of available audiotapes:

- *Sell Yourself without Selling Your Soul: Secrets to Becoming a Media Sensation*

- *How to Use Sound Bites in Business—to Get What You Really Want*

- *How to Grow Your Business—without Selling Your Soul*

- *How to Promote Your Book to the Top of the Best-seller List*

- *Publicity Secrets to Create a Wildly Successful Book—without Selling Your Soul*

- *How to Be a Publicist's Dream—and Sell More Books*

- *Top Publicists Tell You How to Create a Blockbuster Book*

- *How to Sell Your Writing—but Not Your Soul*

- *Promote Your Book Boldly: Write, Speak, Teach*

Also available on my Web site is the new book called *The Ultimate Guide to Getting Booked on Oprah: 10 Steps to Becoming a Guest on the World's Top Talk Show.*

I welcome your input and will make every effort to include your ideas in my newsletter or in my new books, as often as possible.

I relish you!

Warmly,
Susan

P.S. A portion of the royalties from this books goes toward supporting organizations for mindfulness, women, children, and the arts. Wishing you well!

ABOUT THE AUTHOR

America's top media coach and marketing strategist Susan Harrow has helped thousands of people achieve their dream—to get on *60 Minutes, Oprah,* CNN, CBS, *Howard Stern, Good Morning America, Larry King Live,* and dozens of other top talk shows. Her clients have appeared in the *New York Times,* the *Wall Street Journal, Inc., Forbes, Time, Wired,* and many more of the most respected print publications nationwide.

She coaches executives, elite e-businesses, best-selling authors, and successful entrepreneurs whose projects have a lot of passion and heart. Her diverse clientele include iVillage, PlanetRx, Random House, Gillette/Oral B, Pacific Bell Directory: The Yellow Pages, and many best-selling authors.

A beloved speaker, she offers keynotes, workshops, training, and consulting to corporations, executives, associations, and individuals. Contact her to speak to your organization, corporation, or college, or for personal one-on-one consulting.

Susan Harrow
Harrow Communications
4200 Park Blvd.
PMB 333 S
Oakland CA 94602-1312
Susan@publicitysecrets.com
http://www.publicitysecrets.com
510.419.0330